TWAYNE'S WORLD AUTHORS SERIES
A Survey of the World's Literature

GERMANY

Ulrich Weisstein, Indiana University

EDITOR

G. W. F. Hegel

TWAS 461

G. W. F. Hegel

G. W. F. HEGEL

By CLARK BUTLER
Indiana University - Purdue University at Fort Wayne

TWAYNE PUBLISHERS
A DIVISION OF G. K. HALL & CO., BOSTON

Library of Congress Cataloging in Publication Data

Butler, Clark, 1944 -
  G. W. F. Hegel.

  (Twayne's world authors series ; TWAS 461 : Germany)
  Bibliography: p. 199 - 208
  Includes index.
  1.   Hegel, Georg Wilhelm Friedrich, 1770 - 1831.
I.   Title.
B2948.B85   193   77-6809
ISBN 0-8057–6298–1

To Dallas Willard

Contents

About the Author

Clark Butler, born in Los Angeles in 1944, holds a B.A. and Ph.D. from the University of Southern California. He has also studied at the *Université de Tunis*. He has taught in the Indiana-Purdue Fort Wayne Philosophy Department since 1969, where he is currently Associate Professor. His specializations are metaphysics and social philosophy as well as Hegel. He is a member of the *Internationale Hegel-Vereinigung*, the *Internationale Hegel-Gesellschaft* and the Hegel Society of America as well as the American Philosophical Association. In 1974 he was the holder of a Fulbright Summer Travel Grant to do research at the *Hegel Archiv* in West Germany, and during 1975 - 76 he was a guest researcher at the *Archiv*. In 1974 - 75 he was a Visiting Lecturer at Trent Polytechnic (Nottingham).

Professor Butler has published several articles in professional journals, including *Inquiry*, *Philosophy and Phenomenological Research*, *Idealistic Studies*, *Hegel Jahrbuch* and *The Personalist*. He is presently working on an English edition of Hegel's correspondence, and is also writing a book on Hegel in relation to the major post-Hegelian thinkers. Professor Butler is Coeditor of *CLIO: An Interdisciplinary Journal of Literature, History and the Philosophy of History*.

Preface

It is a fair estimate that an average of one book a week is currently being published somewhere in the world about Hegel. Yet the vast majority are precisely that: books *about* Hegel. They testify to the immense influence of the nineteenth-century German philosopher, but they also show that, despite this impact, there are relatively few individuals who would wish to call themselves Hegelians. What the Lutheran theologian Karl Barth noted a few decades ago continues to be largely true: Hegel has not yet fulfilled what once seemed his promise to become the Thomas Aquinas of the modern Protestant world.[1] There is a resigned attitude among many Hegel scholars that, even if defensible, Hegelianism is too esoteric to gain wide acceptance. But Hegel himself wished nothing less than to give the world another esoteric mystery philosophy reserved for an elite of initiates. The present volume was undertaken in the hope that the Hegelian philosophy could be communicated to a wider public. The book is, moreover, written by one who sees this philosophy as a live option today, and thus as something more than a vastly influential museum piece.

If I were to choose a subtitle, I think it would be *God, Revolution and Philosophy*. Ever since the French Revolution, the modern world has been torn asunder by the opposition between *God* and *revolution*. Thus America, by all accounts a most religious nation, consciously aligns itself against world revolution. Yet the American spirit is not impervious to the creeping nihilism of the age. Many seek a way to assuage doubts, to justify their religious instincts in an apparently alien world. It is just possible that what they seek, without knowing it, is a way to *philosophy* as Hegel conceived it. Philosophy, which for Hegel is a bond capable of uniting the most extreme opposites, provides the hidden link between religion and revolution. The opposition between the two extremes, an opposition from which the world suffers, defines the world's need for knowledge of their inner identity. It is this need which constitutes what Hegel considered the modern world's essential need for philosophy. But if in the Communist world we would be compelled first to talk of revolution in order to speak of God, in America we must first speak of God in order to talk of revolution. The recent American Bicentennial, however, provides occasion for the realization that religion in America is, at its deepest level, inseparable from revolution. The civil rights movements of the 1960s have reminded us that the American Revolution, though now more than two centuries old, is still very much alive. The time may thus be opportune for a small book which seeks to communicate something of Hegel's philosophical comprehension of God, revolution, and their inner identity.

The volume seeks to be elementary and accessible without being oversimplistic. There is no denying that Hegel is a difficult philosopher for beginners. To solve the pedagogical problem I decided early not to write another book on the relation between Hegel and other philosophers such as Plato, Aristotle, or Kant. Thus Hegel's lectures on the history of philosophy have not been extensively drawn upon. The reason is simply that the book is addressed to, among others, readers who have no previous knowledge of philosophy and its history. A book which primarily dealt with Hegel's relation to other philosophers, of whom the reader knows nothing, would likely either bore or frustrate. On the other hand, it may be presupposed that even nonexperts have some notion of the world's history, great religions, and art. The book, accordingly, draws heavily on Hegel's lectures on the philosophy of history, the philosophy of religion, and aesthetics. Indeed, the volume is as much about China, Hinduism, Buddhism, classical Greece, Rome, and Christianity as about Hegel. This certainly is not a book about Hegel in a biographical sense. It seems more in conformity with the spirit of Hegelianism that the main emphasis should be placed on the objective historical and cultural realities which absorbed Hegel's attention, not on Hegel as an individual. An effort has been made to interest the reader in the Hegelian philosophy by showing how it enables him to better comprehend topics to which he has already been introduced on even a preuniversity level.

But Hegel's method of comprehending history, art, and religion involves the use of a battery of abstract logical concepts usually included under the label of the famous Hegelian "dialectic." These concepts, elaborated by Hegel in his *Logic*, no doubt constitute the most difficult part of the Hegelian philosophy, but they are indispensable. Where the attempt is made in the following pages to epitomize the essential core of Hegel's logical concepts, both their difficulty and importance are stressed. The reader is warned that he may not find the dialectical concepts very meaningful on a first reading, but it is hoped that they will become more intelligible through repetition, through rereading, and through seeing their use in the comprehension of more concrete subject matter.

In remaining faithful to the elementary nature of this book, very little use is made of Hegel's philosophy of nature. This part of his philosophy has been considered a chief stumbling block for those who would wish to be Hegelians in the twentieth century. One could not very well consider oneself a Hegelian without accepting, at least in principle, the philosophy of nature which Hegel took over from Friedrich Wilhelm Joseph Schelling and elaborated in terms of the natural science of his day. The basic principle is, simply stated, that our knowledge of nature is a knowledge which is *of* mind *(Geist)* as well as *by* mind. In other words, the physical world is only in appearance merely physical: the knowing mind shares a common nature with the physical world which is known. Although I accept this principle, I would wish to make a concession to my own time by elaborating it in terms of the natural science of this century. And in doing so I gratefully follow the lead of Alfred North Whitehead and Charles Hartshorne, even though Whiteheadian panpsychist cosmology has yet, for the most part, to discover its Hegelian vocation.

The present volume has led me to inquire into a range of subjects which goes well beyond the kind of expertise in analytic argumentation and the history of philosophy in which I received my special training. The hazards that arise when one undertakes to speak of the Whole are great, as Bertrand Russell noted long ago.[2] But if one is to evaluate what Hegel says from a Hegelian standpoint and thereby suggest a noninfantile alternative to the nihilism of the age, it is of the Whole that one must speak. At a number of points in the pages that follow, Hegel's understanding of empirical topics is criticized in the light of more recent knowledge. It is hoped that it will come as a surprise to some readers to find how essentially alive Hegelianism remains despite some errors and gaps in Hegel's knowledge. But it is too much to hope that the present book is free of similar errors and gaps of its own. The most that can be hoped is that the future will not want for researchers who will show what is perennial in Hegel's work by correcting and completing it according to the historical and scientific situation of their times. Fortunately it need not be feared that the errors of this slim volume will seriously discourage them.

The book is written from a standpoint which seeks to be at once Hegelian and faithful to the general viewpoint of the late twentieth century. Footnotes referring to Hegel's texts naturally indicate that the views expressed are explicitly Hegel's own. But the absence of such footnotes in passages where I do not explicitly take issue with Hegel on questions of secondary importance should not be taken as indicating an expression of my own views independently of Hegelian ones; rather, they should be construed as an attempt to explain Hegel in an idiom intelligible to readers approaching him from the institutional, scientific, and cultural standpoint of the present. Purists will accuse me of falsely abstracting Hegel's thought from its original historical context. But to view historical context as a kind of prison is to preclude the very recognition of universal philosophical genius which was the original justification for historical erudition. No doubt it is our job as scholars to show that there never has been more than one Hegelian, and that he died over one hundred and forty years ago. But we cannot as philosophers allow the power of disciplined abstraction and transcontextual generalization to lie permanently fallow.

CLARK BUTLER

Indiana University - Purdue University at Fort Wayne

Acknowledgments

Gratitude is expressed to the West German Fulbright Commission for a travel grant which permitted me to work at the Hegel-Archiv during the summer of 1974; to Professor Otto Pöggeler and the staff of the Hegel-Archiv for making possible the 1975 - 1976 sabbatical year which I spent at the archive; to Miss Monica Bradley of Trent Polytechnic (Nottingham) for enthusiastic discussion of the developing manuscript; to Mike Ellis and Jan Hoagburg of Indiana University - Purdue University at Fort Wayne for help with typing, bibliography, and notes; to Professor Norbert Schedler for reading and commenting on Chapter 8 from the perspective of a trained theologian; to Professor Ulrich Weisstein whose numerous and patient editorial suggestions resulted in significantly greater clarity of style; and to my wife Rose-Aimée who inspired me to write a small book which would explain to her why I was always talking about Hegel, and who generously accepted the hardships of a year in Germany at reduced salary.

Chronology

1770   August 27, Georg Wilhelm Friedrich Hegel born in Stuttgart, Württemberg, the son of a government finance official.

1773   Enters German primary school.

1775   Enters Latin school.

1780   Enters *Gymnasium illustre*.

1781   Death of his mother, Maria Magdalena.

1785   Begins keeping journal in German and Latin.

1788   Graduates from *Gymnasium* and enters Lutheran seminary in Tübingen. Writes "Über einige charakteristische Unterschiede der alten Dichter" ("On Certain Differences between Ancient and Modern Poets").

1790   Receives master of philosophy degree. Forms friendship with Hölderlin and Schelling.

1793   Passes theological examinations in Tübingen; becomes house tutor in Bern, Switzerland. Begins fragments on folk religion.

1795   Writes *Das Leben Jesu (The Life of Jesus)*. Writes *Die Positivität der christlichen Religion (The Positivity of the Christian Religion)*, completed in 1796.

1797   Becomes private tutor in Frankfurt am Main.

1798   Anonymously publishes translation of letters by Cart condemning repression by aristocratic government of Bern. Writes *Der Geist des Christentums und sein Schicksal (The Spirit of Christianity and Its Fate)* and notes on economic history, completed in 1799.

1800-   Writes *Die Verfassung Deutschlands (The German*
1802   *Constitution)*.

1801   Publishes *Differenz des Fichte'schen und Schelling'schen Systems der Philosophie (The Difference between the Philosophical System of Fichte and Schelling)*. Defends thesis on planetary orbits. Becomes *Privat dozent* at the University of Jena. Lectures on Logic and Metaphysics.

1802   Lectures for first time on natural law. Publishes *Kritisches Journal der Philosophie (Critical Journal of Philosophy)* with Schelling, including *Glauben und Wissen (Faith and*

Knowledge) and *Über die wissenschaftliche Behandlung des Naturrechtes (On the Scientific Treatment of Natural Law)* by Hegel, completed in 1803.

1805 Promoted to *Ausserordentlicher Professor* on Goethe's recommendation. Lectures for the first time on the history of philosophy.

1806 Completes *Phänomenologie des Geistes (Phenomenology of Spirit)*. Leaves for Bamberg after the Battle of Jena disrupts university life.

1807 Becomes newspaper editor for French-controlled *Bamberger Zeitung*. Birth of Hegel's illegitimate son, Ludwig. Publishes *Phänomenologie*. Break with Schelling.

1808 Named director and philosophy professor at Nuremberg *Gymnasium*.

1811 Marries Maria von Tucher of Nuremberg.

1812 Publishes *Wissenschaft der Logik (Science of Logic)*, completed in 1816.

1816 Becomes *Professor* at University of Heidelberg. Coedits *Heidelberger Jahrbücher*. Illegitimate son joins Hegel household.

1817 Publishes *Enzyklopädie der philosophischen Wissenschaften (Encyclopedia of the Philosophical Sciences)* and articles on Jacobi and Württemberg. Teaches aesthetics for first time.

1818 Succeeds Fichte in philosophy chair at Berlin University.

1819 July, Henning, his assistant, imprisoned on suspicion of demagoguery. November, Hegel defends debarment of Professor de Wette for condoning assassination of the reactionary Russophile writer Kotzebue by the German patriot Sand. Friction with Schleiermacher on the issue.

1820 Becomes state examiner in Brandenburg.

1821 Publishes *Philosophie des Rechts (Philosophy of Right)* Lectures on philosophy of religion for the first time.

1822 Tours Belgium and Holland. Teaches philosophy of history for the first time.

1824 Travels to Prague and Vienna. Intercedes with Prussian government to free Victor Cousin, French philosopher friend with liberal reputation.

1826 Denied admission to Prussian Academy of Sciences, Hegel presides unofficially over foundation of Society for Scientific Criticism.

1827   Travels to Paris. Visits Goethe. Second edition of *En-zyklopädie*.

1829   Becomes rector of Berlin University. Publishes self-defense against charges of pantheism.

1830   Reacts apprehensively to July Revolution in France. Revises *Logik* for second edition.

1831   Begins revision of *Phänomenologie*. Dies suddenly in November, presumably of cholera, in Berlin. Last publication: an essay on the English Reform Bill.

CHAPTER 1

Life and Times

I   *Germany, Hellenism, and the French Revolution*

IT has been said that Hegel's life—the conventional life of a German professor—lacks intrinsic interest. But he lived from 1770 to 1831, the era of the French Revolution; and Hegel has more title than anyone else to be called the philosopher of that Revolution.[1] It is true that he was German rather than French. But it is unlikely that a Frenchman, immersed in a revolutionary political environment, could have possessed the detachment needed to comprehend so well the events through which he was living. Hegel gazed—sometimes enviously, sometimes nervously—on events transpiring on the political stage which was France. But he did so essentially as a spectator, until the success of French arms and nationalism made Germany into an importer of revolutionary institutions and led Hegel to proclaim the new order as nothing less than the kingdom of heaven on earth.[2]

Hegel's first intellectual stirrings revealed a despair about his own land which was not uncommon in his age.[3] The duchy of Württemberg in which he was born and raised was one of hundreds of sovereign states and principalities in the old Holy Roman Empire. But the atomization or fragmentation of German life was not merely political. Hegel's family, chiefly one of civil servants, teachers, and ministers, moved to the duchy several generations before Hegel's birth for the sake of their Lutheran Protestantism. Württemberg was a Protestant enclave in Swabia, surrounded by Catholic territories. Protestantism had been Germany's greatest contribution to modern culture, but since it converted only a part of the German populations it aggravated political divisions with divisions of a religious nature.

An essay surviving from Hegel's school days in Stuttgart reveals

19

his early preoccupation with the misfortunes of his country.[4] It contrasts ancient Greek poetry with that of modern Germany. Striking a theme popularized a few years later by Friedrich Schiller,[5] Hegel describes how the Greek poets coined words to formulate their experience directly and spontaneously; they were *original,* while the Germans, by contrast, lived off a borrowed Greek and Latin culture and language. This circumstance highlights a further division afflicting German life. Hegel was not the first to note that German culture, through a process of Hellenization and Christianization, was alienated from its own primeval roots in the Teutonic forests. And this cultural division reflected a further, social division: Greek and Latin culture was most deeply ingrained in the educated elites, a fact which separated them from the masses. Whereas a Greek poet enjoyed as his public the entire citizenship of his city-state or polis, German poets such as Friedrich Gottlieb Klopstock could address themselves to a sophisticated audience only at the price of sacrificing popular appeal. But Hegel did not conclude, like some romantics, by urging a retrieval of Teutonic culture and removal of foreign influences; for he felt that the loss could no longer be undone. Moreover, it was a loss which he was not inclined to bemoan, since he was already persuaded—as were most of his teachers—that the culture of ancient Greece provided an unsurpassable, classical model for all humanity. Thus Hegel commenced his intellectual Odyssey under the banner of Hellenism.

After he went to the Tübingen theological seminary in 1789, in accordance with the wishes of his father, his enthusiasm for things Greek led him to draw further contrasts between Greece and contemporary Germany. What understandably preoccupied him as a theology student was the difference between Greek religion and the Christianity to which he was exposed. He concluded that the main difference was that Greece enjoyed a *folk religion* which appealed to the imagination and engaged the heart and aesthetic sense of the individual, while Christianity was a predominantly *private religion* consisting in a set of dogmas and rituals externally imposed on the individual, thus leaving the heart cold.[6] But, most importantly, Greek folk religion elicited the individual's full participation in his city-state, while the Christianity Hegel knew was "private" in promising the individual a personal salvation unrelated to the collective fate of his people. The Christian religion thus served to detach the individual from his social environment, and to reinforce the atomization of society.

Such were the ideas germinating in Hegel's mind when the news of revolution crossed the Rhine from France. Hegel's initial enthusiasm for the Revolution can only be explained in the light of his Hellenism. He imagined he saw in the democratic ideals of the Revolution a rebirth of his classical Greek ideals of citizenship and popular political participation. Hegel's enthusiasm was shared by fellow students at the seminary, including the precocious Friedrich Wilhelm Joseph Schelling and the poet Friedrich Hölderlin. According to a story which is probably apocryphal but which still accurately reflects the revolutionary character of Hegel's views at the time, Hegel and a number of his friends ceremoniously planted a "liberty tree" outside Tübingen.[7] The enthusiasm remained unrestrained until the Reign of Terror of 1795, when Hegel, having managed to avoid parish work after graduating from the seminary two years earlier, was a private tutor in the Swiss canton of Bern.

But it was not only the latest news from France which seems to have persuaded the young Hegel that the Greek ideal could not be restored in the modern world. Despite his derogatory designation of Christianity as a "private" religion, it could not be denied that it—and not the pagan religion of Greece—remained the religion of the modern world. This realization seems to have caused Hegel to investigate the possibility of reforming modern Christianity and restoring primitive Christianity viewed as a folk religion. Hegel displayed his realistic bent by trying to realize his ideals by working within the established Christian framework. He wrote a "Life of Jesus," unpublished until this century, which portrayed Jesus as a reformer of the legalistic authoritarian religion of the Old Testament in the name of a Greek-like folk religion based on the spontanaeity of love.[8] But he soon concluded from this investigation that the failure of Jesus to convert the Hebrews to such a folk religion was inevitable because political conditions had changed. The decline of the city-state and the rise of imperial Rome made the folk religion of the city-state obsolete.[9] The private religion of orthodox Christianity suited better the political conditions of the Roman Empire. The individual Christian could not identify with the remote bureaucratic state and thus pinned his hopes on a private salvation in a transcendent heaven.

II *From Romanticism To Philosophical Realism*

The young Hegel we have described so far could aptly be called a romantic. He strove after the realization of a distant dream which he himself finally recognized as utopian. The attitude contrasts sharply with the extreme realism of the mature Hegel. The transition occurred in the last years of the eighteenth century, when, from 1796 to 1800, he was employed as a private tutor in Frankfurt. There is reason to believe that the crucial lesson was learned from the Scottish economist Sir James Steuart:[10] it was that there are necessary, inevitable stages in the economic development of society. Steuart distinguished successive pastoral, agrarian, and commercial-industrial societies. In other words, the earliest form of wealth consisted in herds; this was followed by an era in which wealth chiefly consisted in cultivated lands; and finally there occurred the age of commerce in which wealth was chiefly constituted by manufactured goods.

Hegel adopted this schema from Steuart and interpreted biblical history in terms of it. Abraham, according to Hegel, became the father of the Jews by revolting against the agrarian fate of his people, by trying to restore the obsolete pastoral way of life, thus becoming a wanderer on the face of the earth.[11] But eventually the Hebrews were obliged to follow the pattern of the peoples around them and to settle on the land. This they did by occupying the promised land and establishing a kingdom. Similarly, Jesus rebelled against the commercial fate of his age in the name of a declining agrarian culture, but the Christian church which followed was obliged to recncile itself with the inevitable rise of the commercial world.

In Hegel's own age the industrial revolution was transforming social relations; and the pursuit of private wealth regardless of public welfare was introducing a new factor of division. Yet history had taught Hegel the futility of turning one's back to the real world, of trying to escape into the past. He resolved to embrace the world and make a home for himself in it despite its apparent inhumanity. In the image he would use many years later, he resolved to discover "the rose in the cross of the present."[12] If the world seemed a sinister place, he would nonetheless stare it down. He would conquer his fate by smothering it with his embrace. It is not too much to say that the entire mature philosophy of Hegel is a vast elaboration of this single theme of reconciliation with an apparently alien world.

III   The Hegelian Dialectic

In 1801, at the invitation of his friend and Tübingen classmate Schelling, Hegel left Frankfurt for the university town of Jena.

Schelling, five years Hegel's junior, had already made a considerable reputation for himself. He stood at the center of the revolutionary philosophical movement in Germany initiated by Immanuel Kant and developed by Johann Gottlieb Fichte. In going to Jena to teach philosophy for the first time, Hegel implicitly admitted a change which had just recently come over his thinking. For the first time he now conceived his life work to be that of a philosopher, rather than merely that of a critic of society and religion. He wrote to Schelling that his goal was now to express the "ideal of his youth in reflective form."[13] By the ideal of his youth he meant the ideal of reconciliation and oneness with the social environment. It was an ideal which had been realized imaginatively by means of art and myth in classical Greece; but, in the modern world of nation states vastly larger and economically more developed than the Greek city-states, the ideal could only be realized philosophically, that is, conceptually rather than aesthetically.

The modern world suffered from division or alienation, and it was the experience of division, Hegel wrote, which engendered the need for philosophy.[14] But philosophy could both account for the origin of this division and provide the means of overcoming it. Explanation of how this is possible requires introduction of the difficult "dialectical" concepts forged by Hegel. The division between oneself and one's environment, between the self and the "not-self," subject and object, has its ultimate source in the human faculty of abstract thought. The self feels unable to identify with its environment because it *thinks*, because thought is abstract, and because by means of thought the self *abstracts* itself from the primitive union with the environment characteristic of the nonhuman animals. The self abstracts itself from the environment and then becomes *fixated* on this abstract self-concept. It absolutizes its abstract self apart from the world. But because the self is really inseparably bound up with its environment, it fails to escape the environment, but rather experiences it as something essentially *other* than itself. Because the self is fixated on itself in abstraction from the environment or "other," it seeks to repudiate or *negate* the other. However, because the self is nonetheless essentially related to the other, the attempted negation of the other is really *self-negation*. Negation of the other calls forth negation of the self by the other. This self-negation of the self can be overcome only if the self surrenders its fixation on an abstract self-concept and comes to redefine itself less abstractly, more concretely, as essentially related to its environment or other. This more concrete redefinition of oneself in relation to the other or "not-self" is, in accordance with Hegelian terminology, called *negation of the negation*. The self's negation of its other—and hence of itself—is itself negated. Negation of the negation is a philosophical act of "concrete thinking" which solves the problem of division (alienation) created by abstract thinking. Through concrete thinking philosophy is capable of solving the human problem.[15]

These are the central thoughts to which, in Jena, Hegel sought to give ever more satisfactory systematic development. But it must not be supposed that the ideal of reconciliation of self and other, subject and object, was unique to Hegel. Its germ is detectable in the philosophy of Kant, and as we move from Kant to Fichte, Schiller, Hölderlin and, finally, Schelling it becomes ever more prominent. Hegel, building on Schelling, brings in the harvest sown by others.

Schelling had developed a romantic philosophy of nature which sought to overcome the division between man ("spirit") and nature by reinterpreting nature as "slumbering spirit," and thus as only apparently alien to man. Hegel embraced this philosophy of nature, which expressed his own belief as to the underlying identity of subject and object.[15] But, unlike Schelling, he was not content to consider this belief merely the result of a conceptually inarticulate *intuition*. The intuition was really the conclusion of a logical process of thinking, and Hegel felt that the whole logical process by which abstract thinking created oppositions and then passed into concrete thinking in order to resolve them needed to be articulated and made explicit. He was thus led to create a "logic" as an essential division of a complete system of philosophy. This division preceded and prepared the way for the philosophy of nature. Finally, he did not believe that man's ability to recognize his identity with even "inanimate" matter through a romantic philosophy of nature constituted a complete realization of the ideal of subject-object identity. Nature may in reality be spirit, but it is only slumbering spirit, not spirit awakened to full life. This awakening occurs only beyond the realm of nature, in the specifically human realm of history, institutions, and culture. The oneness of man with nature is most truly appreciated, not by speechless communion with nature, but by the realization that nature is the necessary condition of the emergence of human life, of "spirit" in the proper sense. Thus Hegel was led to make room for a philosophy of spirit as the third and crowning division of his system of philosophy.[17]

The mature Hegelian philosophy is thus divided into three

branches: logic, philosophy of nature, and philosophy of spirit. The logic explains the meaning of concrete thinking; the philosophy of nature shows how nature, despite its apparent "otherness" in relation to man, is really spirit in disguise; and the philosophy of spirit shows how man finally realizes himself in the realm of institutional and cultural history. All three branches of the system are developed from the Schellingian standpoint of the identity of subject and object. The nonidentity or opposition of thought and matter (nature) is indeed allowed to develop within the system—that is what happens when the logic passes into the philosophy of nature—but since the opposition is developed within the system, it is known from the start to be a nonabsolute or nonultimate one. It is developed because ultimate self-realization, that is, self-recognition in the other, is essentially the overcoming of alienation, that is, of nonself-recognition in the other; thus self-realization presupposes alienation.

It is only from the standpoint of abstract thought which has not yet developed into concrete thought that the opposition between thought and matter appears as absolute and unbridgeable. The problem of "introducing" the ordinary man to the Hegelian philosophy is the problem of leading him from abstract to concrete relational thought. It is Hegel's claim that abstract thought pushed to its logical conclusion itself leads to the standpoint of concrete thinking. During the Jena years, Hegel struggled with the attempt to provide an introduction to his system, tracing the gradual transition to concrete thinking. The ultimate result of this struggle was his first full-length book, *The Phenomenology of Spirit* (1807).

IV   *The Progress of a Career: 1806 - 1831*

Completion of the *Phenomenology* coincided with the close of Hegel's career in Jena, which ended with Napoleon's historic victory over Prussia at the battle of Jena. The war disrupted university life and obliged Hegel to seek employment elsewhere: in Bamberg, where he became a newspaper editor. And in the following year he accepted an appointment, which he held for several years, as director of a *Gymnasium* in Nuremberg. During all these years, Hegel maintained a consistently pro-Napoleonic attitude. Prior to the battle of Waterloo he wrote in a letter that if he saw any hope of success for Napoleon he would take a rifle and join him in Paris.[18] This enthusiasm can only be explained by his belief that Napoleon was trying to introduce modern, rational, and constitutional institutions—the best fruit of the Revolution in France—in politically backward Germany. And it is important to remember that his later Prussianism was conditioned by the belief, which perhaps was not so wild in the 1820s, that Prussia was the most politically advanced state of Europe and had appropriated the cause of the French Revolution.

Hegel's exile from university life came to an end in 1816, when he went to the University of Heidelberg. Two years later he moved to Berlin University, where he taught until his death in 1831 and where he attained world fame. After having published his *Logic* between 1812 and 1816, he brought out an overview of his entire system, the *Encyclopaedia of Philosophical Sciences* (1817), in Heidelberg, while his *Philosophy of Right* (that is, *Philosophy of Law* to use more idiomatic English) followed in 1821. Only these three books plus the *Phenomenology* were published during his lifetime. The substantial remainder of his complete works consists in early unpublished writings, shorter essays, occasional writings, and, especially, in several series of lectures on the philosophy of art, the philosophy of religion, the history of philosophy, and the philosophy of history.

The years in Heidelberg and Berlin did not bring any far-reaching revision of his system. They were years of continuous and confident elaboration. Hegel knew in his last years a success beyond the dreams of most philosophers. He enjoyed the support of highly placed persons in the Prussian government, and, although his position was not uncontested, he gained the reputation of being the "official" Prussian philosopher. Yet Hegel was probably the most ambitious philosopher who ever lived, and in terms of his own goal of establishing a philosophical civilization to rival the aesthetic civilization of ancient Greece he must be counted a failure. He began his teaching career in Jena with the claim that philosophy had become the chief requirement of the age. It is only in relation to the ambitiousness of this claim that one can appreciate the full pathos of his admission in 1830 that philosophy was, after all, only for the isolated few.[19] Despite his unswerving criticism of ordinary religious images and modes of representation he came to the conclusion that most people were content to assimilate the truth in this inferior form. Yet Hegel's impact on the intellectual world of the past one hundred and fifty years has been unrivaled. Different philosophical movements of the post-Hegelian era—Marxism, existentialism, pragmatism, analytic philosophy—may fruitfully be viewed as a series of reactions to Hegelianism. Each of these schools of thought self-consciously opposed Hegel, but except for the analytic movement—which took its start with Bertrand Russell and G. E. Moore—this opposition was accompanied by considerable (though often covert) borrowing from Hegel.[20] A Hegel renaissance in the present century—beginning in Germany, gaining force in France, already invading American shores—has done much to uncover the Hegelian roots of post-Hegelian thought. But the significance of such a renaissance will remain limited if it does not go beyond historical erudition. The important question is whether the Hegel renaissance is capable of reversing the philosophical loss of nerve caused in the last century by the original decline of Hegelianism. This is the question to which we may expect an answer in the years to come. The question is posed as to whether the driving ambition of Hegel's life, in which he himself, perhaps somewhat impatiently, confessed failure, many not be capable of posthumous realization.

CHAPTER 2

Hegelianism: The Problem of an Introduction

I T might fairly be supposed that this volume should offer an "introduction" to the Hegelian philosophy. In the case of thinkers less systematic than Hegel, an introduction to the man's life and intellectual development, such as was sketched only briefly in Chapter 1, would count at once as an introduction to his philosophy. But Hegel was one of those rare philosophers whose life was not spent in the vain pursuit of a satisfying system, and this imposes on us the responsibility of considering this philosophical system in and for itself, apart from the facts of Hegel's biography.

Our task would thus seem to be to provide an introduction to the Hegelian system. And in fact, ever since Hegel himself billed his *Phenomenology of Spirit* as the introduction and first part of his system[1] much has been written on the topic. But if we consider the matter more closely, it will appear that the very idea of an "introduction" to the Hegelian system is a contradiction in terms. For it is of the nature of this system that, if its claim to truth and *completeness* is to be sustained, no standpoint can really be external to it.[2] Hegel's system is essentially one of alternative standpoints arranged in a series leading from the less truthful and complete to the more complete. And each standpoint except the first is to arise out of an internal self-analysis and self-criticism of the previous standpoint. This means that what passes for an "introduction" to the system can, in fact, be nothing more than the discovery that one's thought already is, and has been, operating from within the system. In other words, an introduction to the Hegelian system can only be an *internal* introduction. But if one is already inside the system the question of being introduced to it can no longer arise. This explains why the idea of an introduction to Hegelianism is really a self-contradiction. What is called an introduction is, from

28

the Hegelian standpoint, more properly described as the system's own self-discovery. For Hegel this self-discovery of the system is a momentous and even cosmic event. We shall see that for Hegel the system of philosophical thought is the highest achievement of the universe or—as he himself would put it—of the "Absolute." What is in question is nothing less than the universe's own self-discovery. Because man is part of the universe his consciousness of the universe is at once the universe's awareness of itself.

It might now seem that we should go ahead and try to explain with Hegel how everyone has already been a Hegelian all his life, but did not know it! But because of the large variety of individual standpoints this is impossible to do within the compass of the present volume. We cannot take the time to start from the most incomplete or "abstract" standpoint and follow it all the way to the final point of view. Instead, this book begins with the most primitive *religious* standpoint, in order to show how it, according to Hegel, is already encompassed within the perspective of his system. Hegel's perspective is that of philosophy. He takes philosophy to be the ultimate standpoint. In selecting religion as my starting point, I am considerably simplifying the task of developing the Hegelian standpoint. This is because religion for Hegel is penultimate; in other words, it is surpassed only by philosophy itself.

In a broad sense, religion is defined by Hegel as the universe's or the Absolute's consciousness of itself.[3] In this sense, philosophy is also religion. More narrowly interpreted, however, religion is distinguished from philosophy: in religion, the Absolute attains self-consciousness in the form of myth, image, and symbol, while in philosophy this same self-consciousness dispenses with imagery and articulates itself in the form of pure imageless thought.[4] But it must not be supposed that religion arises in a historical vacuum. On the contrary, it presupposes and encompasses specific natural, economic, social, political, and artistic conditions. Thus in expounding the religion of a people all the essential aspects of its social existence come in for discussion.[5] In Hegel's view, the art or politics of a people is finally comprehended through its religious context in a way in which the religion is not comprehended through art or politics. Religion is a concrete *organic whole* of which art and politics are but essential *aspects*, and to comprehend the whole is impossible without explicit reference to these aspects, while the attempt to comprehend each aspect without explicit reference to the whole fails even as a comprehension of the aspect.

Thus in taking the religious standpoint as our starting point we shall be obliged to bring apparently nonreligious aspects of life into the discussion, and this will serve the purpose of acquainting the reader with Hegel's understanding of much else than religion narrowly interpreted. It may be asked how it will be possible for one to understand a complex phenomenon such as religion before its various constituent aspects have been studied separately and for themselves. The answer is that familiarity with both religion and its aspects may be presupposed on the part of the reader. For, after all, we have been raised in what is known as the Christian civilization, and this civilization presupposes previous religious traditions out of which it has grown. Thus Hegel's philosophy does not pretend to teach one what he does not already know, but only to help one become intellectually aware of what he previously knew more dimly by way of myth, allegory, poetry, imagery, and symbolism.[6] The objective is that one should come to *think* what previously he only *felt*.

It is of interest that when Hegel himself, as a philosophy teacher in a German *Gymnasium,* was faced with the problem of expounding his philosophy on an elementary level to students approximating what in the United States would be the high school to junior college level, he decided against beginning with the seemingly arid abstractions of pure logic. He found that he had more success presenting problems and concepts of social ethics and religion, which had the advantage of already seeming relevant to the students.[7] But if one keeps in mind the intimate connection which Hegel postulates between social ethics and religion, between the institutions (for example, family, state) which define a people's life-form and the religion in which it attains consciousness of itself and its relation to the universe, it will appear that the approach adopted in this book is very close to Hegel's own approach in a similar situation.

What we must do is distinguish between the *objective* starting point for the exposition of Hegel's philosophy and the *subjective* starting point. The objective starting point is *absolute,* whereas the subjective starting point is not absolute but *relative* to the situation of the person to whom the system of philosophy is being expounded for the first time. The objective starting point in Hegel's view is the most abstract standpoint, that is, the one whose concept of reality is the most *abstract,* least rich in many-sidedness, least *concrete.*[8] It is axiomatic for Hegel that wealth of content, differentiation, articulated complexity, what Hegel calls "mediation," is the result of a process of development or derivation. Objectively or, as Hegel sometimes says, *in itself* (as contrasted, in this case, to *for the beginner*) a complex (that is, concrete) whole of essentially related aspects can only be articulated on the basis of the prior articulation of the simple (that is, abstract) aspects of that whole. Thus, objectively, Hegel's exposition of his own system begins with those arid abstractions of logic which do not, even in his own view, recommend themselves as the starting point of an exposition directed to beginners. To be sure, philosophy moves in the rarefied atmosphere of conceptual abstraction, and thus I would not be giving an exposition of Hegel's philosophy if I did not at some point expect the reader to begin to breathe at those giddy heights. But within my subjective exposition the plan will be to lead the reader *toward* the secrets of Hegel's *Logic*, not to start off profaning them by what might well seem mere gibberish. What is most holy must be treated with due reverence, and not casually wasted on a hearer not yet prepared to understand it. It is for that reason that the summary of Hegel's dialectic was given in Chapter 1 only with some reluctance. It may bear some rereading as one progresses through the text.

CHAPTER 3

Oriental Despotism or Paradise Lost

I   *The General Nature of Religion*

ACCORDING to Hegel, religion is rooted in the abiding human condition. It is of the very essence of religion to affirm the omnipotence of the spirit of man.[1] This belief is common to all forms of religion and is enshrined in myth and ritual. Yet the belief appears in flat contradiction to the testimony of ordinary experience, which would seem to demonstrate that man is essentially insecure, vulnerable, finite, dependent on an alien environment which he can never completely control, and born into a hostile world on which he nonetheless vitally depends.[2] But there is something in man which makes him unable totally to accept this apparently obvious fact of human finitude. Man, according to Hegel, has intimations of his own essential divinity and infinitude.

Hegel's conviction as to the deep-lying infinitude or divinity of man's self-identity has attained striking confirmation in our own century from an unsuspected source. Sigmund Freud held that man's unshakable tendency to believe in his essential invulnerability and omnipotence has its basis in the *postnatal* reminiscence of the *prenatal* experience of total security which the human infant presumably had in its mother's womb.[3] The human species is distinguished by a prolonged prenatal life in the womb, and it is not unreasonable to suppose that these nine months of relative bliss, protected as one is from the rude shocks of this world, should exercise some appeal on one in postnatal life. The intimation of one's infinitude Freud calls the "oceanic feeling." To say, with Hegel, that man by nature tends to identify himself with a being such as God may, in fact, amount to little more than the assertion that the oceanic feeling is natural to man by virtue of his biological situation.

Freud considered himself an atheist. He wished to explain

32

religion away. Hegel, on the other hand, regarded himself as a believer in the existence of God and, in fact, wished through his philosophy to give a rational justification of Christianity. It is thus worth noting that the atheistic conclusion that there is no God does not logically follow from the theory of the oceanic feeling. A Hegelian can point out that there really exists a reality which is independent, infinite, and unlimited. This divine reality is what Hegel calls the Absolute.[4] And it is identical with the universe, which is also unlimited; for if the universe were not all-encompassing, if it were relative to something outside it, it simply would not be the universe. However, if we identify the Hegelian Absolute with the universe and leave it at that, we open the door to *pantheism*, that is, to an identification of God with nature, the world of physical or material reality. Hegel strenuously objected to the suggestion that he was a pantheist.[5] And there was more in this objection than the desire not to be associated with what in the Christian world was considered a heretical belief. Hegel was an *idealist*, not a *materialist*. He insisted that the Absolute is ultimately spirit, not matter. For him the universe is not truly understood as long as it is conceived in purely material terms.

II   *The Religion of Magic*

So far we have been speaking of religion in extremely general terms. We have identified a common feature of all religion: man's intimation of his own infinitude. But if we restrict ourselves merely to this, we shall have a very poor, undeveloped notion of religion. Nonetheless, in accordance with Hegel's method of proceeding from the simple (immediate, abstract) to the complex (mediation, concreteness), it is with this undeveloped notion of religion that we must begin. In the remainder of this book I shall follow Hegel's method—the so-called dialectical method.[6] I shall reconstruct the development of religion from its most primitive to its final, most developed form. We shall see how the religions of the world tend to follow one another in a logical order, and this order will largely be that of their historical development. We begin with the chronologically earliest of religions, that of prehistorical man.

The only place within Hegel's mature system where he treats human prehistory thematically is the section in his lectures on the philosophy of religion dealing with the "religion of magic," which he takes to be the earliest and simplest form of religion.[7] But the

religion of magic has itself a complex development. In its first form
it arises out of primitive man's experience of "undisturbed unity"
with his natural environment.[8] This distant, original condition of
man had, ever since Jean - Jacques Rousseau's celebration of the
"noble savage," exercised an attraction on the romantic sensibility
of Hegel's age. The Garden of Eden in which Adam and Eve lived
before the Fall was equated with Paradise, so that the Fall of man
was, in turn, equated with the *loss* of Paradise. In the pessimistic,
forlorn outlook of some romantics, the history of man has been one
of degeneration, of an irreversible *falling away* from a primitive
Golden Age in which man lived wisely and happily in unison with
nature. The original, natural state of man was seen as one of
childhood, innocence, and moral purity.

Hegel was highly critical of this romantic vision. It must not be
supposed, however, that he rejected the ideal of oneness with
nature. On the contrary, this oneness, expressed as the "identity of
subject (spirit) and object (nature)," stands at the very center of his
own philosophical vision. Hegel even agrees that this identity existed at the prehistorical beginning of man's career. What he denies
is simply that this original identity was the true or perfectly realized
identity of man and nature.[9] It is basic to Hegelian logic that *identity* also entails *difference.* In other words, two things cannot really
be known to be identical until they have first been distinguished.
The prehistorical identity of spirit and nature is thus an immediate,
unrecognized one. For the truth that man and nature are one to
become known—for spirit's identity with nature to become self-
conscious—it must first be denied. Man must first attempt to rise
above nature and assert himself against it, in order to discover the
ultimate futility of the attempt and the necessity of reconciliation
with nature. The Garden of Eden cannot, Hegel says, have truly
been Paradise, since if it had it would never have been lost.[10]
"Paradise Lost" is a contradiction in terms. The Fall was necessary
for man's ultimate self-realization. To be sure, man was not evil
before the Fall, but Hegel insists that he was not really good either.
Before the Fall, man lived in a plantlike or animallike state of innocence, but because this vegetative state leaves potentials which
set man apart from other living beings unfulfilled, it is a guilty innocence, an innocence which contradicts man's peculiar good.[11]
Human goodness lies in the overcoming of evil. Evil must therefore
be committed in order for good to be done. *Evil*, for Hegel, essentially consists in man's use of his free will to assert himself, his

private interest, apart from the welfare of some larger whole in which he is contained.[12] *Goodness* consists in denying this egotistic, exclusive self-assertion through discovery of one's inseparability from this larger whole.

But while insisting that the Garden of Eden was not really Paradise, Hegel still holds that, in a sense, it really once existed and indeed was man's original state. Viewed economically, Adam and Eve before the Fall were food gatherers. They were provided with a plentiful supply of natural vegetation which made toil unnecessary.[13] Needs were simple, and they were as a rule easily satisfied. However, it is not to be excluded that occasional emergencies or states of deprivation occurred even in Eden. In such emergencies, when he does not know how else to cope, man resorts to magic. Hegel calls the magic practiced at this most primitive stage of human development *immediate magic.*[14] What this means is that man, in resorting to magic, seeks to control a temporarily hostile nature by means of his own hidden powers, without any reliance on the magical powers of external objects or beings. One may, for example, attempt to cause rain by orally commanding the skies, by uttering a magical formula which is supposed to cast a spell over natural processes.

Yet it is doubtful to Hegel whether this immediate magic—which he also calls direct magic—really merits the title "religion."[15] To be sure, it resembles religion in that it displays a belief in the supremacy of the human spirit over the forces of nature. It reflects what we have seen to be, for Hegel, a basically religious belief in the omnipotence of the human spirit. However, a second essential element of true religion is missing: awareness (objectification) of God as a power distinguished from the finite, conscious human individual. Whereas in religion the individual characteristically seeks to escape natural threats and deprivation by putting himself in the hands of God, in direct magic the individual rather attributes all power of control over nature to himself.

Still, even if immediate magic is not yet religion, we should reflect that it is not *yet* religion, for it is within it that truer religion emerges. Within immediate magic a distinction gradually emerges between the individual who uses magic when he is viewed as a natural, ordinary, finite iindividual and when he is viewed as identified with the extraordinary creative, cosmic power which he taps through the use of magic.[16] The practice of magic requires that the individual, shaman, or witch doctor incorporate within himself ex-

traordinary creative power, that is, "mana." And once this extraordinary magical power is *objectified,* once it becomes something the
magician is aware of, it becomes possible to speak of a "religion of
magic." Still, this religion of immediate magic, in which the magician solicits possession by the extraordinary but normally hidden
power of the cosmos, is a very imperfect realization of the idea of
religion because the individual's motives are largely utilitarian and
self-centered. The individual *uses* the extraordinary power more
than he *worships* it. The element of "free adoration," of faithful
reverence, is missing. [17]

III   *The Fall From Paradise*

So far, we have been discussing the emergence of religion in the
idyllic Garden of Eden. Now let us look at what happens with the
Fall. In the first place, man is condemned to live by the sweat of his
brow. In other words, *labor* becomes the necessary basis of human
life. [18] What distinguishes labor from primitive food gathering as the
basis of life is the making and use of tools, such as the bow and
arrow and other weapons which were invented as man became a
hunter. The introduction of tools created a new relation between
man and nature. Man as a user of tools falls away from his prior
unity with nature. He withdraws from nature in order to
manipulate it, making it into his *other,* the other of spirit. [19] For the
first time, man begins to see nature as a despiritualized system of interacting things. [20] Previously, at the stage of food gathering and
direct magic, nature was alive with spirit. The food gatherer, into
whose idle hands ripened fruit naturally falls, experiences nature as
autonomous and self-creative. This primitive spiritism is, further,
presupposed by the attempt of direct magic to control nature by
commanding it or imploring it with magical formulas. (Yet direct
magic does not consist in the "worship" of these nature spirits; they
are poorer than the spirit which man musters in controlling them.)
But as man develops into a tool user, he begins to calculate that if
he performs such and such an operation, a given result will
mechanically follow. Man becomes a disembodied *subject* over
against nature; his task now is to be a thinking thing, and to master
nature as reduced to the level of a mere *object.*

The mental outlook of the tool user produces a corresponding
form of magic. No matter how hard the user of tools labors, there
will be times when even he needs to resort to magic. But the con-

cept of magic natural to a user of tools will be broader than the merely immediate or direct magic of a primitive, nontool-using gatherer. Immediate magic will be supplemented by the resources of mediate or *indirect magic*,[21] which implies the use of the magical power of "means" or external objects as well as that of the magician. Stated otherwise, the magic of a tool user will be broadened to allow for a variety of *magical tools:* charms, amulets, medicines, totems, and fetishes. But we must not suppose that there is a neat division between magical tools and ordinary implements such as a bow and arrow. For the way in which many an ordinary and quite efficient tool works is mysterious to its user and thus magical.[22]

In discussing direct magic, we saw how the distinction emerged between the ordinary man who resorts to magic and the extraordinary magical, creative power which must possess him if he is to succeed in the use of magic. A similar distinction now occurs in the realm of indirect magic between the ordinary natural object and the extraordinary power which it manifests when used as a magical tool. The religion of indirect magic qualifies as a religion because it objectifies the divine or extraordinary power which selected natural objects may manifest. It is the awareness of this power as something more than a mere natural object which is religious. Yet it must not be supposed that the distinction between the divine power and the ordinary object in which it resides is clearly made at the level of indirect magic. It must be remembered that we are still dealing with a very primitive form of religion. The distinction may, at most, be felt, but it is not yet made conceptually. Thus it may appear to an outsider who does clearly make the distinction that the hunting tribe worships ordinary finite objects, in contrast to the infinite cosmic power which may be accidentally manifest in those objects. But this is a misunderstanding due to the fact that the outside observer is imposing on the primitive experience of the world a conceptual distinction which has no place in that experience.

The range of natural objects which can function as fetishes is quite broad: inanimate objects, animals, even human beings. The possibility of a human being serving as a fetish or magical tool is of particular interest because of its importance in the transition from the religion of magic to the more advanced "religion of substance," illustrated by the emperor worship of China.[23] The socioeconomic condition of this transition is the domestication of animals and the agricultural revolution, which for the first time created durable wealth, a need for servile labor, and an authoritarian-hierarchical social structure. With the creation of durable wealth—herds and farmlands—under patriarchal control, the community as a whole loses its former freedom and subjects itself to the patriarchal leader. Individuals other than the leader come to view themselves as essentially dependent. They cease to attribute any magical power to themselves and, innstead, turn to the patriarch-priest for the paternal, protective exercise of magical power on their behalf.

Yet at the first stage of this religion of priest fetishism we can no more speak of genuine reverence for the father-priest-magician than we can speak of reverence for any fetish. The father-priest is at first merely used as a magical tool, and is tossed away in favor of some one else when his magic seems to work no longer.[24] True fidelity to the priest would seem to emerge only after he has acquired the political power to punish infidelity, that is, only when he has become a patriarch. But further consideration of patriarchy—the political rule of the father-priest—would take us beyond prehistory and its religion of magic into the historical realm of the state and the higher religion of substance based upon it. Our purpose thus far has merely been to restate briefly Hegel's views on prehistory, and that purpose has now been essentially accomplished.

Reflecting on the views I have just summarized, one is struck by the degree to which Hegel's views on prehistory anticipate evolutionary theories which were to develop later in the nineteenth century. And this is so even though Hegel did not adopt the theory of biological evolution which was later to be made scientifically respectable by Charles Darwin. The evolutionary interpretation of human prehistory has been widely criticized since the last century, and the possibility of establishing a single necessary evolutionary sequence such as the one which Hegel suggests has been frequently discounted. The very attempt to do so is often dismissed as "speculative." It is true that the hypothesis of a "Garden of Eden" marked by an immediate unity between man and nature is incapable of empirical verification. Although there are primitive peoples who, at least until very recently, lived principally from food gathering, it is surely hazardous to identify such peoples as survivors of a primordial stage of man's existence upon his descent from the trees. The arguments for the "Garden of Eden" hypothesis are theoretical rather than empirical (for example, the apes from which man descended are not hunters), but they are not therefore to be neglected.

One final reflection on Hegel's treatment of prehistory has to do with his anticipation of another movement of late nineteenth-century thought: Marxism. In the above exposition we have deliberately made explicit Hegel's often implicit or casual references to the economic conditions underlying religious evolution. Karl Marx was himself highly critical of Hegel for having denied the economic basis of all higher spiritual life. Friedrich Engels recounts that Marx found Hegel standing on his head and proceeded to set him back on his feet.[25] But the truth seems to be that Hegel was standing on his feet all along, but simply did not stare at them as intensely as Marx desired.

IV   *Political Despotism in China*

With a quick survey of the Hegelian view of prehistory behind us, the stage is now set to examine the first form of historical civilization taken up by Hegel in his *Philosophy of History*: the so-called "Oriental despotism" of ancient China. Hegel labored under the misapprehension, which was general in his time, that China was the oldest, as well as the longest surviving, of world civilizations.[26] He was misled by China's own historians, whose traditionalism led them to look for a model for the present in the original and most ancient stage of Chinese history. Since the historians of imperial China found it hard to believe that the Golden Age was an age of political disunity, they tended to project *contemporary* ancient kingdoms into successively more remote and hence more venerable pasts. In this way they could retain their belief that China was originally a full-blown and unified empire. Today we know that China, though perhaps the longest continuously existing civilization, is certainly not the oldest: historians date the beginning of the first dynasty not much before the middle of the second millenium B.C.

If Hegel had presented himself as a historian, his mistake as to the antiquity of China would no doubt be a serious flaw. But because he claimed only to be a philosopher of history the error is less damaging than might be thought. China merits its position as the first civilization to be treated in his philosophy of history not because it is the oldest civilization, but because it illustrates civilization at its most primitive stage. This most primitive stage is patriarchy[27] or, to use a less neutral expression used by Hegel himself, despotism.[28] And because China serves as his prime example of despotic government, Hegel speaks of "Oriental despotism."[29] It is a phrase which continues to enjoy rather widespread currency.

It should be remembered, however, that except for the fact that the Aztecs are no longer around to illustrate for us civilization at its most primitive Hegel might have been as justified in speaking of "middle American despotism." There is certainly no reason to suppose that the Oriental mind is somehow intrinsically or peculiarly despotic. For if Hegel is right, all more advanced civilizations, including those of the Western world, originally inherited and built upon a despotic basis. At a certain level of abstraction, China gives the Western nations an image of their own past. Hegel would have been better advised to avoid the potentially racist overtones of "Oriental despotism" and to have simply spoken of "despotism" or, better still, "political patriarchy."

V   *Freedom: Prehistorical and Posthistorical*

Hegel's philosophy of history conveys the notion that civilization "goes West," that is, that it originates in China, migrates to India, from there moves to the Middle East, Greece, Rome, and then northern, Germanic Europe, until it finally jumps across the Atlantic to America.[30] If the "world spirit" indeed follows the sun in this way, we might expect it by this time to be preparing a gigantic leap across the Pacific back to China again![31] But although there is some historical basis for saying that Rome, for example, took over and further developed Greek civilization, or, more obviously, that the United States inherited the civilization of Europe, there is no basis whatsoever for saying that India took over and developed the civilization of China. The truth is, rather, that for the most part India and China developed autonomously. And what borrowing did take place between the two cultures went from India in the West to China in the East rather than the other way around: no Chinese influence on India is comparable with the impact of Buddhism on China.

The more defensible of Hegelian claims, and the one which lies more at the heart of Hegel's philosophical vision, is thus not that European civilization historically grew out of the civilization of China, but that it grew out of despotic beginnings *somewhere*. But what is despotism? It is, to begin with, a political system in which only *one man* is explicitly recognized to be free: the despot himself. History then moves, for Hegel, to a condition where *some* but not all are free, and finally culminates in universal freedom: the *universal* recognition of man by man.[32] Thus history moves on this model—which is by no means peculiar to Hegel—toward ever broader extensions of freedom.

But this way of putting it suggests that Hegel was an "evolutionary optimist" who thought that the passage of time automatically spells progress toward the abolition of human suffering. To correct this impression, it is sufficient to recall that, although Hegel believed that *history* begins with despotism, human evolution did not for him begin with historical recollection. I have already discussed his view of prehistory, and it may be said that the first stage of prehistory—the Garden of Eden before the Fall—was a stage of implicit universal freedom. There then reigned the freedom of the prepolitical state of nature, of the noble savage of whom Jean - Jacques Rousseau spoke. Since there was no durable wealth to speak of when man was a food gatherer in Eden, there was no economic inequality. Nor, without wealth, was there any need for servile labor. The need for such labor emerges only with the domestication of animals and the agricultural revolution. For the man who has more land or a larger herd than other men is apt to have more than he can tend to himself. He is apt to require the labor of others less fortunate than himself. But the *servitude* of one man means the *despotism* of another. The transition from prehistory to recorded history presupposes the agricultural revolution and an accompanying autocracy. It is the despot who creates recorded history, by employing historians to record and transmit his achievements. Thus for Hegel human history, which advances toward universal freedom, begins with a tragic *loss* of universal freedom.

This is not to say, however, that history, for Hegel, is a circular movement which eventually returns to the point from which it originally departed. For the *post*historical freedom toward which history moves is qualitatively different from the *pre*historical freedom from which it departs. In Hegel's view, the real Golden Age does not lie in the prehistorical past, but *before us* as the culmination of history. And what makes the difference between the prehistorical freedom of the noble savage and posthistorical freedom is the intervening reign of despotism. Servitude is the historical cross which man must bear in order to be resurrected in a life of genuine freedom. It is through acquiescing in servitude, through the acceptance of despotism, through learning obedience,

that one eventually learns to command oneself, to channel the flow
of natural impulse. Whereas the noble savage knows only the
freedom of impulsiveness, of doing what he wishes, posthistorical
man learns the freedom of autonomy or rational self-determination.

VI   Despotism: Political and Domestic

An aspect of Hegel's idea of despotism which deserves further
attention is its connection with patriarchy, that is, with the
authoritarian rule of the father. Most sociologists and
anthropologists will tell us that there has never been such a thing as
matriarchy. Authoritarian or despotic rule thus seems restricted to
societies with a male-dominated patriarchal family structure.
Patriarchy is found in nomadic prehistorical (that is, prepolitical)
societies, for example, among herding tribes. But in his philosophy
of history Hegel is not concerned with such societies. What distinguishes patriarchy as a *historical* reality is its political organization into a territorially fixed state. It is in a stable agricultural state
that a literate leisure class capable of historical record-keeping can
come into existence.

We are now in a position to restate in a more illuminating way
Hegel's concept of political despotism. A despotic state, whether it
exists in the West or the Orient, today or hundreds of years ago, is a
state which is modeled on the idea of the patriarchal family. The
principle of the patriarchal family is transferred to the political level
and applied to the state as a whole. The despot assumes in relation
to the people the position of a father in relation to his underage
children.[33] Despotism is the most primitive form of the state
because what distinguishes the state from the more ancient institution of the family is not yet clearly perceived. What is new and un-
familiar is falsely modeled on what is old and familiar.

To understand more exactly Hegel's concept of despotism, we
must look more closely at the patriarchal family on which it is
modeled. What needs noting is that the patriarchal family *as such*
assures no rights whatsoever to the children or wife.[34] Unless the
state intervenes in the life of the family, the father has the right to
do whatever he pleases with any member of his family, even to the
point of killing him. But if the state itself is modeled on the
patriarchal family, it is not yet sufficiently independent of the family to assure protection of the children and wife from the father. A
despotic state is an imitation family, the despot an imitation father,

with the result that all his subjects become imitation children. The despot may well decide in any given case to exercise his paternalistic right to protect his subjects from their biological fathers, but the point is that he has no obligation to do so, and his subjects have no legal rights.

A legal right is a politically recognized and protected claim to some freedom of action, to freedom from interference by others. It is obvious that there are many rights enjoyed by adults which children do not have, if only because they do not yet know how to stake out claims upon the respect of others. Despotism means treating all subjects, even adults, as dependent children without rights. At the other extreme from despotism is a state in which all individuals, even children, are raised to the level of adults with legally protected rights with respect to one another. If despotism models the state on the family, the opposite extreme is to remake the family in the image of the (nondespotic) state, that is, of a political society of adults, so that even babies are endowed with "putative rights" claimed by the state on their behalf until they are old enough to claim the rights themselves.

Hegel would no doubt subscribe to the widely held view that an important difference between the Orient influenced by China and European civilization is that the family is far stronger in the Orient than it is in the West. The Chinese practice of ancestor worship is merely an extrapolation of a deeply ingrained respect for age and, in particular, for one's own parents. A traditional Chinese son would not think of putting his parents in a state nursing home, nor would a traditional Chinese parent think of putting his son out on his own in the school of hard knocks at eighteen with a handshake, a pat on the back, and a five-dollar bill (or loan repayable with interest). The American family, with its paper routes and savings accounts for each child, is a self-consciously temporary affair, a kind of training in financial self-reliance. The West German university student can sue his father for financial support. A widowed French father knows that he does not own his house, but merely holds it in trust for his children. In a number of ways we see how, in the West, the model of the business world—of "civil society" to use Hegel's own expression—insinuates itself into the family and modifies parent-child and husband-wife relationships. We sometimes hear the complaint that business relationships have no place in the family, that they undermine the natural bonds of trust and love. But the family may have to be undermined in this way if individual freedom (for example, the freedom of job choice or marriage) is to be protected. It may not be possible to have both individual rights and maximally strong family bonds or identification with the family group. One suspects that another name for what is called "strong family ties" is "despotism." Note, however, that despotism need not be experienced as a yoke around one's neck. It is possible to be quite happy with despotism, which can provide far greater security to the individual than a nondespotic society.

VII   *Chinese Emperor Worship*

For Hegel, China is a land of strong family ties, and thus not a land of individual freedom. The individual can succeed in winning his independence from his father only by falling into a similar dependence on the emperor. The religion of China in Hegel's view centers around the emperor, who is a priest-magician-ruler paternalistically mediating between the cosmos and his people.[35] As the Chinese philosopher Tung Chung-She explained nearly two thousand years ago, in a well-ordered society the people subject themselves to the emperor, and the emperor subjects himself to the law of the cosmos (called "Heaven"—*t'ien*—in Chinese philosphy). The emperor secures the prosperity of his realm in part by the moral example he sets, but popular superstitition attaches a great importance to the meticulous performance of magical rites and sacrifices. The emperor is the "Son of Heaven," but natural disasters are a sign that the "Mandate of Heaven" has been withdrawn from him due to some failure in his conduct.[36] The situation of the emperor in relation to Heaven is thus ambiguous. On the one hand he enjoys magical power over the cosmos, and to this extent the Chinese religion resembles the religion of magic discussed in a previous section. But, on the other hand, he can exercise such power only to the extent that he subordinates himself to the "Way" (*Tao*) of Heaven, and to this extent the Chinese religion anticipates the Indian "religion of substance" discussed in the next chapter: Heaven appears as the sole substantial reality, while the emperor is merely an accidental vehicle for the expression of its cosmic power.

VIII   *Confucius*

In identifying the religion of China with the emperor cult we have just described, Hegel is identifying it with Confucianism in the form it assumed as the official state religion of imperial China from the Han dynasty of the second century B.C. to the revolution of 1911. The chief support of this official religion was the Mandarin class of literate civil servants or bureaucrats. The class may well have evolved out of an earlier priest class. Confucius himself (551 - 479 B.C.) was contemptuous of the superstition and magical practices of the lower classes. He rationalized the primitive animistic world view inherited from the past: in the place of personal nature gods he saw mere abstract forces of nature, all ultimately encompassed under the cosmic concept of Heaven. His rationalistic despiritualization of nature may be seen as reflecting the growing will and capacity of the governing classes to control nature technologically (for example, dikes, irrigation) without recourse to magic. In fact, the public works revolution forms the economic basis of political despotism.

But Confucius' main interest was ethical and practical rather than cosmological and theoretical. He lived in a time of political disarray and disunity in China, and he sought a way back to social order. His solution of the crisis was an elitist form of humanism. He advocated the revolutionary principle that political rule is merited by virtue rather than inheritance. He thus proposed the substitution of an aristocracy of virtue for the traditional blood aristocracy. To follow the path of virtue meant to maintain five essential ethical relationships in good equilibrium: (1) to the love of the father corresponds the piety of the son; (2) the protection of the ruler is balanced by the obedience of the subject; (3) the benevolence of the older brother is to be matched by the respect of the younger brother; (4) the justice of the husband is to be met by the obedience of the wife; and finally (5) the faithfulness of one friend to a second calls for the favor of the second with respect to the first.[37] The patriarchal character of the Confucian code is obvious.

The idea of balance or equilibrium is so basic to Chinese culture that Hegel called the religion of China a "religion of measure," that is, of proportion.[38] The idea gained cosmological significance in the Chinese dualism of *yang*, which is one, active, masculine, and heavenly, and *yin*, which is divided or two, passive, feminine, and earthly. Hegel saw in the opposition of *yang* ("the one") and *yin* ("the two") an abstract, remote anticipation of his own dialectical triad of thesis, antithesis, and synthesis.[39] This more abstract side of Chinese philosophy, Hegel tells us, was developed more by the Taoists than by the practical Confucianists.[40]

The concern of the Confucianists was chiefly ethical. Yet, despite his humanistic rationalism, Confucius wished to preserve traditional ritual, interpreting it as an external expression of virtue rather than as the exercise of magical power. But belief in magic did not disappear among the masses, and the emperor was able to put the popular belief in magic to political use in maintaining the social order.

IX   *Hegel's Exaggeration of Chinese Despotism*

Hegel seeks to bolster his view of China as a despotic state by documenting a general lack of individual freedom or autonomy in China. He mentions in this respect the Chinese practice of attributing one's accomplishments to one's parents, one's ancestors, and ultimately to the emperor.[41] He refers to the widespread practice of corporal punishment, suggesting that the Chinese relate to social authority as something external and thus are insensitive to the pangs of conscience.[42] In the same vein, he notes the practice of punishing even unintended deeds, implying that the Chinese are somehow unaware of intention as something distinct from execution.[43] The custom of punishing an individual's relatives for his misdeeds is brought in to suggest that the Chinese are unaware of the true locus of responsibility in the soul of the individual. Hegel even repeats, rather unfairly, the reports of European travellers to China, especially businessmen, that the Chinese are double-faced.[44] In keeping with his image of China as a stagnant, backward-looking society, he belittles such Chinese inventions as the printing press and gun powder, again quite unfairly.[45] He also claims that there is a lack of theoretical curiosity in China, and he finds this deficiency expressed in the hieroglyphic language of the Chinese: the characters of the Chinese language, he says, tend to channel thought into pre-established patterns by providing ready-made composite pictures of reality.[46]

It is not surprising that Hegel has been criticized for exaggerating the absence of individual freedom, inwardness, or subjectivity in China. It seems clear that he identified Chinese civilization as a whole too closely with the official Confucian state religion. Alongside the despotic-patriarchal ideology of official Confucianism, numerous individualistic and even anarchistic tendencies existed, especially in times of social unrest between two strong dynasties. Hegel's identification of Chinese civilization as essentially despotic may have been influenced by the fact that he was largely dependent on the reports of Jesuit missionaries from the seventeenth and eighteenth centuries, a time in Chinese history when despotism was especially prominent. The Mongolian occupation of China during the fourteenth century left a strong imprint on the Ming and Mandschu dynasties of the following centuries. But we should not forget that despotism did not go uncontested, and that Chinese history is strewn with periodic, if unsuccessful, peasant uprisings. And when Hegel identifies the religion of China with Confucianism he fails to give recognition to the fact that, alongside this public religion, private Buddhist and Taoist religious convictions were tolerated, even though Confucianism attempted, to some extent, to integrate them. The very possibility of private, nonofficial convictions contradicts any claim that imperial China was totally despotic. Hegel himself betrays the falsehood of this claim by calling attention to the institutionalized existence of censors who exercised the right to criticize even the emperor.[47] And it did not escape Hegel's notice that there is a long tradition of lyric poetry in China.[48] As we shall see in a later section, Hegel interprets lyricism as a reflection of individual freedom of feeling and expression. Still, none of these facts contradicts the claim that China was *predominantly* despotic, especially in the seventeenth and eighteenth centuries, and it is not clear why Hegel should need to make any stronger claim.

X *Mao Tse Tung*

The twentieth century has, of course, put an end to the imperial China which Hegel described. The revolution led by Mao Tse Tung was, in its original inspiration, a revolution against the Confucian ethic of respect for authority which, in the nineteenth century, led China all too easily into foreign hands. The recent anti-Confucius campaign in China (1973 - 1974) was essentially consistent with the original inspiration of Maoism. Seen in this light, Mao appears as a Westernizer who introduced the sense of individual dignity along with the Western ideology of Karl Marx into China. Hegel said that someday China, like India, would fall under Western domination.[49] (What he could not know was that China, via Marxism, would fall under the influence of his own dialectical philosophy!) And Hegel saw the Chinese practice of corporal punishment as evidence of a deficient sense of individual dignity. It is thus interesting to learn that a decisive turn in Mao's own life as a young man was his rebellion against such punishment as imposed by his father.[50] But

Mao certainly cannot be understood merely as a Westernizer. He is also deeply Chinese. His assimilation of dialectical principles was doubtless facilitated by traditional Chinese views about the opposition and unity of *yin* and *yang*. And despite Western ideological influence, it is certainly doubtful that the Maoist revolution has brought despotism to an end in China. The cult of personality surrounding Mao himself bears a suspicious resemblance to the traditional Chinese cult surrounding the emperor. The necessity of discipline for the sake of rapid economic development seems to have forced China to fall back on the traditional supports of bureaucracy and respect for authority, although it has been against Mao's wishes if we are to judge by the Cultural Revolution.

CHAPTER 4

India and Mysticism

I   Mysticism as an Escape from Unstable Despotism

IN discussing China we have been chiefly preoccupied
with the despotic political basis of Oriental civilization. In
Hegel's view, it was China more than any other Oriental society
which developed the political principle of the Orient.[1] As we move
from China to India, the Oriental principle of political organization
remains unchanged. India, too, is organized despotically.[2] Even the
most endearing of the great historical rulers of India, King Asoko,
based his claim to moral leadership on a paternalistic relationship to
his subjects. Yet Hegel was probably right in holding that Indian
history does not exemplify the meaning of despotism for us as purely as Chinese history does. The reason is in part that China maintained, throughout its history, a semblance of imperial unity far less
sporadically than India. Although the dream of central rule haunted
India as well as China, the far more usual state of affairs in India
was one of feudalism and splintering into a plurality of smaller
states.[3] But this is not the whole reason. At a deeper level, this very
political disarray calls for explanation. The cause is essentially
religious. We saw that the Chinese emperor was at once a political
and religious leader. It is here that the greatest contrast with India
is found. Paradoxically, the Indian political regime is a despotism in
which the despot, because he does *not* exercise supreme religious
authority in a land in which the prestige of religion is greater than
that of politics, does not enjoy the greatest social prestige. In the
traditional caste system of India, the political rulers do not belong
to the highest, Brahmanic caste.[4]

The Indian political regime is thus a degenerate or impure
despotism tempered by the despot's incapacity to exercise absolute
power over the religious life of the land. Even a despot must respect
the sacred cows. Because of the tremendous influence which

49

religion in India has on social life, being responsible, as it is, for the country's caste system, the power of a despot, however enlightened, to reform the social system is strictly limited. Mrs. Indira Ghandi, in assuming despotic powers in 1975, allegedly to effect needed reforms, was laying claim to a challenge of truly historic dimensions.

From what has been said we can understand Hegel's claim that, whereas China is the prime example of the political principle of the Orient, India is preeminent in the religious life of the Orient. Indian civilization assumes a despotic basis and proceeds to build a vast religious superstructure on that basis. Despotism as we came to know it in China is at once preserved and transcended. The justification of Hegel's treatment of India as a more advanced stage of civilization than China lies precisely in this fact that Indian civilization represents a first attempt to go beyond despotism. We find in Indian religion a first attempt to overcome the insecurity, suffering, and bondage of despotic rule, although admittedly the way in which despotism in India is transcended religiously may be called "escapist" since it leaves despotism intact here on earth. Nonetheless, this very mystical escapism gives eloquent testimony to a desire for freedom emerging in the heart of despotism itself.[5] The religion of India is the negative reflection of the despotism of India. It was Hegel who, before Marx, spoke of religion as the "opium" of the people, but it was more specifically of Indian religion that he was speaking.[6] Marx took over this view of Indian religion and generalized it into a view of all religion. Whether this Marxist generalization is tenable is a question which we must postpone tackling until we take up other religions, in particular Christianity. But what is interesting here is that Marx was able to appropriate Hegel's view of a given religion into his "historical materialist" framework. This he was able to do because Hegelianism, without being the physicalistic type of materialism which Marx himself rejected, is already a *historical* materialism in Marx's sense. "Historical materialism" affirms the thesis that economic conditions determine the political structure of a society, and that the political structure, in turn, determines the religious consciousness of the land. Patriarchy or despotism, we saw in the preceding chapter, is the political consequence of an economic revolution: the herding-agricultural revolution. Indian religion is a religious expression of (unstable) despotism and thus, indirectly, of the agricultural revolution.

II *Hinduism and Buddhism*

So far we have been speaking of "Indian religion" in very general terms. At a certain level of abstraction this is permissible, since Hegel holds that the two major religions whose homeland is India—Hinduism and Buddhism—are in agreement as to basic principle.[7] But when we proceed to make a distinction between these two religions, a problem arises which is unavoidable because it is expository. In his lectures of 1823 Hegel treated Buddhism subsequently to Hinduism, but the very next year he reversed this order. Since, in subsequent years, he continued to make changes in his order of treatment, and since his last lectures on the subject (1831) have not been preserved, the problem of determining his ultimate view of the matter remains unsolved.[8] In what order, then, should we treat these two religions in our exposition of Hegel's philosophy? It seems best to treat them in their historical order; that is, to consider the Brahmanistic-Hindu tradition first. At the time Hegel wrote, research on Buddhism was not very far advanced and it was still not clear whether Buddhism preceded or followed the Brahmanistic-Hindu religion. Thus Hegel was, at least on occasion, tempted to treat Buddhism as a primitive, undeveloped form of Hinduism. But he was also, on other occasions, tempted to consider Buddhism, more accurately as it turns out, as a simplification of a prior Brahmanistic Hinduism; and this is how we, who are presumably more interested in seeing to what extent the real world can be comprehended from the Hegelian standpoint than to pursue the intricacies of Hegel's intellectual biography, shall consider it here.

III *Hinduism: Religion of Fantasy*

In fact, in alluding to India's caste system, we have already begun our treatment of India with a discussion of Hinduism. For Buddhism separated itself from the Brahmanistic-Hindu tradition, at least in part, by rejecting that very system. But a word of explanation for my use of the term "Brahmanistic-Hindu tradition" instead of simply "Hinduism" is in order. The distinction between the earlier Brahmanism, which was based on the Vedic writings including the *Upanishads,* and Hinduism, which grew out of Brahmanism and centers around certain epic writings postdating the *Upanishads,* was one which was not made by Hegel, and indeed one which was not yet generally made in his time. Hegel amalgamates both Brahmanism and Hinduism, despite their partly incompatible elements, under the title "the religion of fantasy,"[9] a phrase which conveys something of the bewildering impression which this amalgamation necessarily made on his mind.

But the phrase conveys much more than a possible confusion in Hegel's mind. Fantasy is the province of *poetry* over against *prose*, and Hegel persuasively argues that the contrast between India and China is precisely that between poetry and prose.[10] "Prose" connotes the despiritualization of the natural world which is a necessary consequence of the despotic will to power over the forces of nature. The prose world is the world of scientific and technological discourse, and Hegel's very attempt to belittle the technological achievements of China serves to highlight those achievements. The prose world is also that of historical discourse, and to a remarkable degree even ancient China achieved a historical consciousness of the concrete unrepeatability or uniqueness of at least political or dynastic events. By contrast, the evolution of India's past is shrouded in myth, fabulation, and imprecision.[11] This seems to be ultimately due to India's essentially prehistorical view of time as an *eternal return*, the wheel of fate turning endlessly on its axis.[12]

The poetic quality of Indian civilization gave it a favored place in the hearts of the German Romantics of Hegel's own lifetime. The Age of Reason and Enlightenment from Leibniz to Voltaire was capable of being impressed by the hardheaded administrative achievements of China, but beginning with Herder thinkers and writers were attracted by the softer tones of the Indian poetic sensibility. Friedrich Schlegel, in the first decade of the last century, learned Sanskrit in Paris and for a time looked for a renewal of Western civilization through contact with India similar to the renewal through contact with Greece in the Renaissance. Hegel was not insensitive to the infinite delicacy and charm of Indian poetic feeling:

There is a beauty of a peculiar kind in women, in which their countenance presents a transparency of skin, a light and lovely hue, which is unlike the complexion of mere health and vital vigor—a more refined bloom, breathed as it were by the soul within—and in which the features, the light of the eye, the position of the mouth, appear soft, yielding and relaxed. This almost unearthly beauty is perceived in women in those days which immediately succeed child birth. . . . Such a beauty we find also in its loveliest form in the Indian world, a beauty of enervation, in which all that is rough, rigid and contradictory is dissolved.[13]

Yet Hegel ultimately forsook the temptations of romanticism. Indeed, part of the interest of what he has to say about India derives, as we shall see, from his assimilation of the Indian experience to the romantic world view and his presentation of a thinly veiled critique of romanticism *via* an ostensive critique of India.

IV   *The Hindu Caste System*

But the poetry of Indian life calls for some explanation. India, after all, is not the Garden of Eden. It is a land of great suffering, a despotism in which nature is as despiritualized as in China. Hegel was well aware of the underside of Indian civilization. He preferred to draw upon the reports of the English who, after the implantation of the East India Company in India, knew the country firsthand, rather than relying on the romantic excogitations of a Friedrich Schlegel. The organization of economic production and the process of government necessarily depoeticize and "thingify" the natural world. But although this process occurs, indeed although Indian political life was marked by a surprisingly modern, Machiavellian realism hundreds of years before Machiavelli demystified political realities in Europe, the process occurs in the background of Indian culture and is not accorded the highest importance. The reason for this is the already mentioned rigid caste system, which ranks despots second to the priestly Brahman class. The latter has a ritualistic and meditative function. It, so to speak, reigns without governing.

The nature and origin of the Brahman caste is of the highest interest, although little of the origin is known. Brahmanism grew out of an earlier religion which goes by the name of Vedism. Vedism was a life-affirming religion introduced into India some time in the second millenium B.C. by the invading Aryans. The Aryans were a seminomadic race of herders from the north. They originally conquered the pre-Vedic Indian civilization due to their superior chariots, technology and mobility. But some time after this conquest there would seem to have been a loss of nerve on the part of the Aryan rulers. Apparently part of the ruling class forsook the responsibilities of government, retreating from problems of technology and administration into a priestly and ascetic preoccupation with ritual and magic. Surprisingly, however, the part of the ruling class which abdicated rule did not fall thereby into social insignificance, but, on the contrary, increased its prestige. One cannot escape the impression that this emergence of the Brahman class represented a certain decadence in the ruling Aryan class. It would seem that the despots themselves became ill at ease with their despotism.

One of the great themes which runs through the Hegelian philosophy is the "dialectic of lordship and bondage."[14] Hegel shows that even the lord, master, or despot is ultimately unfree and unhappy, since he finds himself surrounded and bounded by a servile mass of alien humanity with which he, as a lord, cannot identify. If it is true, as Hegel holds, that Indian religion is essentially escapist, then in the emergence of the Brahmanistic caste it is remarkably the despots themselves who wish to escape from the severities of despotic rule. Of course, the Brahmanistic retreat from rule was by no means a forsaking of class society. The caste system served to repress the masses. It may well have been an "opium" of the people. But it is well to remember that the Brahmans repressed themselves as well. Hegel was mistaken to say that every Brahman is a born god, his merit like his caste membership being a natural attribute independent of any exertions on his part.[15] Among Brahmans it was the ascetic life of ritual, meditation, and study which was most admired.

The ultimate form which Brahmanism took is found in the *Upanishads,* which were apparently written to justify and rationalize the elaborate magic ritual of the Brahmans in an age in which belief in magic was in decline. The justification which was given was that by means of the rituals a Brahman attains mystical identification with the ultimate principle of the universe, that is, with "Brahma." We see here how Indian religion is escapist. Life is defined as suffering, and religion is offered as the remedy, a means of eluding the misery and insecurity of life in a despotic state where no legal rights are recognized. According to the ordinary experience of man, the self, *atman* in Sanskrit, is limited by an environment which bears down upon it from the outside. But the central message of the *Upanishads* is that this external restriction is an illusion (*maya*), and that ultimately the self is identical with the ultimate reality, the infinite substance and might of the cosmos: *atman=* Brahma. Since Brahma, the infinite substance, is without internal restriction, for the self to realize its identity with Brahma is to escape the concrete limitations of ordinary life. Indians of all castes seek realization of oneness with Brahma. However, since in this life only those born into the Brahman caste are capable of actually realizing the goal, the others are left to fall back upon the doctrine of reincarnation, according to which one stands a chance of being born into a higher caste in one's next life if one performs conscientiously the duties of one's caste.

V *Indian Pantheism and Spinoza*

But what is escapism and decadence within the framework of despotism is progress within the larger framework of the human spirit. The renunciation of worldly power by the Brahman caste is at once a turn inward, the discovery of an inner realm of freedom of thought and fantasy. Detachment from the outer world unlocks a new world of inner subjectivity. The discovery is made of a pure abstract subject of consciousness, a totally free consciousness capable of identifying with everything, indeed with the entire cosmos, because it is nothing in particular. Some of the stranger flights of the Hindu fantasy, where it is a question of a Brahman or yogi becoming a natural object or traversing the farthest reaches of the universe, are to be explained in terms of this Hindu experience of cosmic availability and empathy. Hegel detects an increased inwardness in the poetic imagination of India over the prosiness of China.[16] Nature is poetically elaborated by a dreaming, delirious imagination, and the imagination, although less inward (that is, more parasitic on external perception) than pure imageless thought, is still more inward than external perception itself.

Yet, in its highest reaches, the Indian religious consciousness rises even to the level of pure thought, the normal atmosphere of European philosophy.[17] The central concept of Brahmanism—Brahma—transcends anything imaginable. The concept reappears in Western philosophy in a far more systematically abstract and less poetic form as the unique, all-encompassing "substance" of Spinoza's philosophy. Both Spinozism and Brahmanism, according to Hegel, share the same central pantheistic principle of substantiality.[18] Spinozism was abhorred as being tantamount to atheism and materialism during most of the eighteenth century. But many of the German romantics developed, by contrast, a remarkable sympathy for what they took to be Spinoza's pantheism. Hegel himself, as a young man, did not escape this enthusiasm, as is shown by the following quotation from an early poem which he addressed to his friend Hölderlin:

> My eye rises towards the vault
> of the eternal heaven,
> towards you, oh brilliant star of the night,
> and the forgetting of all wishes

and all hopes
rushes down upon me from your eternity,
consciousness is lost in contemplation,
what I called mine disappears,
I abandon myself to the infinite
I am in it
I am all
I am only it.[19]

But the mature Hegel finally went beyond the pantheist position by claiming that the absolute reality is not the empty substance of Spinoza of the romantics and Indian religion, but is rather the self-determining, self-developing, self-articulating Holy Spirit of the Christian religion.[20] Yet because of the importance which the pantheistic concept of substance has as a key signpost along the road of Hegel's intellectual development, we must give more careful attention to its logical features.

VI   *The Concept of Substance*

Whoever speaks of "substance" invokes a time-honored concept of Western philosophy. The classical sense of the term was established by Aristotle, for whom a substance was distinguished by its *essential independence* of all else.[21] A substance is thus capable of standing on its own. It is not an *abstract aspect* of a larger whole, but is itself a complete whole. It subsists in and through itself alone. It is nonrelative or absolute. But Aristotle also established the usage which makes a substance, although *essentially* self-subsistent, *accidentally* related to other things. Thus a substance has, besides its essential properties which cannot change without entailing a change in its very identity, certain accidental properties which may come and go or alternate without the substance's self-identity being jeopardized.[22] In the Aristotelian view, the world is conceived as a plurality of interacting substances, where a substance's accidental properties depend not on it alone, but on the chance relations of interaction in which it stands to *other* substances.

Now it was the achievement of Spinoza in the European metaphysical tradition to point out a basic incoherence in the concept of substance as it comes down to us from Aristotle. For it was Spinoza who forced the recognition upon us that a substance as Aristotle identified it could not really be essentially independent of all else as claimed. Aristotle admits that although a substance is essentially independent it is accidentally dependent on something else. Thus a blade of grass is accidentally moist due to the effect of the morning dew. The question, however, is whether it is really possible to distinguish so neatly between essential and accidental properties. It is to be noted that a substance possesses *some* accidental characteristics *essentially*, by its very nature. A blade of grass which is neither moist nor not moist, which does not stand in *some* relation of causal interaction with other things, is indeed inconceivable. From this consideration alone we can already conclude that the Aristotelian hypothesis of a *plurality* of essentially independent substances is untenable. If we are really in earnest about the search for what is essentially independent and self-subsistent, for what is self-intelligible because it is conceivable through itself alone, we must conclude that in reality there can be only one substance.[23] This in fact was the conclusion which Spinoza drew. Spinozistic *monism* was thus posited in the place of Aristotelian pluralism.

But if we now try to conceive the single all-embracing substance, it is clearly not to be identified with our modest blade of grass. On the contrary, the blade of grass can only be conceived as a momentary manifestation of a substantial reality, the awe-inspiring thought of which transcends anything accessible to the senses or even the imagination. Yet this cosmic substance is not quite so sublime as totally to abjure sensory manifestation. Indeed, every sensory phenomenon is such a manifestation. The substantial reality must, by its very nature, manifest itself.[24] It cannot hide. Yet no single manifestation or imaginable set of manifestations can exhaust its infinite power of expression.

The concept of substance, as we have seen, is essentially relative to that of accident. What is substantial must have nonsubstantial properties. A substantial reality is thus essentially related to what is other than it, if only to the human mind to which it manifests itself. But, at the same time, it is conceived as self-subsistent, existing in a withdrawn state of self-repose, its accidents being unessential to it. What this means is that the concept of substance is, as Hegel concludes, essentially self-contradictory; a substance is explicitly conceived as being both absolute or nonrelative and relative or nonabsolute.[25] One no sooner attempts to conceive infinite substance than one realizes that it cannot remain a mere object of conception, but must appear in sensory form: otherwise it would not be infinite or unlimited, but would rather be limited by the sensory domain. The absolute substance conceived as independent of its accidents suddenly collapses as the substance passes into its present sensory manifestation, becoming momentarily identical with that manifestation. Thus what was nothing as long as we contemplated the substantial reality in its supersensory magnificence—for example, the individual blade of grass—suddenly becomes everything. The accident becomes suddenly essential. This particular accident becomes momentarily the substance itself. But only momentarily, since any single manifestation is essentially relative to the infinity of other manifestations. The supersensory self-concealment of the substance indeed collapses, but as long as the category of substance is maintained the substance must reassert itself as essentially independent of its accidents. Thus the blade of grass which was momentarily everything suddenly becomes nothing again, hurled back into the oblivion of the infinite substance.

The Indian experience of the world is, in Hegel's view, determined by this dialectic of substance and accident which we have just recorded.[26] We see here a good example of the intimate connection which Hegel postulates between history and metaphysical logic. Indian experience is based on the use of a logical category even if there is no explicit awareness of the fact. The Indian mind is fixated on the concept of substance. This is the concept which it uses to interpret reality. We speak of a "fixation" because the Indian does not typically drop the concept of substance and go on to a more adequate definition of reality when contradiction is discovered, but rather reaffirms it and thus experiences a repetition of the collapse of substantiality into accidental appearance, and thus of the same resultant contradiction over again. This collapse, however, does not come as a surprise. Because substance is essentially relative to what is nonessential, because it is an absolute which is explicitly relative and thus self-contradictory, the exhibition of its contradictoriness is an integral part of the Indian experience of the world which, we may say, wallows in self-contradiction. Here, then, is the deeper source of Hegel's description of the Hindu religion as a "religion of fantasy." A world of fantasy is one which is full of contradictions or wildly inconsistent juxtapositions, for example, of the most otherworldly asceticism and the grossest sensuality.[27]

The category of substance is internally void, empty. But since there cannot be anything outside the absolute substance (otherwise it would not be absolute), every empirical phenomenon is an appearance, incarnation, or revelation of the substantial reality or

Brahma. The smallest suddenly becomes the greatest and the greatest the smallest, as one reels as if in a drunken stupor from the extreme of absolutizing what is relative to the other extreme of totally negating it. All is flux, an endless process of becoming and annihilation. Thus Hindu poetic feeling can savor the infinite charm and delicacy of the least significant detail of nature, clasping it to its breast, for it, too, is an incarnation of Brahma. Indeed, a great ethical institution such as the family or the state, even a human person, is, as such an incarnation, placed no more highly or lowly in this respect than a blade of grass.[28] India, Hegel tells us, has hospitals for old cows, but none for aged human beings.[29] Thus the Hindu lacks a sense of relative values and proportion. Every phenomenon is equally real as an incarnation of Brahma and equally unreal or illusory insofar as it purports to have independent, absolute existence.

VII *Hindu versus Christian Trinity*

Hegel finds his analysis of the Indian experience confirmed by a consideration of the Hindu trinity (*trimurti*) of Brahmā, Vishnu, and Siva. These three gods are incarnations of Brahma, the absolute substance. Thus it is important to distinguish between Brahma, which is an impersonal ground or principle, and Brahmā, who is a personal incarnation of Brahma.[30] Following the report of James Mill, Hegel takes Brahmā to be the creator, Vishnu to be the preserver, and Siva to be the destroyer.[31] Hegel's chief interest is in a comparison and contrast of the Hindu trinity with the Christian one. He takes the *trimurti* to be an anticipation of the Christian trinity, which is, in turn, interpreted as an anticipation of his own triadic philosophy of spirit. It must be granted, however, that there are considerable differences between the Christian trinity of Father, Son, and Holy Spirit and the Hindu *trimurti.* The latter, unlike the Christian trinity, has no central place in worship. It is largely the result of a speculative attempt to integrate the two major Hindu sects: Vishnuism, centering around the worship of the god Vishnu, and Sivaism, centering around the worship of Siva. Yet Hegel would probably not care to deny this difference between the two trinities, for he himself contrasts them. The greatest difference is to be seen, according to Hegel, in the third member of the trinity.[32] The third member of the Christian trinity is Spirit, which *preserves* particular determinations or incarnations of the Father—of the absolute substance—even in transcending them and canceling their absoluteness; the Siva of the Hindu religion, on the other hand, is a mere nonprogressive, repetitive becoming, a monotonous alternation of arising and vanishing, universality (substantiality) annihilating particularity (accident) with one swing of the pendulum, universality itself collapsing into particularity with the other swing. But this category of becoming is devoid of development, of any preservation of the past determinations, which are rather cast into oblivion.

VIII   *The Symbolic Art of Hinduism*

The Christian and Hegelian concept of history as a progressive-preservative development is foreign to the characteristic Indian experience. Hegel interprets the Hindu *trimurti* as at most an anticipation of the trinitarian self-development of spirit. The *trimurti* is symbolized in Hindu art by three-headed figures.[33] For Hegel the ultimate content symbolized by such a figure is the truth: the Christian-Hegelian teaching of the Holy Spirit. The sculptural figure thus has a genuine cognitive or revelatory function. It is a sensory symbol of a thought reality which transcends the mere senses. Indian art, in Hegel's interpretation, is typically *symbolic*.[34] Such art, the characteristic art of the Orient, hints at a truth which has not yet been conceptually articulated. The symbol is a sensory analogue which anticipates thought, providing token compensation for the present defect of thought, for its abstractness. The two other types of art recognized by Hegel are first *classical* art and finally *romantic* art. If symbolic art is ahead of thought, at the stage of classical art thought has become more concrete and thus has caught up with art. Classical art, whose historical locus is ancient Greece, gives sensory expression to an articulate concrete idea, as we shall see in a later chapter. At the stage of romantic art, the typical art of the Christian world, thought becomes so concrete that it leaves art behind, which it has overtaken, outstripped. The romantic artist is a disillusioned artist; having formed the idea of Spirit, he knows he is trying to express what is by nature beyond aesthetic expression.

The external and accidental incarnations of the substantial reality which are represented by three-headedness in Hindu art are really, in Hegel's view, *internal* determinations of that substantial reality, which is thus in truth self-developing subjectivity rather than mere empty substantiality.[35] Although Indian thought remains ignorant of the fact, substance, cosmic power, is implicitly and in truth subjectivity. A human being exercises finite power in throwing a stone; his power is an expression of his subjectivity as a human agent. The absolutization of mere power or substance is, unconsciously, implicitly, the absolutization of subjectivity, of spirit. The absolutization of subjectivity in Hinduism is unconscious because thought here apprehends subjectivity abstractly. Subjectivity abstractly apprehended is substantiality; while substantiality concretely apprehended is subjectivity. When subjectivity is apprehended unconsciously and confusedly through symbolic art, subjectivitiy is being apprehended abstractly as substance.

Hegel has been criticized for basing his interpretation of Hinduism too much on Brahmanism and the later philosophy of Sankara.[36] It is true that the Brahmanistic insistence on an impersonal ultimate principle, in relation to which the separate individual is merely accidental, is not characteristic of all forms of Hinduism. The theistic worship of a personal God and the dualistic insistence on the irreducibility of the self to a mere accident of Brahma are only two countertendencies to be found in the Hindu tradition. Hegel assigned these countertendencies only a subordinate role within his essentially Brahmanistic view of Hinduism. But in Hegel's defense it must be said that Brahmanism is in fact the decisive element in Hinduism. After all, it is Brahmanism which was responsible for the Hindu social system, a system in which the Brahmans enjoyed the highest position. Brahmanism is the orthodox Hindu position, although it must be remembered that "orthodoxy" does not mean quite the same thing in Hinduism, which places greater value on tolerance, as in Christianity. The Hindu "holy revelation" includes the Brahmanistic *Upanishads*, but not the later more theistic epics. The latter are distinguished as forming part of the "holy tradition" but not of "revelation."

IX *Buddhism: Mahayana and Hinyana*

We now pass on to Buddhism, a religion about which Hegel knew rather less than about Hinduism. If this did not stop him from talking extensively on the subject, one reason is that his critique of the Buddhist concept of Nirvana was really a covert critique of views held in the Germany of Hegel's own day, in particular romantic pantheism and the "subjectivistic" theology of Friedrich Schleiermacher. According to Hegel, Schleiermacher, in grounding religion in a dumb feeling of dependence on an ultimately indescribable and thus Nirvana-like cosmic absolute, was advocating an essentially Oriental position, and doing so in the guise of Christian theology.[37]

In principle, Hegel took Buddhism and Hinduism to be identical.[38] In his view, the difference between them was superficial. Hinduism, we have seen, asserts a provisional polytheism, but ends up grounding the plurality of gods in Brahma, an impersonal cosmic absolute. Buddhism, however, does not affirm polytheism even as a provisional truth. Everything but the single substantial reality is unreal and illusory. Buddhism fixes upon substantiality to the exclusion of the accidents. Because the absolute does not become incarnate in the accidental lesser gods of mythology, Buddhism cannot be called, like Hinduism, a "religion of fantasy." Because substantiality is totally divorced from the accidents, it is totally empty, and is characterized only negatively as "Nirvana" or nothing. Nirvana is to Buddhism as Brahma is to Hinduism, or so Hegel surmises.[39] The supposition is not so much wrong as it is limited in its validity to a certain variety of Buddhism: Mahayana Buddhism. Hegel failed to distinguish, in particular, between Mahayana and Hinyana Buddhism, describing the former as if it were Buddhism in general.

Buddha himself repudiated metaphysical speculation. It seems clear that the metaphysical concept of a substance out of which all phenomena arise and into which they return was foreign to the original thought of Buddha, to which Hinyana Buddhism remains more faithful. The purpose of the concept of Nirvana was not to explain the phenomenal world. It was rather practical: to point the individual toward the path of salvation. If Buddha insisted on the illusoriness of the world, it was not because the world was an accidental manifestation of Nirvana conceived as the ultimate substantial reality. On the contrary, Buddha was opposed to the idea of *any* abiding or substantial reality, whether it be a material object, a soul or Brahma. The reason for denying the reality of this world is thus quite different from that given by the Hindu. Whereas Hinduism *absorbs* the things of this world into the one substantial reality, Hinyana Buddhism decomposes or *dissolves* them into a myriad of minute momentary events. In Hinduism the blade of grass is ultimately unreal because it is relative to other things. In Buddhism it is unreal because it is ultimately a mere aggregate or series of "blade events."

X   *Hegel and Hypostatization: A Buddhist Critique*

This Buddhist view is surprisingly close to the so-called "quantum view" which has arisen in twentieth-century physics. Quantum theory is pluralistic like classical atomism, but it goes beyond the traditional theory of atoms in postulating a plurality of *successive* as well as *simultaneous* ultimate "quanta" or units of reality. Whereas an atom as traditionally conceived was eternal, a physical quantum of energy is a momentary event. The apparently enduring blade of grass is really a series of grass events in which the present event is essentially independent of the one which follows. The view of the world which results is aptly called the "motion picture" view of reality. Continuous existence and motion are in general explained on the model of the motion picture, that is, as illusions resulting from the rapid succession of separate motionless occurrences. In this century this "Buddhist" view of the world has been developed extensively in the philosophy of Alfred North Whitehead, and in fact it has much to recommend it. (It makes it possible, for example, to accept the famous arguments of Zeno against motion[40] without accepting the conclusion for which Zeno thought he was arguing, namely that this world, in which things move about, does not exist. As a Buddhist or Whiteheadian might put it, things only *seem* to move about.)

In any case, what is interesting in the present context is that Hegel, although he criticized pantheism, did not seem to distance himself from it sufficiently, at least for the Hinyana Buddhist taste. He accepted the pantheist claim that the absolute is substance, merely adding that this is not the whole truth. For the absolute is also *spirit*.[41] Hinyana Buddhism appears to reject the monistic (antipluralistic) basis of both pantheism and Hegelianism. The Hegelian absolute as usually interpreted is, from this traditional Buddhist standpoint, a "hypostatization," that is, a collection which is spoken of as if it were an entity existing in its own right over and above the members of the collection.

XI   *Buddhism on Suffering: A Hegelian Critique*

It must be admitted, however, that there are Buddhist thinkers, of the Mahayana tradition, who do identify Nirvana with a cosmic absolute. Yet this absolute is more typically seen in the Buddhist writings not as a substantial ground (*Grund* in German) of phenomena, but as an abyss (*Abgrund*) lying beneath phenomena which are in fact *groundless*. To attain Nirvana, one must realize the groundlessness of the world in which we normally live, of the desires which propel us and of the "substantial" realities to which we cling. All is in flux, shifting beneath our feet like the sands of Araby, and there is truly nothing on which we can hang our hat. Life is normally marked by suffering precisely because of our attachment to false absolutes. We absolutize what is relative and suffer pain and disappointment when it passes away into something else by virtue of its very relativity. In more Freudian terms, we become *fixated* upon some partial object and thus *repress* (or suppress) whatever is opposed to it; yet what is repressed does not therefore go away: it takes revenge on us in the form of what Freud called "the return of the repressed."[42]

But the same Buddhist insight can also be translated into the language of Hegel's own dialectic. In *abstracting* and *absolutizing* what is *relative* we *negate* its other, and in so doing we call forth upon ourselves *self-negation*, that is, negation of the false absolutization by the negated *other*. This possibility of translating the Buddhist diagnosis of human suffering into the language of Hegelian dialectics points to an area of agreement between Buddhism and Hegelianism apparently unsuspected by Hegel himself. But it also points to the critique which Hegel, had he seen the partial agreement, would no doubt have gone on to make of the Buddhist position. Buddhism has accurate insight into the source of human suffering, but its achievement remains purely negative. The negative, exclusive, one-sided or abstract absolutization of what is relative is self-negated; it negates itself; but the possibility of the *concrete* redefinition of the absolute to include the other which it previously excluded is not perceived. Buddhism negates abstract thought, but fails to see that not all thought is abstract, that there is also such a thing as concrete thinking, a kind of thinking which overcomes the suffering caused by abstract thinking and the consequent absolutization of the relative. And precisely because concrete thought—which Hegel also calls "speculative reason"— is capable of overcoming the suffering brought on by abstract thought (that is, "dogmatic reason"), the suffering is not for Hegel *futile*. It is not futile because speculative reason is possible only through the overcoming of suffering. Thus while Buddhism seeks to end suffering by stilling abstract thought and the consequent rigid fixations, Hegel seeks the same objective by giving free play to abstract thought and the resultant suffering, by holding to the Christian thought that suffering is salutory, the means to its own overcoming. Once again, in the case of Buddhism as with Hinduism, we see how, in Hegel's view, Oriental thought is fixated upon the recognition of contradiction which it fails to resolve. Thus the Oriental ultimately despairs of thought and turns *mystical* in the decidedly un-Hegelian sense of cherishing the *wisdom of silence*, of a nondiscursive *seeing*.

When a Buddhist claims that nothing abides as a substantial reality, the Hegelian reply cannot be repressed: nothing, which abstract thought falsely absolutizes. Hegel, in pressing the claims of concrete thought, claims the right to reintroduce a substantial reality which, precisely because it is truly substantial or absolute, will not prove deceptive. This substantial reality, comprehended by concrete thought alone, is spirit, in German *Geist*, sometimes translated as "mind." But Hegel does not mean by "spirit" any individual mind; nor does he mean a limited group mind or national spirit. Hegel's spirit is a *cosmic* spirit. Thus although it attains its highest manifestation and self-consciousness in the human spirit, it is broader than humanity. The very possibility of accepting the Hegelian definition of the Absolute as spirit thus depends on acceptance of the "panpsychist" romantic philosophy of nature which Hegel took over from Schelling even in going beyond it. In a recent book on Hegel, Charles Taylor maintains that a chief reason why we cannot be Hegelians today is that this romantic philosophy of nature—which makes possible communion with nature, cosmic empathy, and the overcoming of the normal dualism of mind (man) and matter (nature) through attributing feeling even to inanimate nature—is no longer believable.[43] But, not to mention Teilhard de Chardin, Taylor seems to have forgotten the Whiteheadians who, like Charles Hartshorne, advocate panpsychism as well as the Buddhist doctrine that nothing in the world really endures.[44] (Still, it must be said that these Whiteheadians have for the most part not yet discovered their *Hegelian* vocation and destiny!)

XII *Is Hegel Guilty of Vicious Hypostatization?*

Nature is "slumbering spirit." In human history, Hegel continued the metaphor, the slumbering spirit of nature awakens to self-consciousness. Man, after all, is part of the natural universe. He is, furthermore, aware of himself. It therefore follows, Hegel is telling us, that in man the universe, the absolute, is becoming aware of itself. And it becomes completely aware of itself only when man becomes aware of himself as inseparably bound with the universe, as *one* with it. But the conclusion really depends on more than the acceptance of panpsychism and the consequent oneness of man with the universe which surrounds him. It also depends on the legitimacy of the very hypostatization of the universe which Buddhism calls into question.

In defense of hypostatization, it may be said that it is practically unavoidable even for Buddhists. It is not practicable to stop talking about enduring persons and natural objects and start talking instead about the momentary events (the *dharmas* of Buddhist doctrine) which make up so-called persons and things. Even a hardheaded physical scientist who holds that even atoms are aggregates of interacting elementary particles still speaks of atoms, molecules, cells, organisms, and even the universe. We can hardly, therefore, refuse Hegel the right to speak of the universe or "Absolute."

There is really nothing wrong with hypostatization so long as one remembers what one is doing. The danger arises onnly when one begins to believe in the independent existence of what is hypostatized. Whether Hegel avoided this danger, however, is debatable. The hypostatization and personification present in the following quotation is so blatant that one doubts Hegel could have been entirely unaware of it: "I adhere to the view that the world spirit has given the age marching orders. These orders are being obeyed. The world spirit, this essential reality, proceeds irresistibly like a closely drawn armored phalanx, with imperceptible movement, much as the sun through thick and thin. . . ."[45]

Hegel's right to speak of the universe or Absolute, however, might still be challenged. It is one thing for commonsense language or even natural science to refer to the universe, and quite another for metaphysics to do so. For it is the job of metaphysics to be more meticulous about its "ontological commitments" or assertions of what exists than either common sense or natural science. To say that it is metaphysically appropriate to speak of the universe, that is, of the Absolute, is to say that it really exists, or has "ontological status." But if the universe is finally a mere aggregate of externally related entities it does *not* have any existence as an entity in itself. It is, then, a mere logical fiction, convenient for common sense and science, but not to be presupposed by metaphysicians. What justification, then, is there for a Hegelian metaphysician to refer to the Absolute? Let us suppose that the pluralistic interpretation of

Hegel (put forth in the next section) is right and that the Absolute is a cosmic community of mutually sympathetic but essentially independent individual spirits. In that case, reference to the Absolute would in fact be inappropriate in any metaphysical system developed purely from the detached cognitive standpoint. However, Hegelian metaphysics is not pure knowledge for its own sake. It presents itself as a union of "theoretical reason" and "practical reason." It serves a practical function in promising a road to salvation. The term "Absolute" belongs more to religious than to strictly metaphysical language. Reification of the universe as "the Absolute" is necessary if the individual is to relate to it religiously. Although the Absolute is a fiction, it is good to remember that, unlike Santa Claus but like George Washington, it is a well-founded fiction. And just as we must speak of George Washington (instead of individual cells and biographical moments) if we are to relate patriotically to the purpose organizing those cells and moments, so we must speak of the Absolute if we are to identify religiously with the purpose organizing the independent constituents of the universe which alone exist.

XIII *Hegelianism Pluralistically Interpreted*

Although in popular conception Hegel is thought to espouse the monistic theory of the "block universe,"[46] the British philosopher John M. E. McTaggart has argued that Hegelianism is really pluralistic.[47] The Hegelian Absolute, spirit, is essentially a community of minds. The very need for overt communication with other minds, for *deciphering* their messages, argues strongly for the basic privacy and essential independence of the communicating minds. Yet to the extent that communication succeeds, the individual mind, without necessarily surrendering its ultimate privacy, the incommunicable secret of its existence, approaches other individual minds empathetically, internalizing their viewpoints in such a way as to make each individual mind a "microcosmic" mirror of the total community. For example, an individual mind, expanding through communication to encompass the viewpoints of fellow countrymen who altogether make up the nation, becomes one with what may be called the "spirit of the nation." Indeed, until the different viewpoints are internalized and related within an individual mind, they constitute a mere aggregate, and the national spirit cannot yet be said to exist. Thus the expansion of the individual consciousness to include the community *constitutes* the spirit of the nation.

In much the same way, the individual mind which, by cosmic empathy, expands to identify, however haltingly, with the universe, may be said to constitute the cosmic spirit, which thereby first attains actual existence, however fleeting and tenuous. Thus in and for the individual mind the cosmos may come to exist in a way in which in itself, as an aggregate, it never exists. The cosmic community, in itself an aggregate, may become so internalized within participating members that through the socialized consciousness of the individual member it may attain an existence which makes it for the first time something more than a mere hypostatization or convenient fiction. The universe, in becoming conscious of itself in man, thereby comes into being. In the post-Copernican world, nobody takes the earth to be the *physical* center of the universe. There is no physical center. But Hegel, basing himself on reflections such as the above, was able to believe that the earth, because it cradles man, is nonetheless the *spiritual* center of the universe.[48]

But it would still have to be admitted that the universe remains in itself an aggregate and hence a convenient fiction. In a world in which empathetic identification with other human beings remains problematic, we should not delude ourselves into thinking that such identification with the universe can become anything more than a crude, although salutory, approximation. The Whiteheadian type of pluralism is a healthy corrective to illusions about the "block universe." And this Whiteheadian insight, as already noted, bears a close similarity to Buddhist doctrine. It would seem that Whitehead was talking about Buddhism when he wrote that his philosophy "seems to approximate more to some strains of Indian, or Chinese, thought, than to Western Asiatic, or European, thought."[49] Whitehead explicitly distinguishes his view from the Spinozistic-Brahmanistic view we examined in the last section:

In all philosophic theory there is an ultimate which is actual in virtue of its accidents. . . . In the [Whiteheadian] philosophy of organism this ultimate is termed "creativity". . . . In monistic philosophies, Spinoza's or absolute idealism, this ultimate is God, who is also equivalently termed "The Absolute." In such monistic schemes, the ultimate is illegitimately allowed a final, "eminent" reality, beyond that ascribed to any of its accidents. . . . Spinoza bases his philosophy upon the monistic substance, of which the actual occasions [that is, the momentary events, the "dharmas" of Buddhist doctrine] are inferior modes. The philosophy of organism inverts this point of view.[50]

It is evident from this quotation that Whitehead is assimilating Hegelianism ("absolute idealism") to the Spinozistic philosophy of substance. But this is to forget that Hegel is critical of the doctrine of substance. Hegel as well as Whitehead insists that the monistic "ultimate" is inseparable from the process of "accidents," so that, in the ultimate analysis, it is the "accidents" that are essential or substantial.[51] Hegel calls the process of accidents, of momentary events, "necessity." In Hegel's terminology Whitehead's "actual occasions" are "facts," and he defines "substance" as the abiding inner self-identity of necessity, that is, of the natural process of events.[52] The crucial question for Whitehead is: Which is more concrete, the events or the cosmic substance? He replies by assigning ultimate concreteness and independence to the events, the abiding self-identical "substance" being redefined as an abstract feature universally exhibited throughout the process, as "creativity." The events are self-creative. Substance, creativity, is an abstraction, and thus is neither creative nor active.

But Hegel would not dispute this: "Substance," he writes, "is the totality of the Accidents."[53] He distinguishes his position from Spinoza (and hence from Brahmanism) precisely through his insistence on the incoherence of the concept of a cosmic substance subsisting in essential independence and self-repose. The "accidents" are substantial; they are essential to the supposedly independent substance.

XIV   *Buddhism as a religion of Substance*

In conclusion, it appears that Hegel may have been right after all in considering Buddhism a religion of substance. For, as we now see, Buddhism is a religion of process, and "substance" is merely the inner abiding identity of the process of events. It helps to distinguish between two variations of the concept of substance, depending on whether the emphasis is placed on the abiding substance or on the accidents. If the emphasis is put on the abiding substance, we have a Spinozistic-Brahmanistic view of substance as the ground of the accidents. But if the accent is placed on the "accidents" we have a Buddhist-Whiteheadian view of "substance" as the abyss (*Abgrund*) of groundless accidents which, precisely because they lack any ground outside themselves, are really substantial. Hegel himself shows how the accidental or unessential becomes substantial or essential, and vice versa. Still, this is not to say that he could rest content with Buddhism or the Whiteheadian cosmology. The cosmic process of substantial events is but the "negative reflection," the inverted expression, of the Spinozistic philosophy of a single substance.[54] What is necessary from the Hegelian standpoint is to see how the cosmic spirit eventually achieves self-realization in the specifically human world of ethical institutions, art, religion, and philosophy. And to see this we must leave the Orient behind us and look to the West.

XV   Hegel's Western View of the East

Hegel's view of the Orient has been criticized as overly negative and prejudiced. One well-known Orientalist, Helmuth von Glasenapp, argues that in trying to refute the romantic opinion that India is the source of all wisdom Hegel fell into the opposite extreme of falsely denigrating the moral integrity and scientific achievements of the Chinese and Indians.[55] Hegel's usual powers of empathetic appreciation allegedly failed him here, and he thus missed the chance to construct a truly universal philosophy capable of synthesizing the civilizations of East and West. Two comments are in order here. First, it is arguably not true that Hegel's view was one-sidedly European. If Hegel deplored the lack of individual rights and dignity in the East, he also deplored the exaggeration of individualism in the West. What he strove for may thus, after all, be described as a "synthesis between East and West." Still, Hegel's synthesis is one in which Western individualism, however much it may have become one-sided in bourgeois economic and political life, is viewed as progress in relation to Eastern collectivism.[56] But—and this is the second point—Hegel is arguably right in rating the West more highly than the Orient. Despite the end of the colonial order, the Orient is today, as Hegel predicted it would be, increasingly under the influence of Western economic and political forms. Glasenapp's point of view itself betrays a certain romanticism. The traditional Orient which he contrasts to the West is slowly disappearing before our very eyes.

CHAPTER 5

Persia, Judaism, and the Despotic God

I The Persian Empire

H ISTORICALLY and geographically, East and West meet in the ancient Middle East. In his philosophy of history, Hegel calls this transitional sphere "Persia."[1] But if the Chinese world is China and the Indian world India, it must not be supposed that the Persian world is simply Persia. It includes much more. It is the world we encounter in the Old Testament, including the Egyptians, Assyrians, Babylonians, Hebrews, and several other peoples as well as the Persians. The Persians were simply the people under whom the ancient nations of the Middle East finally attained political unification prior to the conquest of the area by the Greeks under Alexander the Great.

It is characteristic of this ancient Persian empire that cultural and religious diversity survived among its various subject peoples. The Chinese empire was Chinese not merely on the political level, but linguistically and culturally as well. In India, Hinduism absorbed and relativized religious differences between the population groups. But the Persian empire created by Cyrus did not attempt any such linguistic, cultural, or religious unification. That is why Hegel takes it to be the first empire in the modern sense of the term.[2] Like the Roman Empire which came after or the short-lived Napoleonic empire of Hegel's own day, the empire of the Persians was a purely political conglomeration of culturally diverse elements. Such an empire, despite the political leadership of a single nation, tends toward a federation. National identity tends to be depoliticized.

The Babylonian empire, which was finally toppled in 537 B.C. by the Persians, was, by contrast, an empire more in the old Oriental sense. Thus the Babylonians, upon conquering Jerusalem, destroyed the Hebraic temple and carried the Jews away into captivity. But one of the first steps taken by the Persian emperor after the conquest of Babylon was to free the Hebrews, allowing them to return to Jerusalem and rebuild the temple.[3] The motive behind this Persian show of tolerance seems to have been a desire to win the allegiance of oppressed populations by granting religious, linguistic, and cultural autonomy in exchange for recognition of Persian political supremacy. If so, it was a political supremacy purchased perhaps too cheaply, one which lacked the staying power of the Chinese or Indian fusion of the political system with a whole nonpolitical civilization. The Chinese and Indian civilizations are still with us today, while the Persian empire is but a memory.[4] The Persian religion—associated with the name of Zoroaster—failed to establish itself as the universal religion of the Persian empire, and it survives today chiefly in the region of Bombay,[5] where a community of Persians sought refuge from Islam in the twelfth century.

II The True Beginning of World History

But it is the very cultural pluralism of the Persian world which gives it its unique place in the Hegelian view of world history. It is with it that, in his eyes, world history actually begins.[6] In part this is so because each of the world-historical peoples since the Persians—the Greeks, Romans, and modern Europeans—was conscious of its historical continuity with the Persians, of having directly or indirectly inherited its mission of world leadership from them. The ancient Greeks were conscious of having achieved their supremacy through an ultimately victorious struggle against Persia. India, by contrast, entered into Greek consciousness only by vague rumor, and China might as well have not existed.

But the reason why Persia was the beginning of world history is not merely that this history became a continuous development only beginning with the Persians; for the cultural pluralism of the ancient Middle East made it intrinsically historical. The succession of ethnically diverse empires over the centuries—Egyptian, Assyrian, Babylonian, Persian—gave the area an intrinsic historical self-consciousness of its own. The Persians were aware of the existence of imperial civilizations before them, and must have suspected that there might be yet others to come.

III Zoroastrianism

The Zoroastrian religion of Persia, we have noted, never grew to the status of a world religion. It nonetheless enjoys, according to

Hegel, an important transitional position between the nature religions of the Orient—in which the notion of the human personality has not yet been abstracted and differentiated from matter or nature—and the religions of the West which, beginning with Judaism and the Greek Olympian religion, succeed in differentiating the human spirit from matter.[7] What is divine for the Persians is light, a material element. But the Persian religion is not simply a natural religion because light is, in Hegel's view, the most immaterial of material elements.[8] Modern science, in defining light as massless energy, seems to lend Hegel some support here. Light is infinitely light. It is this quasi-spiritual nature of light which permits its deification in Zoroastrianism to be at once the deification of ethical attributes such as goodness, truth, or justice.[9] Light here is not a *symbol* of goodness, for this would suppose that it had been distinguished from what it symbolized. Light, for the Persians, *is* goodness.

But while goodness is identified with light, it is also superficially personified as Ozmad,[10] of whom the ancient Persian kings saw themselves as servants.[11] What this view ruled out was the Chinese (or Egyptian) belief in the divinity of the emperor. In this respect, there is a resemblance between Judaism and Zoroastrianism, and in fact the two religions have been frequently compared. They are both fundamentally ethical, and they both replace the idea of an emperor-god with the concept of a sacred kingship itself subject to divine authority. But important differences remain. Judaism succeeds in conceiving God in abstraction from all matter as a purely spiritual being, and is thus what Hegel calls a "religion of spiritual individuality" rather than a natural religion like Zoroastrianism.[12] Connected with this is the fact that the Judaic God is not merely a superficial personification of an essentially nonpersonal being, but a highly individualized person with a definite biographical record of past actions and future plans, as related in the Old Testament. A final difference is that Ozmad, unlike the God of the Hebrews, is not all-powerful. Over against the forces of good personified in Ozmad stand the forces of evil identified with "Ahriman."[13] Every man is called upon to join in a cosmic struggle to combat the forces of evil and darkness, and to spread the empire of light and good. But the complete victory of good over evil is postponed to the end of time. As Hegel says, Ozmad *should* be all-powerful, but in actual fact his realm is limited.[14] Zoroastrianism is thus interpreted as a form of *dualism:* goodness is absolutized apart from evil, life apart from death.

Hegel, of course, takes this dualistic standpoint to be false and indeed inherently self-contradictory. Goodness is in truth inseparable from evil, since it is its overcoming. And life is inseparable from death, since it is essentially an eternal rebirth or reproduction, that is, death and resurrection. (Think, for example, of the constant breaking down and rebuilding of living tissue in the process of metabolism.) Ozmad is not a convincing person because he does not include any evil, falsehood, death or, in a word, "negativity" within himself, but rather explicitly excludes it.[15] Like the heroes of certain first-generation Westerns, he is too good to be true. The believability of the Hebrew God as a person depends in part on the fact that He is subject to violent emotions, can repent some of his acts, and on occasion can even be challenged by man on moral grounds.

IV *The Egyptian Religion*

In Hegel's view, Zoroastrianism is not even the highest form of natural religion. Within nature, "negativity" appears as death. A conception of divinity which, without leaving natural religion, is more adequate than the dualistic Zoroastrian religion is thus one which represents the death of the god himself. This advance appears in the Syrian cult of Adonis and in the Egyptian cult of Osiris.[16] In Adonis or Osiris we have a god who dies and is resurrected. But this apparent anticipation of the Christian conception of the death and resurrection of Christ should not blind us to important differences. The Syrian or Egyptian god is essentially a vegetation god, whose death and rebirth signify the passage of the seasons, in particular, the transition from winter to spring. Further, he is only one among many gods, and thus is not all-powerful. Christ, by contrast, is no mere vegetation god. The death and resurrection of Christ do not chiefly signify the passage of the seasons or, indeed, any natural process, but rather answer to an essentially ethical or spiritual need for reconciliation between the supernatural Old Testament Lord and his creatures. Christianity is thus not a natural religion. Its originality consists in identifying the dying god with the supernatural, omnipotent Lord of the universe.

Still, the Egyptian Osiris may be interpreted as a natural symbol of the yet undiscovered spiritual reality and process.[17] Hegel takes ancient Egypt to be the land of symbolism par excellence. Among the natural religions of the Orient, it is the Egyptian religion which, more than any other, develops a culture of symbolic art. Symbolic art, like all art, presupposes that nature is not by itself experienced as divine.[18] If, as in Hinduism and pantheism in general, all natural processes are experienced immediately as revelations of the divine, art in the Hegelian sense cannot exist. True art, as Hegel conceives it, has a religious function. It is not mere ornamentation; it is not art for art's sake but is revelatory. An artist, then, is moved to transform natural objects into works of art only because he senses that the natural object is devoid of divinity and profane until it has been aesthetically transformed and transfigured.

V Symbolic Art and its Egyptian Homeland

It follows that Hegel does not consider Chinese or Indian art to be true art. Chinese art tends to be decorative handiwork in which the minute detail work shows more technical skill than artistic depth.[19] As for Indian art, it fails to be true art because it is more *sublime* than *beautiful*.[20] A genuine work of art allows spirit to manifest itself in sensuous form, and that is what makes it beautiful. Natural religion, which fails to differentiate spirit from nature, is thus incapable of producing genuine works of art. What Hinduism produces instead are grotesque deformations of natural objects (for example, a multiplication of heads and arms). This deformation serves the purpose of heightening awareness of the infinite cosmic substance which appears through the object. The deformation prevents us from viewing the object as merely a finite ordinary thing, and thus imbues it with sublimity.

True art, it is argued, first insistently emerges in Egypt. For it is in Egypt that we find a dawning awareness of a distinctly spiritual or nonnatural reality. Yet the first form of this awareness is symbolic. One is conscious of the nonnatural reality only through the sensuous, natural symbol. Because the artist who creates the symbol is not aware of what is symbolized apart from the symbols he uses to represent it, he is not really aware of his use of symbols. The symbolism is thus unconscious.[21] A symbol represents a nonsensuous reality by bearing some resemblance to it. If the artist were aware of his symbolization, if he were able to distinguish his meaning from the sensuous symbols he uses and thus to see the resemblance between symbol and meaning, he would not really need the symbols in order to be conscious of his meaning. And in that case the use of symbols would be contrived, artificial, or mechanical. True symbolic art is unconscious of its symbolism. The genuine symbolic artist does not consciously translate abstract ideas into symbols. He does not yet have abstract ideas, and thus he takes his symbols seriously because they are his only access to the ideas. If he already had clear abstract ideas, the symbolization would amount to making what is clear less clear. The conscious attempt to disguise one's meaning may characterize some degenerate or secondary forms of art (for example, allegory),[22] but it is in principle excluded at that stage where art is still a vital search for greater clarity and understanding on the artist's part.

The symbolic artist may not even realize that there is some hidden meaning which he is trying to represent by means of his work. In painting a sun, for example, he may be thinking of his painting as nothing more than an image of the sun, and thus may fail to recognize its symbolic ambiguity. But if the artist finally does realize that he is trying to represent something or other by means of a symbol, the symbol becomes for him an enigma, a puzzle.[23] However, if he solves the puzzle and discovers by abstract thought what is being symbolized, the symbol loses much of its interest for him, and he goes on to express his meaning in its own proper terms without the use of symbolism.

What is symbolized by means of the animal forms, pyramids, and other typical works of Egyptian art is, in Hegel's view, man, that is, spirit. The pyramids were tombs, houses for the dead, that is, for those who have left the natural realm, for spirits. But it is the Sphinx which is Hegel's favorite example of Egyptian symbolism. He even calls it the "symbol of symbolism."[24] Half human and half animal, it presents itself as a riddle whose solution is the transition from Egypt to Greece, from nature to man, from symbolic art to classical art, from the ambiguous allusion to spirit as distinguished from nature to the adequate expression of this spirit in the grace of the human form, as in a Greek statue. The Sphinx symbolizes symbolism because its human head, emerging from an animal body, symbolizes the spirit of man working its way from bondage to nature to free self-consciousness and self-expression.

VI   Hegel on the Persian World: An Appraisal

A seductive reconstruction! But we must avoid the practice of taking Hegel's interpretations as a closed system, restricting ourselves to paraphase. Even after Hegel reached his mature systematic standpoint he continued, as we have seen, to extend his empirical knowledge and revise his historical constructions. We should assume that if he were writing today he would at least attempt to integrate the results of the most responsible living investigators. Hegel's articulation of his own system remains, even from the Hegelian standpoint, an open system, and *it* is decidedly not the "Absolute" of which he himself speaks.[25] The Absolute is all reality, the historical-cultural and natural universe onto which the system in its present stage of development opens. The system must remain in vital contact with this universe and receive unceasing nourishment from it if it is not to rigidify and die.

It is thus always necessary to ask what revisions of Hegel's constructions may be needed in the light of today's knowledge. In the first place, it would seem that Hegel's view of Zoroastrianism as an ethical dualism of good and evil can still be maintained, despite the presence of secondary countertendencies in the Persian religion. The Zoroastrian concept of history as a series of unrepeatable events with a beginning, direction, and goal, as a world-historical and fateful battle between good and evil, in fact provides a sharp contrast to the Indian ahistorical view of time as an eternal return.[26] In this respect, Zoroastrianism appears in fact to represent, as Hegel thought, a stage on the road from East to West. At the same time, Hegel's identification of Ozmad, the good, with an abstract notion of light conceived as an invisible power of making things visible has been criticized as a distortion of Persian theology, which Hegel viewed through the eyes of Western philosophy. No equivalent for Hegel's rather Platonic concept of light has been found in the Persian language.[27] It has even been suggested that his view of the Persian religion of "light" initially resulted from a transposition to the Eastern world of concepts derived from his reading of Jakob Böhme, the German mystic.[28]

Hegel seems correct in insisting that Ozmad, who excludes all evil, fails, for that reason, to be a convincing person. It is, moreover, true that what is missing in the Persian concept of Ozmad is found in the Egyptian concept of a dying god. The more concretely personal concept of the gods which can be found in Egypt is accompanied by greater insistence on the importance of the human person as well. Herodotus, the Greek historian, claimed that the Egyptians were the first to conceive the idea of an immortal soul.[29] Immortal souls were recognized in China, but they remained bound up with the powers of this world, both wielding power over natural forces and, in turn, yielding to the superior earthly power of the emperor.[30] And, as for Hinduism and Buddhism, we found them to harbor more an aspiration for the annihilation of individual personal identity than for individual immortality. The Egyptian practice of mummification and of stocking tombs with food provisions does suggest something new. However, this very concern for the preservation of the dead body shows that, although the Egyptians may have formed the concept of individual immortality, they had not clearly differentiated the soul from the body.[31] That step, which was taken in Herodotus' own Greece, required that the sphere of natural religion be left behind.

We may even go along with Hegel when he interprets Egyptian art as essentially symbolic. Further, Hegel makes an intrinsically interesting distinction between the symbolism of an artist who is unaware that he is using any symbolism and that of an artist who is aware of this without yet being able to tell what is symbolized, so that his symbols become enigmas to him. Yet it seems doubtful that Egyptian religion was so much marked by the consciousness of enigma that we are warranted in calling it, with Hegel, the "religion of mystery."[32] Still, it must be admitted that Hegel did not create the image of Egypt as a "land of mysteries," for that view was common even in ancient times. Plutarch, for example, took Egypt to be a land of mysterious symbolism at least in part because his Greek refinement prevented him from taking literally whatever appeared offensive in Egyptian religion (for example, the dismemberment of the god Osiris). Such crudities were attributed to a hidden but undoubtedly more wholesome meaning. This general image of ancient Egypt remains in force even today. Although Egyptian hieroglyphics were decoded in Hegel's own time, the term "hieroglyphic" still connotes mystery. Hegel's view was probably also influenced by the fact that the literature of ancient Egypt was practically unknown in his time. He believed that it was significant that the Egyptians had no Homer or Bible.[33] He concluded that they were a puzzle even to themselves, unable as they were to give any verbal account of themselves. But since Hegel's death numerous literary and religious works have come to light, and they have in part dispelled the contrast which Hegel sought to establish in this respect between Egypt and Homer's Greece or the biblical Hebrews.

VII   *The Spirit and Fate of Judaism*

Politically speaking, the Persian world of which Hegel speaks is no longer with us. A possible exception, however, is Israel. But

Israel exists today because of its religion. Judaism, the religion of a minor nation of the ancient Middle East, survived the political eclipse of the Persian world and went on to assume, in Hegel's view, a world-historical importance far exceeding the political importance of the ancient Hebrew state. This religion, by preparing the way for Christianity, served as an essential link in the transition from East to West. Much of Hegel's interest in the Hebrew tradition is due to his conviction that the Christianity of his own time retained the definite imprint of its Judaic origins. We shall thus see once more how Hegel's preoccupation with the past, with history, conceals a concern with the present.

Hegel's most lively preoccupation with Judaism falls within the early, formative years of his development. In Frankfurt, in the late 1790s, he was concerned to study the Hebrew tradition in order to understand the background of the rigid Lutheran Protestant orthodoxy to which he had been exposed in his seminary years. Following the example provided by Herder, he sought to view the Old Testament nondogmatically as the literary revelation of the unique Hebrew experience of the world.[34] Persuaded that the essence of Judaism was to be found in what today, following Sartre, we might call the "existential project"[35] of Abraham, its founder, Hegel sought to sketch empathetically an "existential biography" of Abraham, showing how a free choice, constituting Abraham's identity as a person, became a seemingly unavoidable destiny for the people which traced its origins to him.[36]

Abraham's choice was essentially one of alienation or divorce from nature. Forsaking his urban, commercial roots in the Sumerian civilization of Ur, Abraham reverted to a more primitive nomadic past. He assumed the life of a herdsman and became a wanderer on the face of the earth, divorcing himself from the bonds of affection which previously held him to the natural and cultural environment of his father.[37] He turned his back on his ancestors and their polytheistic worship, placing himself instead in the hands of an all-powerful Lord, conceived as the immaterial Creator of the material world.

The meaning of Abraham's choice is best understood if it is placed in the context of the alternatives which it excluded. Hegel interprets the Hebraic decision as one of different, alternate responses to a situation of extreme need, of natural catastrophe and the consequent rupture with nature. Such a catastrophe was the biblical flood. The usual response is precisely the Oriental despotism which we have examined in previous sections, and whose classical model is China. In the Old Testament, this path is attributed to Nimrod. Nimrod succeeded in subjugating the people by promising security against a hostile nature.[38] He then sought to subject nature to the control of despotically organized masses. The originality of the Hebrew response is illustrated by the semimythical figure of Noah. Instead of subjugating himself to a human or natural despot, or perhaps seeking despotic control over nature for himself, Noah subjugated himself to God, that is, to a supernatural despot. He perceived that no natural despot is omnipotent, so that absolute security is not possible by placing oneself in the care of a human king or emperor.

VIII   *The Hebrew Concept of Sacred Kingship*

All despotism, as Thomas Hobbes realized, is based on a covenant or "social contract" in which the subjects promise obedience in exchange for security.[39] What we have in Judaism is, in a sense, the ultimate development of despotism. In Judaism, patriarchal despotism enters human consciousness to the point of serving as the model for conceiving ultimate reality, that is, God. For the first time, the Absolute itself is defined patriarchally. Whereas the Brahma of Hindu thought or the Heaven of Confucianism is personified only superficially, the Lord of the Old Testament, the God of Abraham and Isaac, is a highly individualized person, complete with a biographical record of plans and humanlike actions relative to his people. God promises his people prosperity in his kingdom if only they will obey his law. If a human despot rules nature through his abstract patriarchal intelligence, a divine despot realizes absolute intelligence and wisdom.

But if, in one sense, Judaism is the ultimate form of despotism, this very elevation of despotism to the supernatural level is, in another sense, a step toward its abolution. Despotism is magnified beyond human proportions and is thereby in principle transcended as a human institution. It is no accident that the early Hebrews, newly settled in the promised land, long resisted the temptation of following the pattern of neighboring nations by establishing kingship.[40] When Gideon was offered a crown, he refused, reminding Israel that it already had a heavenly king. And when the Hebrews finally succumbed to the temptation, the form of kingship established was historically original. Solomon, despite his legendary splendor, was not a despot in the Oriental sense. Unlike the Chinese emperor, he was not considered divine. He was rather the anointed of God. Even if he was a king, he was also, like his own subjects, the subject and servant of God. The Hebrews thus gave the West the idea of sacred kingship. It is the idea of a king who serves not his own ends, nor even those of his people, but rather the larger purposes of God.

IX *Judaism as an Ethical Religion*

The Chinese emperor, it may be recalled, served the Mandate of Heaven. But, unlike the Hebrew God, Heaven by itself was an empty abstraction for the Chinese. The requirements of Heaven were determined either by the harmonies of existing social relationships or, as long as the empire remained prosperous, by the will of the emperor. The deification of the emperor consisted in his identification with the impersonal might of the cosmos, and natural or political disaster called this identity into question, thus leading to the overthrow of dynasties. In Judaism, on the other hand, the will of God is presumed to be, in itself, quite definite, even if it is inscrutable or not definitely known, and even if it brings about apparent disaster. Thus Judaism, unlike ordinary despotic religion, could survive and even grow in moral inwardness and strength during the decline and destruction of its political base. Judaism reached its ethical pinnacle in the era of the prophets who preceded and accompanied the destruction of ancient Israel and Judea. Trust in the supernatural patriarch was so great that it could not be destroyed by temporal misfortune. If God punishes the wicked and rewards the virtuous, the misfortune of his people suggests that there is more to virtue than meets the eye, or perhaps that virtue is its own reward.

Thus the history of the Jews brought out the essentially ethical character of their religion. Obedience to the will of an all-powerful and just God is necessarily rewarded, by virtue of the covenant between Him and His people. If the fortunes of history turn against His people, faith will lead them to conclude that obedience to His will is more than external compliance with ritual, or that material rewards are not genuine, or both. But, even on a lower moral plane, the Hebrew relation to God is necessarily ethical because it is, even if ritualistic, a contractual relationship of commitment, obligation, fidelity, and dedication to an ever-renewed task. Such a statement could not be fairly made about either Brahmanism or Buddhism. It is true that the Hindus seek reincarnation in a higher caste by proper conduct, and that Mahayana Buddhists value charity and love of one's neighbor. But in both cases ethical conduct serves an ulterior purpose which is distinctly nonethical: the extinction of one's personhood through union with Brahma or attainment of Nirvana. To be a person is to place obligations upon oneself, to promise, and to live in the gnawing disquietude of unfulfilled tasks. Both Hinduism and Buddhism ultimately aim at a mystical state of depersonalization in which consciousness of such disquietude is laid to rest. Judaism, on the other hand, heightens this consciousness because it conceives God to be essentially personal, and man's relationship to Him to be essentially contractual and thus inherently ethical.

X   *The Metaphysical Originality of Judaism*

But Hegel, in pointing out the world-historical importance of Judaism, stresses more its *metaphysical* than its *ethical* originality. Of course, the Hebrews never developed a native tradition of speculative metaphysics such as arose in Greece. But metaphysics in the sense of an implicit view of reality, what Hegel calls a "definition of the Absolute," is common to all men and does not require the existence of a group of self-conscious metaphysicians. What is striking is that the ordinary, untutored Hebrews conceived the highly abstract idea of a totally disincarnate, disembodied spirit, for it is this being of pure thought, present everywhere and nowhere, whom they worshipped as God. Judaism is a popular metaphysics, and in this it differs from the Greek metaphysical tradition. Greeks such as Plato, Aristotle, and Xenophanes developed a critique of popular polytheism which tended to monotheism, and which was thus somewhat analogous to the Judaic critique of polytheism. But the Greek critique, unlike the Judaic one, remained essentially aristocratic, the property of an intellectual elite. Whereas the Platonic-Aristotelian dualism of Being and Becoming, pure form and material substance, was restricted to the few, the Judaic dualism of immaterial Creator and created world was the common property of the people as a whole.

It would not be too difficult to defend the thesis that Western civilization is, to a large extent, a result of the convergence and mutual reinforcement of these two dualisms. If spirit is conceived in abstraction from matter, the matter which is left over will accordingly be conceived as spiritless. The idea of pure spirit thus calls forth the opposite idea of mere matter, and it is no surprise that the same Hebraic culture which came up with the theistic idea of a transcendent immaterial God should, along with Greek metaphysics, have also produced the metaphysical materialism and physical science of our civilization.

But Judaism goes beyond the mere dualism of matter and spirit by conceiving the relation between God and the world to be one of "creation." Yet the effect of the creation doctrine is to reinforce the despiritualization of matter inherent in any mind-matter dualism. In the first place, if the world is created it follows that it is non-creative.[41] Thus any creative power which the creatures of this world have is ultimately *borrowed* from God. Moreover, if, as John Locke holds, ownership derives from labor, [42] God's labor in creating the world entitles Him to ownership of the world. But ownership implies control. Ultimately only dead matter can be truly owned because only it can be fully controlled. Once again Judaic theology leads to the despiritualization of the natural world, which as God's handiwork, the objectification of his labor, is a thing owned by Him.

The worship of natural objects is condemned as *idolatry* by the Hebrews because it implies the autonomy, creative power, and spiritual dignity of nature and thus constitutes a denial of nature's status as God's property.[43] To appropriate is to "thingify." Where the polytheist adores a statue of a god as the sensory incarnation of the divine spirit, all the Hebrew sees is the senseless and humanly degrading worship of a merely material thing. The Hebrew depoeticization of nature is also evident, as Hegel notes, in the Old Testament concept of *miracles*.[44] The very idea of a miracle presupposes that nature is by itself a merely material domain of mechanically interacting things. Although the Hebrews did not create natural science, they did hold the view of the world which makes natural science possible. A miracle is for them an exceptional divine intervention in the order of nature. Hinduism lacks the idea of miracles because it lacks the idea of a despiritualized mechanical order of nature. In Hinduism every natural phenomenon is an incarnation of God; or, to put it another way, for the Hindu everything is miraculous. But if every natural event is a miracle, ultimately nothing is miraculous. Indian religion generally fails to rise to the level of *pure* thought, of thought totally abstracted from nature. Brahma, the cosmic substance, is indeed a thought object, but it is a thought object which is universally manifest in nature. Thus Hinduism remains for Hegel a natural religion, whereas Judaism, in abstracting spirit from nature, becomes a religion of

spiritual individuality.[45] By "individuality" Hegel means here
something whose unity is derived from its active opposition to
something else.[46] The individual spirit of God is opposed to the
world He created.

XI   The Sublimity of Hebraic Poetry

The despiritualization of the Hebraic world is the reason for
Hegel's claim that Judaism is the most ugly of religions.[47] Hegel, as
we shall see, defines beauty as the sensory realization of spirit. It is
thus evident that in his view nothing can be beautiful for the
Hebrews. However, this rather extreme judgment, reached while
Hegel was still young, was somewhat tempered later in life. He
never abandoned his view that the experience of beauty is closed to
the Hebrew mind, but he did broaden his conception of art to allow
for a specifically Hebraic (and to some extent Islamic) form of
poetry which, if not "beautiful," is at least admitted to be
"sublime." He derived the distinction beween the beautiful and the
sublime initially from Kant,[48] but he went on to develop the concept of sublime art in his own way. If beauty is spirit revealing itself
in sensory form, sublimity marks the aesthetic experience of any
people which fails to define the Absolute as the sort of spirit capable
of revealing itself in sensory form. Beauty, we shall see, is reserved
for the Greeks. What remains for the Orientals is sublimity. But
there are two kinds of sublimity according to Hegel: positive and
negative.[49] Hindu sublimity is positive. By this Hegel means that
the natural phenomenon is experienced as a direct incarnation of
the cosmic substance. The finite becomes sublime to the extent that
the infinite appears momentarily in it. But Hebrew sublimity is
negative. What this means is that since God, as otherworldly or
transcendent, does not directly reveal himself in the natural order,
the characteristic way in which natural things reveal God is by
pointing to what is totally *other* than them. Thus the Psalms of
David achieve negative sublimity by singing praises of a Lord
whose grandeur far exceeds anything which is known to the senses.
Hegel developed an appreciation for Hebrew poetry largely
through the influence of his revered friend and one-time administrative superior (Jena, 1801 - 1808) Goethe.[50]

XII   The Judaic Contribution to Human Freedom

The relationship of spirit to matter in Judaism, we have
suggested, is the metaphysical transcription of the economic

relationship of proprietor to property. It is thus a relation of domination, of what Hegel calls "lordship and bondage."[51] It follows that the religion of the Old Testament would be incomprehensible to a prepastoral society of hunters and food gatherers prior to the invention of durable property (for example, herds) and to the social relations arising therefrom. Thus the economic basis of Judaism turns out to be essentially the same as that of the religions of China and India: the pastoral and agricultural revolutions which led to the creation of the ancient city-states and empires.[52]

But the same general patriarchal economic basis allows for the construction of different religious superstructures. In China the revolutions which led to political despotism led, on the religious level, to a deification of the human despot. In India we find a religious-metaphysical transcendence of human despotism, but it is ultimately escapist because it leaves despotic conditions intact in this world. It is only in Judaism that the religious superstructure reacts upon its despotic base, leading to a genuine reform of political despotism. Judaic theology could not have arisen except in despotic conditions, for earthly despotism, whether of the Pharoah or the Babylonian king, was the model on which God, the supernatural patriarch, is first conceived. But this theology so reacts upon its despotic sociological base as to transform Oriental despotism into the institution of sacred kingship.

Both India and Judaism represent steps on the road to freedom. In India we have a religious-metaphysical freedom joined with political bondage, while in Judaism we have a kind of political freedom joined with religious bondage. The Hebrew institutions of tribal democracy, which persisted prior to the creation of the monarchy, were preserved in the sacred monarchy established by Saul. The history of the prophets shows the exercise of the right of popular dissent even under the monarchy. But the choice between the Indian combination of religious freedom with political bondage and, on the other hand, the Judaic combination of bondage to God with political freedom is not groundless. Judaism represents the higher principle. To export despotism into the otherworldly realm is to expel it from this world. The inner despotism of conscience, of bondage to what Freud calls the superego, is freedom from external social authority. Similarly, the servant of God knows no earthly master. The exchange of an earthly master for a heavenly one represents progress in the history of the realization of freedom because bondage to God is bondage to a purely inward, spiritual principle. To be sure, such bondage is not yet freedom. Indeed, in one way slavery to the voice of God is more tyrannical than ordinary slavery, since God sees all. Yet such bondage is a necessary step toward freedom. The fear of the Lord may not be wisdom, Hegel says, but it *is* the beginning of wisdom.[53] One must learn to obey in order to learn to command, even in order to learn to command oneself.[54]

XIII   *Hegel's Early Criticism of Judaism*

Hegel's preoccupation with Judaism in his early years was, as already noted, part of an attempt to understand critically the legalistic, dogmatic Lutheranism in which he had been trained. His attitude toward Judaism was negative because he interpreted it as the original source of the sort of Christian orthodoxy which sought to prescribe beliefs, actions, and even feelings.[55] In commanding feelings Christian legalism outdid its Judaic model. Hegel eventually came to view the critique of theological dogmatism given by Kant and his follower Fichte as perverted by the very Judaic legalistic spirit which they sought to undermine in the name of human enlightenment and freedom.[56] Kant criticized "heteronomy" (that is, determination by something external) in the name of "autonomy" or self-determination.[57] Kantian self-determination consisted in subjecting oneself to the rational "categorical imperative" of morality. In its simplest terms, the categorical imperative commands one to respect the dignity of persons. But in Hegel's view the idea of obedience to a command, even supposing the command to be moral and rational, and not merely legal, presupposes a divorce between the natural human being who receives the command and the issuing authority.[58] Such obedience thus presupposes the same "heteronomy" or determination by something apart from oneself which Kant presumably wished to criticize. And the essence of the Judaic standpoint is well preserved, according to Hegel, in the Kantian philosophy of Fichte. We find in this philosophy the characteristic Judaic combination of subjection to an inner commanding authority and despiritualization of nature. Nature, according to Fichte, is nothing in and for itself, but is a mere object existing for the human subject, providing a field of action, an obstacle course to be overcome, an occasion for the performance of one's duty.[59]

XIV   *Hegel's Mature Appreciation of Judaism*

In the 1790s, Hegel reacted against this double alienation from God and from nature. He lamented the passing of the Greek polytheistic world-view which, by poetry and myth, made a home for man in nature, attaching man to his environment through bonds of love and trust.[60] But the mature Hegel developed a considerably different attitude toward Judaism. He came to believe that the passing of polytheism and its charms was inevitable,[61] and that the Judaic extreme of alienation from both nature and an authoritarian God was necessary for the eventual and equally extreme transcendence of alienation through Christianity.[62] God had in Judaism to separate Himself from nature, first to *disincarnate* Himself for the Christian doctrine of the Incarnation to have any meaning. Christianity is the solution to the problem of alienation from nature, which is posed religiously and cosmically in Judaism. But the problem is implicitly present in the situation of civilized man as a worker confronting nature as an other to be transformed. The God of the Hebrew patriarchs is the metaphysical absolutization of their own abstract patriarchal intelligence. Nimrod trusted his own intelligence, but Abraham, aware of the finitude of his intelligence, embodied his dream of infinite intelligence and power in the concept of his God.

The basic structure of the entire mature Hegelian system reserves a central place for Judaism. We know that the three parts of the system are the logic, the philosophy of nature, and the philosophy of Spirit. The logic is described by Hegel as the articulation of God as He existed in Himself prior to the creation of the world.[63] The reference to the creation doctrine signifies that it is the Hebraic God, that is, religiously absolutized patriarchal intelligence, who is being articulated in Hegel's logic. The philosophy of nature articulates the world created by this intelligence, while the philosophy of Spirit articulates the Christian reconciliation between God in Himself, a purely thinking being, and despiritualized nature.

But it is evident that Hegel preserves Judaism in his sysem only insofar as it is interpreted from his Christian point of view. The logic certainly does not articulate the Hebraic God as the Hebrews understood Him. Judaism, Hegel holds, assumes the standpoint of the patriarchal *understanding*,[64] which abstracts and absolutizes itself in negation of the sensory world. The God of Abraham is Abraham's idealized, infinitely magnified concept of his own self. God is everything Abraham is not but deeply wishes he could be. Christianity, on the other hand, assumes the standpoint of *reason*, which negates the understanding's neegation of the world, which reconceives God as essentially one with nature. The Hebrews understood their God abstractly and partially. In Christianity the same

God is understood concretely and completely. The God articulated in Hegel's logic is, like the Judaic God, a being of pure thought, but from Hegel's Christian standpoint it is known that the destiny of pure thought is to overcome its original abstraction to such an extent as to achieve reconciliation through "Spirit" with matter. Thus in Hegel's logic God in Himself before Creation is comprehended in anticipation of His destiny as the God of Creation and, ultimately, of the Incarnation. The logic, however abstract, develops the basic conceptual methods of concrete thought by which its own abstraction is to be overcome.

CHAPTER 6

Greece's Religion of Art

I *Greek versus Oriental Civilization*

I N the last chapter, we saw how Hegel distinguished the
Hebrew experience of the world from the more typical despotism
of the Orient in terms of a unique response to natural catastrophe,
symbolized by the account of the flood in the Old Testament. The
typical response of people in the empires and kingdoms of the East
was to place their trust in a paternal despot, an emperor or king.
The originality of the Hebrews, however, consisted in placing trust
in a transcendent but all-powerful God. Only a truly all-powerful
and, hence, superhuman God was truly trustworthy. The Hebrews
thus rejected the pretensions of human despots to divine status.
Still, it must be admitted that the idea of paternal despotism
remains, although it is transferred to the supernatural level.

But, in the same passage in which Hegel distinguishes Hebraism
from ordinary despotism in this way, he also distinguishes both from
the Greek response.[1] Greek religion also contains a flood story. According to Greek legend, the god Zeus was angered by the violence
of a primitive race of mortals, and he sent a flood to destroy them.
Only two mortals, Deucalion and his wife Pyrrha, were spared, having built an ark on the advice of another god, Prometheus. After
nine days the flood receded, and the pair found themselves alone on
the mountains of Thessalia. It is to them that the Greeks traced
their ancestry. What is significant for Hegel, however, is that the
Greeks did not respond to the memory of the flood by enslaving
themselves to either a human or a supernatural patriarch. Despite
the threat posed by natural forces, the Greeks refused to be afraid.
It was their abiding trust in both themselves and nature which, in
the first place, distinguished them from the peoples to the East.

90

G. W. F. HEGEL

II   The Idea of Citizenship And Its Aristocratic Origin

This self-confidence is evident in Greek political institutions. The Greeks treasured their liberties and laws, which they defended in an epic struggle against the Persian king and his vast empire. We have already noted that the Persian empire was considerably less despotic and more tolerant of diversity than its predecessors. The king did not see himself as divine, but rather as the servant of Ozmad, a transcendent ethical principle. Moreover, as in the case of the Jews, he was willing to respect the religious, linguistic, and cultural autonomy of subject peoples so long as they accepted Persian political supremacy. But it was just this political subjection which the Greeks, unlike the Jews, were unwilling to accept. To have accepted it would have meant abandonment of the Greek idea of citizenship. On the basis of this idea, the Greeks claimed the right to participate in the public deliberations and decision-making which affected them. Preservation of the ideal of citizenship required preservation of the small Greek city-state or "polis" from being swallowed up in a vast empire, where the individual's fate would be determined without his participation by an emperor and anonymous bureaucracy in some remote capital.

The Greek ideal of citizenship was eventually expanded, especially in Athens, on an increasingly democratic basis, but it had essentially aristocratic origins. Most of the Greek cities once had kings. Yet the Greek notion of kingship must not be confused with the patriarchal kingship found in the Orient. In a political despotism all but the despot are ultimately treated as underage children. The Greek idea of kingship, on the other hand, was more aristocratic than monarchical. The king was frequently elected. Like Agamemnon in Homer's *Iliad*, he was merely first among equals. He officiated at religious ceremonies, arbitrated disputes, led the army in battle, but in important matters was obligated to follow the counsel of clan heads. These aristocratic family heads thus reserved the right to deliberate and decide public policy as self-confident, self-governing adults.

We can get a fairly good idea of Greek aristocratic kingship by taking a look at the polytheistic society of Olympian gods worshipped by the Greeks. The Olympian religion originated in the aristocratic class of the Greek world, and the relation of Zeus, the reigning Olympian, to the other gods reflects a monarchy tempered by aristocratic liberties. Each of the gods has his own proper sphere, his independent power, privileges, and susceptibilities, to which Zeus must accommodate himself. Zeus is, to be sure, a patriarchal figure, but he is largely concerned with keeping peace in his family, and is content to maintain the forms of his authority by ratifying and solemnizing all essential claims made by the other gods. There is no absolutization of patriarchal authority into an omnipotent Creator. The Greeks knew little of the fear of the Lord.

Yet it must not be supposed that the Greeks completely evaded the dialectic of lordship and bondage which, politically or theologically, determined the entire previous history of civilization. It is true that the early Greek king presided over a confederation of his equals, deriving his authority from their consent. The king thus did not relate to the members of the council of elders as a patriarch. However, the members of this council were themselves patriarchal despots, each enjoying a power of life and death over the members of his family or clan. Agamemnon could not command the obedience of Achilles, who was basically his equal, but he could put his own daughter Iphigenia to death as a sacrifice to the gods. Even in the classical age of Pericles fathers exercised the right to expose unwanted children. The Roman father (*pater familias*) enjoyed similar rights. Yet this despotism of the father over his family was, paradoxically, the beginning of political liberty. The despotic rights of the clan head were the guarantee against the political despotism of a king. A nondespotic, aristocratic king may originally be defined as one who refrains from interfering in the domestic affairs of the family because he respects the despotic rights of the father within his own domain.

The difference between an aristocratic and despotic kingship can be clarified in terms of the difference between a "Lockian" and "Hobbesian" monarchy. John Locke imagined the "state of nature" preceding the creation of government to be less insecure than Thomas Hobbes, who described the prepolitical state of nature as a war of all against all.[2] In Locke's view, war and the threat of violence in the state of nature was more an occasional hazard than a permanent and universal condition. As a result, Locke did not think men would be willing to bargain away all their natural liberties for the sake of the security available through subjection to a monarch. Of course, Hegel, in conceiving the contrasting origins of Greek and despotic society, traces the insecurity of the state of nature to the threat of natural catastrophe rather than, as in Hobbes' and Locke's case, to the threat posed by man to man. Hegel sees the despot (symbolized by the biblical Nimrod) as an organizer of great public works—irrigation, dams, roads—designed to protect man from nature.[3] Yet the threat of natural catastrophe is not unrelated to the threat posed by men to one another. It is when nature is most cruel—in times of famine, flood, and pestilence—that men show themselves the most cruel to one another. But the interesting question is: *Why* were the Greeks more Lockian than Hobbesian? It is a question to which we shall return shortly.

III   Athenian Democracy

The aristocratic institutions of preclassical Greece eventually made Athenian democracy possible. It is far easier to extend the ranks of the free to *several* or even *many* if it is admitted that *more than one* is free than if, as in despotisms, it is insisted that *only one* is free. Thus, from a democratic standpoint, the defense of aristocratic liberties must be looked upon as an essentially progressive cause in its own time. To anyone who embraces what Hegel considers the modern Christian view that *all* are free, Greek civilization represents clear progress over what went before.[4] (Judaism, which achieved the ultimate despiritualization of nature, represents progress of a different kind: the less obvious but more profound progress of positing the ultimate error about the world, necessary for calling forth the ultimate Christian truth.)

Hegel portrays the Athenian polis of the Periclean age as a "political work of art."[5] The Athenian victory in the Median wars with Persia ushered in this classical age, providing the occasion for the full flowering of the Greek genius. The principle which distinguished Athens in the classical age was, according to Hegel, its social ethic. It was an ethic marked by a beautiful balance between Oriental collectivism and Western individualism.[6] The individual was identified with the polis in which he participated, and the polis protected his political and private rights. Hegel designates this ideal ethical harmony by the German term *Sittlichkeit*, which he contrasts to a "morality" based on private conscience.[7] The ethical individual who participates in the life of the polis is guided by institutionalized rules of practice. He thus embodies what Montesquieu, by whom Hegel was influenced, calls republican "virtue."[8] Hegel believed that the modern Western world had lost the sense of the Greek social ethic. According to him, the modern individual is merely moralistic. Guided solely by the inner voice of conscience, which Rousseau calls an infallible and celestial voice,[9] modern man detaches himself from the institutional life of his people and sets his own moral judgment up as an absolute standard of conduct. It was Kant who gave the most systematic articulation to this moralistic standpoint.[10]

There was a widespread tendency in Hegel's time to overidealize Athenian democracy, and even the mature Hegel does not seem to have fully escaped it. His image of Athens as embodying a beautiful balance between the individual and the polis fails to recognize the depth of the party conflicts which existed from the seventh century B.C. on. Hegel invokes a well-known funeral oration attributed to Pericles in justification of his idealized image,[11] although the hymn of praise to Athens was in fact more a patriotic plea than the description of reality for which Hegel took it. Although Hegel's image of the Greek ethical spirit is not without relation to the historical reality, he does tend to view it as an eternal idea abstracted from the conditions of its historical emergence. More generally, it is remarkable that Hegel conceives world history as a series of such largely nonhistorical, national principles. The world-historical transition from Persia to Greece, and from Greece to Rome, is considered, but the transitions taking place within the national history of each people are placed in the background. World history becomes a development whose stages are national spirits, not national histories. The Greek spirit is fifth-century Athens, the Roman spirit the age of Augustus, and so on. Yet the leap across the centuries from Pericles to the Emperor Augustus may be excused if one remembers that Hegel was writing philosophical world history and did not claim to be a historian. What was most important for him in understanding the present was not the gradual rise and decline of the Athenian polis, but rather Athens in its full glory; that is the Athens which remains in the modern consciousness as an essential moment in the process of its own emergence.

Yet even in idealizing Athens Hegel avoided the excesses of uncritical Hellenism. Athenian democracy suffered, in his view, from slavery,[12] from a failure to integrate all those engaged in material production (that is, the members of what Hegel calls "civil society") within the political community of the state,[13] a failure to create universal political rights and citizenship. Citizenship was extended on a somewhat accidental basis, as a reward for special services to the state, and was not justified on general principles. Yet Hegel also recognized, that slavery was a precondition of the citizen's leisure, and thus of the very existence of participatory democracy. It has been charged, however, that he was too complacent in thinking that the modern Western state, by officially abolishing slavery and extending citizenship to all, had overcome slavery in more than a formal sense.[14] It was Maurice Merleau-Ponty who wrote:

> The humanism of the capitalist societies, as real and precious as it may be for those who benefit from it, fails to descend from the level of the citizen to reach the man, does not suppress either unemployment or colonial exploitation, and thus, placed in the context of the history of all men, is, like the liberty of the ancient polis, the privilege of the few and not the property of all.[15]

IV   The Greek Basis of Western Civilization

But despite the limitations of classical Greek civilization, its achievements have inspired admiration ever since. Rather paradoxically, the people who achieved this progress owed it in part to their underdeveloped, backward condition. The empires of Egypt and Mesopotamia, based in the huge river valleys of the Orient, were farther removed than the Greeks from the tribal democracy of nomadic hunters and herders. When the Indo-European Greeks invaded the Mediterranean in the second millenium B.C., vast agricultural city-states and empires had already existed in the Middle East for centuries. The mountainous terrain of Greece, which made travel difficult, discouraged the organization of the Greeks into a centralized state and helped preserve traditional tribal institutions. When the Greeks came into contact with the more advanced civilizations to the East, their still vivid sense of individual autonomy and initiative allowed them to take up the Oriental culture in a creative way, producing a highly original culture of their own. Thus the very backwardness of the Greeks may have been a prime (though hardly sufficient) cause of their sudden preeminence.

This preeminence is found in a variety of areas: political life, philosophy, art. Greece has been a source of revolutionary renascences for Western civilization ever since: the medieval synthesis of Christian theology and Greek philosophy, the humanist Renaissance of the sixteenth century, the French Revolution, and German classicism-romanticism in Hegel's lifetime. The modern state, according to Hegel, extended the Greek idea of democracy to all, according to the Christian belief in the equal dignity of all men.

Greece is also the cradle of Western philosophy, although it is easy for philosophers, with their own professional bias, to forget that philosophy represented not the glory but the decadence of classical Greek civilization. It undermined belief in the Olympian mythical religion, and it upset the classical balance between individual judgment and public ethos in favor of the former. Hegel was always quite clear that, although philosophy was born in Greece, it existed there first as a marginal and ultimately as a destructive force.[16] Philosophy, he was persuaded, came into its own only in his own time, ultimately in his own philosophy.[17] The Hegelian philosophy revives the Greek speculative tradition of Plato and Aristotle and seeks to wed it to Christian theology. Attempting to go beyond the medieval "synthesis" of Thomas Aquinas, which finally leaves theology and philosophy lying side by side, Hegel sought to translate Christian dogma into the rational discourse of Greek metaphysics and thereby to justify faith by reason. But the same philosophical tradition which he used to *justify* Christianity *destroyed* the Olympian religion, for it tended toward a monotheistic awareness that God (the Absolute), unlike the Greek gods, could not be finite or limited by an external "destiny." Yet if philosophy was more the self-dissolution than the glory of Greek civilization, nonetheless glory there was. It was to be found in the art of Greece. Though the idea of citizenship originated in Greece, the degree to which it was realized there was to be surpassed, according to Hegel, by the modern state. Similarly, the potentials of Greek philosophy were to be realized by the modern Germans more completely than by the Greeks themselves. Only the beauty of Greek art remains, in Hegel's view, unequaled.[18]

V *The Religion of Beauty*

To understand the unique artistic achievement of Greece we must, Hegel believed, realize that art for the Greeks was more than art. It was their religion, so much so that Hegel called the Olympian religion the "religion of beauty."[19] He noted that, no matter how much we today may admire the grace and beauty of a Greek statue, we are incapable of worshipping it as a god.[20] And that is part of the reason why we are incapable of producing classical statues which, being more than imitations, surpass those of ancient Greece. Art for us is not religious revelation. We know that God cannot be made to manifest Himself by means of the sculptor's chisel or poet's imagination. Any god who can be made to manifest himself outwardly to the senses in a work of art is not God, not the Absolute. It is not divine because it is not infinite. Even the Greeks had a presentiment of the limitation of their gods. There was a vague aura of fate which hung even over their gods, casting a shadow of sadness and resignation over even the most beautiful works of Greek art.[21].

The aesthetic culture and religion of the Greeks was seen by Hegel as standing midway between the Oriental and modern Western civlizations.[22] In world history, Greece is a halfway house. The underlying principle of the Orient is substantiality. The individual human being is swallowed up in the sublimity of the cosmic substance. The principle of modern culture, on the other hand, is individual subjectivity. The individual detaches himself from the substantial social or cosmic whole through the caprice of private judgment. In ancient Greece the individual had already detached himself from nature, although the superstitious dependence of the Greeks on oracles and natural omens shows that they did not reach the level of self-confidence generally prevailing today.[23] But the effect of the flood, of natural disaster, was to destroy all *naive* trust in the forces of nature. The typical Oriental response, we have seen, was an attempt to subject nature to human control. (Interestingly, such despotism has enjoyed a singular revival in the century since Ludwig Feuerbach, in 1843, called upon man to replace the God of the Old Testament.[24] The Communist planners and Western, technocratic systems analysts have heard the word.) The Hebrew response was for man, not daring to rule the world on his own, to place himself in God's hands. Unlike the Orientals, the Greeks sought to restore a relation of trust with nature. Of course, it was impossible to return to the naive trust which prevailed before the cataclysm. Instead, the Greeks sought to establish a relation of self-conscious, artfully constructed trust. They sought poetically to produce a second nature more beautiful than the first, a humanized nature in which they could feel at home, developing a self-confidence based on confidence in nature.[25] The very fact that ancient Greece was an aesthetic civilization implies that a rupture with nature had taken place. For one does not set out to remake nature through art unless a divorce has occurred between oneself and nature in its aesthetically unreconstructed form. The poet who imaginatively reconstructs his material surroundings has detached himself from them in order to do so.

But whereas in the Orient man withdrew his trust from nature to place it in a king, in God, or in mystical release from the finitude of the human condition, the Greeks restored their trust in nature through art. God's separation of the waters of the Red Sea to permit the Hebrews to escape from Egypt was an unusual direct intervention in nature. But for the Greeks *every* natural phenomenon was the direct result of the action and rule of anthropomorphic gods. The thunder and lightning were, for the most part, the harmless raving of Zeus. A live volcano was the smokestack of a subterranean metal shop run by the Cyclops, a race of tame one-eyed monsters in the service of the Olympians. A mountain range was the site where Zeus had buried vanquished giants under masses of clay and stone. We should suppose that these myths were less attempts to explain natural phenomena than attempts to tame and humanize them poetically. The triumph of the highly individualized and human Olympians over the more brutish Titans, mere personifications of natural forces in most cases, was the mythical expression of Greek self-confidence and trust in nature.[26] And it is precisely this aesthetically produced trust which explains why Greek political life remained free of the despotism of the Orient. The Greeks, we noted, were more Lockian than Hobbesian. They were more secure in their natural environment than the Orientals. The reason is not that natural forces were more benign in Greece. Nor is it that the Greeks were somehow more courageous than other mortals. Greek institutions are to be explained in terms of Greek aesthetic creativity, and not the other way around. Nature was transfigured by an aesthetically captivating polytheism. Thus art for the Greeks was the functional equivalent of technological control over nature. Clearly, in the long sweep of history technological control is indispensable. The security which the Greeks won through art was a false security, subject to repetitions of natural disaster against which art is defenseless. The "Greek miracle" could only be short-lived. But it lasted long enough to give us what Hegel, with numerous others, considered the most beautiful civilization which has ever existed.

VI   *Classical versus Symbolic Art*

Hegel takes sculpture to be the form in which Greek art reached its fullest development. It, more than any other art form, embodies the classical ideal of art,[27] and it is in Greece that classical art achieved a unique flowering.[28] Classical art is distinguished by the perfect harmony which is attained between what Hegel calls "form" and "content," that is, between the work of art as a material object and the meaning possessed by that object.[29] The symbolic art of Egypt, by contrast, is marked by a disharmony between the material form and the aesthetic meaning. The disharmony lies in the fact that the material form fails to be a self-contained whole, since it alludes to some undiscovered meaning which it fails to express. The symbolic work of art is a definite material object which fails to be a self-contained, rounded-off whole because it opens on to a meaning which is still indefinite. Such art is disquieting and unsatisfying, still searching for itself. As long as art remains symbolic, it fails to reveal what it is searching for. This search comes to a happy conclusion only when the threshold from symbolic to classical art is crossed. In classical art, the indefinite meaning of symbolic art becomes definite. The definite material form which is the work is itself the definition of its meaning. The material form encloses the significant content within itself, and the work, instead of refusing to satisfy our quest for meaning by pointing beyond itself, now becomes a self-contained whole and thus satisfies our desire for completion and wholeness of meaning. The spectator at last comes to rest in the contemplation of the aesthetic object.

Now the meaning or content of all art is, according to Hegel, *spirit,* and this is true whether the artist knows it or not. Art has a cognitive function: it is a quest for knowledge of reality,[30] which for Hegel means a knowledge of spirit. Classical art is the happy conclusion of the artistic quest. The material form of the classical work is no longer merely material, but is transfigured and transfused by spirit. However, the sort of spirit revealed by such art is not the *infinite* spirit which is one with the Christian God, but rather the *finite,* individual spirit of a limited, idealized divinity.[31]. When the knowledge which is sought finally becomes that of infinite spirit, art will prove inadequate. The Absolute cannot be encompassed within a surveyable work of art.

VII   *Sculpture: The Most Classical Art Form*

But we are now in a position to understand why sculpture realizes more than any other art form the ideal of classical art. The content of classical art, we said, is the individual spirit of a single human being. But that is also the content or subject matter of sculpture.[32] Sculpture which is not in the human form, for example, animal or modern abstract sculpture, would not be recognized by Hegel as true sculpture. Such sculpture has not yet liberated itself, in his view, from architecture. Even the Sphinx—half human and half animal—is considered as much as architecture as sculpture.[33] What he is saying here becomes clear once we realize the distinction he draws between "independent" and "dependent" architecture. Architecture in the more common sense—houses, churches, theaters—is what Hegel views as "dependent" architecture.[34] It is dependent because it is functional and serves some purpose beyond itself, as a house serves to shelter human beings. Abstract or animal "sculpture" is clearly not architecture in this sense. It is rather architecture in the sense of what Hegel calls "independent" architecture. This is architecture which is not functional, which does not serve to enclose, exhibit, or protect something beyond itself.[35] Examples of abstract or inorganic "sculpture," that is, of independent architecture, are Stonehenge, the Egyptian obelisks, the Tower of Babel, and the Eiffel Tower. They are all essentially non-utilitarian structures, and they are more architectural than sculptural because their form is not human. Yet precisely because independent architecture is useless, a mere work of art, it is a purer realization of architecture *as an art form* than architecture of the more common functional type.

An obelisk alludes, by some similarity of form, to a meaning which remains external to it. Where sculpture is essentially *classical* in Hegel's view, independent architecture is essentially *symbolic*. The subject matter or meaning of the obelisk is, like that of the classical statue, essentially spiritual, but, unlike the statue, the obelisk *refers* to its meaning without *expressing* and revealing it. The Egyptian obelisk, for example, symbolizes a ray of light joining the sun with the earth,[36] but the sun is symbolic of *spiritual* enlightenment. Thus the obelisk shares a spiritual *content* with the statue, but lacks its spiritual *form*. A statue in human form is spiritual with respect to both form and content.

Besides their common content, independent architecture and sculpture are similar in that both are nonutilitarian, that is, they are in a sense useless. Moreover, independent architecture evolves toward sculpture.[37] *Inorganic* form tends toward *organic* and, finally, *human* form. Symbolism evolves toward expression. Thus the organic, animal sculpture of Egypt represents an intermediary stage on the road from independent architecture (inorganic "sculpture") to sculpture in the true sense. Hegel's conviction that true sculpture is in the human form finds some basis in ordinary language usage. We speak more easily of animal "figures" than of animal "sculpture." A truly statuesque figure must be upright, hence human. Animal figures belong to the prehistory of sculpture. The animal figure may express a certain intuitive quickness which belongs to the substantial, nonindividualized animal soul. But a human being cannot achieve full self-consciousness except in the contemplation of what is distinctly human. Because the artist is himself spirit, art, whose subject matter is spirit, is a form of self-knowledge. In sculpture, as in the Greek world generally, man achieves awareness of himself as an individual spirit. (In the inorganic sculpture of the Oriental despotisms—for example, the Tower of Babel embodying the labor of regimented masses—man achieves awareness of himself rather only as a substantial or collective spirit.)[38]

Classical art is more specifically the ideal sensory realization of individualized spirit, and sculpture is the most classical of all art forms because it is in a statue that the *idealized* individual spirit is best expressed. Classical art does not aim at the *realistic* portrayal of living individuals, complete with warts and blemishes, but rather at the embodiment of ideal, beautiful individuals.[39] Of course, there are classical works of art which are not statues, which belong to art forms other than sculpture. There is *classical architecture*, for example, a Greek temple.[40] But the classical Greek temple is not intended to be at the center of artistic attention. It is rather designed to display, highlight, and enclose sculpture, that is, a statue of some god. The temple must not distract attention from the statue. Classical architecture is functional, dependent architecture, and its form is adapted to its function. It has clean lines, is free of excessive ornament, is discreet, economical, and unostentatious.

There is also such a thing as *classical mythology*. Greek mythology is classical because it portrays gods who are vividly drawn and individualized as persons endowed with knowledge and volition, whereas the more primitive Titans are superficial personifications of natural forces, and thus reflect a less classical form of mythology.[41] Classical mythology forms, in fact, the necessary background for understanding classical sculpture. The sculptors took their point of departure in the mythology of Greece.[42] They then proceeded to elaborate the mythical legend of a god or hero in the direction of greater precision and luminous clarity. Hegel recalls the claim of Herodotus that the Greek poets, the creators of literary myth, created the Greek gods. But Herodotus also reports that the

Greeks derived their gods from Egypt. The contradiction, however, is only apparent.[43] The truth is that the poets assimilated Egyptian material creatively. The sculptors related to the poets in a similarly creative way. They were also the creators of gods.[44]

Indeed, it is in the creations of sculpture that the individual spirit of the god attains its highest expression. Classical statuary reveals the abiding ideal character of the god. All that is accidental is elimated. The god revealed in the statue is relaxed and serene, disengaged from external action. The pose of the body contrasts sharply with the rigidity of Egyptian statues which, although technically proficient, always seem to stand or sit at attention.[45] The Greek god stands almost insolently at ease. Whereas in earlier Greek statues this ease is symbolized by a distinctive smile, in classical statues the whole attitude of the body is suffused with life, so that the smile symbolizing life can drop out, the facial expression acquiring a characteristic contemplative severity and a touch of sadness. Classical Greek tragedy eventually forced the gods out of this statuesque withdrawal into interaction with other gods and with men.[46] Aesthetically, the *classical tragedy* of Greece remains unequaled as classical tragedy according to Hegel. But this does not alter the fact that in tragedy the process of dissolution of the Greek religion of beauty is already underway. The dramatic interaction of gods among themselves and with men is the demonstration of their essentially relative character.[47] What is truly divine cannot be finite or relative. Greek sculpture was the highpoint of the religion of beauty because the isolation and mutual indifference of the different statues expressed better than myth or drama the claim to divinity put forth by the individual spirits of the gods. Greek drama rather shows the falsehood of these pretensions.

In these matters Hegel was much influenced by the work of Johann Joachim Winckelmann, an important instigator of German classicism.[48] It was Winckelmann who established the basic equation between Greece, beauty, idealization, classicism, and sculpture. Hegel borrowed the equation. Yet later in life he recognized the limitations of Winckelmann's views. Philosophically, Winckelmann was a Neoplatonist who identified the good with the beautiful and who insisted on the educational value of beauty, which inspires imitation. "The only path which can permit us to be great and, if it is possible, inimitable is the imitation of the Greeks," he wrote.[49] Winckelmann's position, on its simplest interpretation, aims at a restoration of classical antiquity. But the mature Hegel avoided the

pitfalls of an uncritical Hellenism by insisting on the inevitability of
the decline and disappearance of classical Greece.

VIII   The Artist as His Own Work of Art

In the *Phenomenology of Spirit*, Hegel calls the Greek statue an
"abstract work of art."[50] He means that, ultimately, a statue, even
when reproducing a human form, is inorganic, since it is made of
stone. Inorganic matter is more abstract, that is, less complex or
"concrete," than organic matter. The sculptor, who is living, effaces
himself before the god, a thing of stone in which he has invested his
creativity. What happens is a sort of *religious alienation:* the more
beautiful the divine statue, the poorer, by contrast, is the sculptor.[51]
This religious self-effacement before the gods is also evident in the
lyrical choral hymns of Pindar, in which different selves, singing in
unison hymns to the gods, fuse in a single inwardness of feeling.[52]
But in song the artist, unlike the sculptor, becomes one with the
work of art. The singers achieve both a unison with one another and
an empathetic oneness with the god to whom the hymn is addressed: to address a hymn to a god is to identify with the standpoint of that god, in order to formulate the communication so that
he will understand and accept it. But Greek religion did not stop
with the contemplation of statues and the singing of hymns. The
Greeks refused to give everything to the gods and thus went beyond
the religion of temple statues and hymns to create a highly
humanistic culture.

Greek worship, like that of many other peoples, took the form of
animal sacrifices. But what was distinctive about the Greek
sacrifices was that the best part of the meat was consumed by the
celebrants themselves, while the bones were left for the gods.[53]
Sacrifice was thus quite the opposite from self-denial. It took the
form of a feast, a celebration full of joy and self-affirmation. Since
the sacrificed animal was a symbol of the god, the sacrifice united
the worshippers with the god. But it was a union in which the god
sacrificed himself to man rather than the other way around! The
result was the religious celebration of man himself, what Hegel calls
the "living work of art."[54] If a statue or the undifferentiated unison
of a hymn is a self-alienating work of art, the feast of sacrifice is a
celebration of one's own mystical union with the god in which the
celebrants display an "art of living" which is itself revelatory of the
divine.

IX *The Epic Poetry of Homer*

The Bacchic and Eleusinian mystery religions, which practiced such sacrifices, contained, in Hegel's view, an undercurrent of Oriental pantheism.[55] It is this Oriental element which Nietzsche was later to call "Dionysian," and which contrasts with the more distinctively Greek "Apollonian" spirit, embodied in the calm detachment of classical sculpture.[56] But the Apollonian spirit is capable of expressing itself in a living human being, a living work of art, that is, in the form of the athletic heroes of the Greek games as well as in stone statuary.[57] The artist, through physical self-cultivation, becomes his own work of art.

But the inarticulate effusions of the Greek mystery religions and the visible harmony and grace of an Apollonian athlete are opposed to each other as the extremes of dumb inner feeling and superficial outward form. The union of inwardness and outwardness is found only by abandoning the sphere of the living work of art for that of what Hegel calls the "spiritual work of art."[58] The medium proper to the spiritual work of art is neither stone nor human flesh, but language. It is language which is at once equally inward and outward. For speech is by nature the externalization of what is internal. Inner feelings and thoughts become external by being put in the form of words.

The spiritual work of art is what Hegel also calls "poetry" and what we usually call "literature." We tend to restrict "poetry" to what Hegel calls "lyric poetry," while Hegel recognizes three different poetic genres: epic, lyric, and dramatic.[59] The basis on which all further Greek literature arises are the epic poems of Homer, the *Iliad* and the *Odyssey*, which Hegel takes to be the classical models of epic literature in general.[60] The Greek epics are marked by a balance between divine and human action which is missing, he believes, in the great Hindu epics, e.g. the *Bhagavad Gita* and the *Ramayana*.[61] An epic is distinguished from mere mythology by the weight attached to the exploits of human heroes. Hegel claims that in the Indian epics human action is not finely drawn, and is relegated to the background unless the individual is seen as an incarnation of a god, as for example Rama is an incarnation of Vishnu. The Greek balance has not yet been discovered, as the full meaning of human heroism has not yet been understood.

But it is the history of a people which makes a hero. Epic poetry has a patriotic function. It presents the history and life of a nation.[62]

It follows that the poet's individual character must not enter into such poetry. He rather effaces himself before events which are considered to be of an objective, historical, and public nature.[63] Both he and his hearers are chiefly spectators of these events. Quite apart from its aesthetic value, the epic has an educational function. It serves the purpose of assimilating the young into the national tradition. Incidental to relating the exploits of the hero, the epic portrays the total life of the nation. It presents a total human world. The Theogeny of Hesiod fails to be an epic because the world of the gods which it relates is an incomplete abstraction from the total human world.[64] The saga of the generations and dynasties of the gods takes place on the margin of the world of historical human struggles. A geniune epic presents ethical values concretely exemplified in the exploits of individual human heroes. But in the course of relating these exploits, the aim is achieved of presenting a panoramic view of all aspects of the nation's life, including its political and economic institutions, its domestic life and religion. A library of national epics, Hegel says, would be a gallery of national spirits.[65] Unlike drama, the epic unfolds slowly, so that each aspect of the collective life may be contemplated in its turn. All sides are passed in review as if in a parade. The epic knows nothing of "dramatic haste."[66] Hence its prolixity and seemingly endless detail should not be considered a fault. For example, the *Iliad* contains extensive descriptions of tools and artefacts. Such descriptions may seem insipid to us, but that is because we live in a prosaic age in which tools are mass-produced and impersonal.[67]

In the heroic age which is celebrated by Homer, the prosaic is not yet sharply distinguished from the poetic. [68] On a practical level, in a society in which education is still oral, the rhythm and cadence of poetry is an aid to memory. The heroic age of a people is one in which the nation has already awakened to self-consciousness and become at home in its world, but in which life has not yet become highly regimented and institutionalized.[69] And because public institutions cannot be taken for granted, it is a world in which the individual has not become conscious of a private identity and power of judgment capable of setting him against collective values and sentiments. Thus heroic action is essentially naive.[70] It has a childlike character. The epic hero is moved by uncomplicated patriotic feeling and courage. Hegel's idea of such a hero is illustrated by the hero of an old-fashioned American Western who never questions the received values of law and order and is free of psychological problems.

The heroic age of a nation, however, must not be confused with its earliest stage of development. Nearly every people, in its earliest stage, undergoes a foreign influence which precludes the self-confidence and creative freedom necessary for native poetic self-expression.[71] Thus until the second half of the nineteenth century the United States was dominated by European culture. The Greeks, as they first reached the Mediterranean, were exposed for a time to Oriental culture and religion. Hegel calls this preheroic, pre-epic era the "idyllic age" in which the Greek tribes had not yet developed sedentary political life.[72]

In the heroic age the political life of the city-state system exists, but it has not yet been routinized. Social relations are feudalistic, and a feudal king such as Agamemnon must take care not to offend the other chiefs, since he may otherwise find himself without their support in time of war. The heroic age is one in which obedience is not automatic, but is still a morally charged act, motivated more by honor than by the fear of punishment.[73] In the Hindu epic of the *Bhavagad Gita*, as in the *Iliad*, the question of a hero's participation or nonparticipation in battle is a major theme.

An epic poem from a past age holds interest for us today, according to Hegel, largely to the extent that it is the story of a nation's progressive struggle and just triumph over an adversary nation in the advancing course of world history.[74] Homer's epics are the story of the victory of the Greeks over the Orient as represented by the Trojans. By this standard, the German legends of Siegfried and his companions hold little interest for modern Germans, Hegel says, because they are stories of a moribund people and culture, whose heritage the modern Germans had renounced.[75] The Hebrews and Greeks have greater meaning for the Germans of today, he says. In light of the romantic trend of German culture and politics after Hegel, from Wagner to the National Socialists, the judgment was perhaps overly optimistic.

The Homeric epics have an especially great meaning for us, in Hegel's view, because of the universal destiny of Greek culture. Greece received a world-historical mission from Asia, which it later relayed to Rome. World history presents itself as a series of epic struggles; but it would be a mistake to infer that it forms a single protracted epic. An epic is the story of a single hero or band of heroes. World history presents a succession of different individual heroes. The unity of world history is not perceivable in a single individual, but is accessible to thought alone. The Hegelian "world spirit" which progresses through history is not any one individual,

although it may temporarily incarnate itself in a given individual or
great man.[76] Hegel's philosophy of the historically advancing world
spirit has been compared with the educational novels
(*Bildungsromane*) popular in Hegel's own time, which follow the
self-education of an individual hero (for example, Goethe's Wilhelm
Meister) through a succession of trial life-styles.[77] But Hegel, who
denied that the self-education of the world spirit was an "epic,"
would have denied for the same reason that it was a *Bildungsroman*.
The comparison is but a comparison.

If the total life-form of a nation forms the subject matter of an
epic from the pedagogical standpoint, from the literary standpoint
this life form is merely a background or setting. What takes the
foreground is conflict and action. Tragedy, of course, also centers on
conflict and action. The difference is that an epic conflict takes
place between different nations and thus takes the form of war,
while a tragic conflict occurs between compatriots and thus assumes
the form of civil war.[78] From this standpoint, Shakespeare's *Henry
V*, for example, is more of an epic than his *Henry IV*. Connected
with this distinction between epic and tragedy is the assumption
that the epic is concerned with an unambiguous struggle between
good and evil, while a tragedy is concerned with conflicting goods,
a struggle of "brother enemies."

Apart from its essentially patriotic content, an epic resembles an
adventure story.[79] Whereas the emphasis in tragedy is on the
character of the tragic hero and its fateful, inexorable realization in
action, the stress in the epic is not on the psychology of the hero's
aim but on the successive and unpredictable obstacles encountered
along the way toward realization of that aim.[80] The character of a
tragic hero tends to be marked by some extraordinary ambition,
which raises him above the common level of mortals. The epic hero,
of course, also rises above the ordinary—otherwise he would not be
a hero. But he is a total man embodying all the major traits of his
people, and is not dominated by a single all-consuming passion.[81]

To say that an epic is an adventure story is to say that accident
plays a considerable role. Contrary to common opinion, Hegel says,
fate has its proper place more in epic than tragedy.[82] It is in tragedy
that there are no innocent victims. For in tragedy character is fate,
which means that the "fate" of the tragic hero only appears to be
due to external accident. Dramatic haste is necessary to show the inevitable link between character and fate. The epic hero lives in a

more unsettled, unpredictable world where, as for Ulysses on his seemingly endless voyages, the ever-changing environment holds ever-new surprises. Each delay, each detour along the way, is the occasion for a separate episode.

Yet if an epic consists of a series of episodes, we must not suppose that the number of episodes can, in fact, be infinite.[83] Because the series of *Gunsmoke* episodes *can* in principle go on to infinity, *Gunsmoke* fails to conform to the classical idea of an epic. Hegel maintains for the same reason that the *Nibelungen* do not form a true epic.[84] It is impossible to establish single authorship for all the episodes. New writers come along, pick up where other writers have left off, and in principle there is no end to this. But the case is quite different, in Hegel's view, with the *Iliad* and the *Odyssey*. He has no respect for the critics who have suggested that either of these epics lacks single authorship.[85] It is true that the epic poet must efface himself before the panorama which he unfolds before our eyes, but that does not mean that there might as well be different authors for different episodes. A truly classical epic must constitute a single organic whole, something which an endless soap opera cannot do. Hegel's admiration for the Homeric epics and his attention to the cross-references which bind all the episodes into a single whole are such that he considers it aesthetically impossible to deny single authorship to either epic.

The *age of epic poetry* (for example, of Homer) must be clearly distinguished, in Hegel's view, from the *heroic age* which forms the subject matter of such poetry. Epic poetry celebrates the heroic age, but it is removed from it in time.[86] Homer was separated from the Trojan wars by several centuries. The heroic age does not attain the level of artistic self-awareness required for its own self-celebration in the epic. Manners in the heroic age are still too coarse to permit such a level of artistic refinement. Yet the epic poet must participate mentally in the values of the heroic age.[87] He must identify with it and have genuine faith in its greatness. Hegel's point may be illustrated by the American example. The heroic age of the United States occurred in the nineteenth century, during the conquest of the frontier. But the Western as a literary and theatrical genre is more the product of the twentieth century. Yet our century could have perfected the "epic poetry" of the Western only because it still believed in the values of rugged individualism, law and order, hard work, and the simple faith celebrated in the Western.

X *Does Epic Poetry Have a Future?*

The Greek epics of the past celebrated the triumph of Western civilization over the Orient which finds its ultimate justification in the dialectic of world history.[88] It is a triumph of freedom over despotism. But Hegel poses the interesting question as to what the "epic of the future" might be like.[89] His definition of epic poetry leads him to exclude the possibility of a new European epic. Bourgeois European civilization had become too routinized, too institutionalized and rigid. The age of the epic was gone.[90]

One distinctive literary form of modern Europe is, of course, the novel. Perhaps surprisingly, Hegel has very little to say about it, but what he does say leads him to link it with epic poetry. The modern novel, he says, is the "epic of the bourgeoisie."[91] What distinguishes it from the Greek epics is that it presupposes the prosaic, depoeticized world of modern industrial production (that is, of "civil society" in Hegel's terminology). Hegel does not mean that the novel is the epic of the bourgeoisie's struggle and triumph over the aristocracy. He means rather that it is an attempt to restore to the modern world the poetic quality of which bourgeois economic life had deprived it. The novel tends to center around the conflict between the "poetry of the heart" and the "prose of circumstances." The solution may be either tragic or comic, and it consists either in a reconcilation of the heart with circumstances or in a poeticization of circumstances, a new aesthetic transfiguration of the prosaic world.

It is evident that the link between the Greek epics and the modern novel is, despite what Hegel says, really quite loose. The term "epic" in the phrase "epic of the bourgeoisie" fails to be used in the precise sense already defined by Hegel. In searching for the "epic of the future" he must turn away from the stultifying confinement of Europe. Following the Congress of Vienna Hegel observed that the European nations so balanced and limited one another that none of them was able to achieve domination over the others. And as he cast his gaze away from Europe, he surmised that America was the only escape from the "prison" which was Europe. The epic of the future, he said, might celebrate the victory of "American rationalism" over European "moderation" and "particularism."[92]

Hegel does not elaborate on the suggestion. Since "rationalism" is opposed to "moderation" and "particularism," the term seems to convey the idea of a "boundless dynamism" and "pragmatic universalism" rising above ethnic differences. Reference to European moderation and particularism, on the other hand, seems to cast Europe in the role of the Greek city-states, granting that what is considered moderate size for a state today is larger than what the Greeks thought moderate. America is then cast in a role similar to Rome, which was also known for its pragmatic universalism and immoderate size. The American conquest of the West in the last century was a poor imitation of an epic struggle. For the most part, the Indians could not oppose a real challenge to the American march to the Pacific. The struggle was unequal and hence unheroic. Only after the American frontier had been conquered, only when Yankee dynamism began the search for *new* frontiers in the twentieth century, for new markets and spheres of influence beyond American borders, could Hegel's hypothesis be tested.

One of the questions of the century has been, Was America going to strike in the direction of world domination like Rome after consolidation of its Italian base? André Malraux has made the perceptive observation that, contrary to most great powers of the past, the United States after World War II forsook the opportunity of an epic struggle for world conquest. The opportunity to establish *Pax Americana*, which temporarily existed after 1945, no longer exists. But the responsibility does not lie with the United States alone. European colonialism had already sown the seeds of its own destruction by spreading the ideologies of Western humanism to the four corners of the world. The dreamlike affluence of America limited its capacity for comprehending and leading the humanist social and economic revolution in the Third World. For better or worse, it today seems unlikely that the great American epic of which Hegel spoke will ever be written. Indeed, in an age of increasing international interdepedence, there would seem to be little future from any quarter for epic as a literary genre. Even the Chinese speak less these days of "encircling the cities."

XI *Drama*

Quite the opposite from epic poetry, in which the poet effaces himself before the objective, public events which he recounts, is lyric poetry, in which the poet expresses his own emotions and subjective responses to events. Lyric poetry, Hegel says, exists at all stages of civilization,[93] and Greece was no exception. The name of Pindar stands out with particular brilliance in this domain. Whereas the personality of Homer so effaces itself before the epic events that scholars have wondered if there ever were such a man, this question has never been asked about Pindar. When Pindar wrote hymns celebrating athletic champions, it was more the athlete who was honored by being sung by the illustrious Pindar than Pindar by the privilege of singing the champion's praises.[94] We shall have occasion to discuss lyric poetry in greater detail when we take up the romantic art of the Christian world, with which lyric, in Hegel's view, has a special affinity. But in a discussion of what is specifically Greek it is drama far more than lyric which demands our attention. If lyric existed throughout history, true drama originates, according to Hegel, among the Greeks.[95]

The purpose of epic, as we saw, is to reveal the total life of a nation, while that of lyric poetry is to express the poet's own inner subjectivity. Drama combines both the individual subjectivity of lyric poetry and the objectivity of the epic. It takes its start in the subjectivity of the protagonists. (This already introduces an element of objectivity relative to lyric poetry. Drama, unlike lyric poetry, takes its start from the subjectivity of individuals other than the poet.) But this subjectivity of the protagonists, instead of remaining closed within itself and expressing itself only in lyrical effusions, finds release in outward action bringing the individual into conflict with other individuals. An emphasis on external action is common to both drama and the epic. But drama differs from the epic in viewing action not as a mere event but as the externalization of subjectivity, as the manifestation of inner character, that is, by integrating a lyrical dimension, just as it differs from lyric poetry by integrating an epic dimension.[96]

XII *Tragedy*

The Greeks attained a preeminence in drama which, like that attained in other fields, has aroused the admiration of men ever since. Hegel had immense respect for the Greek dramatists, and especially for Sophocles. It is sometimes said that he rated the achievements of the Greek theater as unsurpassable even in the modern world. Hegel does single out Sophocles' *Antigone* as one of the most sublime and, in every respect, most consummate works of art ever produced.[97] However, it has been convincingly argued that he merely means that *Antigone* is one of the most beautiful examples of its type, that is, of Greek tragedy.[98] The Greeks produced, in his view, the first real tragic theater in world history. In the Orient individual subjectivity had not yet attained sufficient independence from the substantial cosmic Absolute to be capable of asserting its claims dramatically.

Tragic conflict arises out of the circumstance that an individual identifies with a finite, limited end with such single-minded passion that other, related ends are blindly ignored and stomped under foot. In the language of Hegelian dialectics, we should say that the tragic hero *abstracts* and *absolutizes* some limited end essentially related *(internally related)* to *other* ends which he thereby *negates*, calling forth his own *self-negation* through those other excluded ends. Thus Antigone identifies absolutely and exclusively with the ancient claims of a family code of ethics which compels her to seek a proper burial for her treasonous brother, and to do so in defiance of the new political principle of the state represented in the person of Creon, who has prohibited such a burial. Antigone's identification with the family ethic is so unswerving that she destroys herself in unbending stubbornness. It is thus stubborn one-sidedness which, in Hegel's view, makes Antigone representative of Greek tragedy.

Modern tragedy, by contrast, tends to culminate in the hero's awareness of guilt, of the finitude and narrowness of his aim. The hero grows in awareness, achieves a final salvation through reconciliation with the force which he opposed and which ultimately and necessarily defeated him.[99] This reconciliation, which amounts to *negation of the negation* in the Hegelian dialectic, serves to soften the specifically tragic character of tragedy. Thus modern tragedy—and Hegel is thinking especially of Shakespeare—is less tragic than its Greek model. Tragedy, the defeat of finite aims, finds justification by serving as a means to reconciliation, to the discovery of a higher, more concrete truth than the one which the hero initially represented. If we mean by "comedy" drama with a happy ending, modern tragedy, we may say, tends toward "tragicomedy." It was of modern tragedy that Hegel was thinking when, using the theater as a model for understanding the ultimate nature of reality itself, he wrote: "The Absolute eternally plays a moral tragedy with itself in which it forever gives birth to itself in the form of objectivity, then in this form of itself gives itself over to suffering and death in order to raise itself out of its ashes to glory."[100] The modern principle in tragedy is illustrated by Othello, who before his death recognizes the depth of his error born of jealousy, or even by Macbeth, who realizes at last the wages which his heedless amibi-

tion have earned for him. The awareness of guilt and the need for
inner reconciliation is for Hegel a distinctively modern, Christian
phenomenon, although he finds it prefigured to some extent in
Sophocles' *Oedipus at Colonus*.[101]
Expressing ourselves dialectically, we may thus say that whereas
the more typical ancient tragic hero is fixated at the level of *absolutization of the abstract* and *negation of the other*, the more
typical Christian hero overcomes such absolutization, achieving
through *negation of the negation* atonement with the *other*. Thus
modern drama attains for Hegel a higher level of spiritual insight
than Greek drama. Another, perhaps related, difference between
Greek and modern tragedy is that, whereas the Greek hero identified with a substantial ethical institution such as the family or the
state, the modern protagonist achieves greater emancipation from
institutions, identifying with little beyond himself, his own passion,
or ambition.[102] It is as if the greater alienation and guilt of the
modern protagonist (for example, Othello) were a condition of the
greater insight and reconciliation which is eventually achieved.

XIII *Comedy*

But the ultimate development of Greek drama was not tragedy
but comedy. In particular, Hegel is thinking here of the comedy of
Aristophanes.[103] It is characteristic of tragedy that the ends pursued
by the protagonists, however limited they may be, are nonetheless
sufficiently weighty to arouse the awe of both protagonists and
spectators. In Greek tragedy these ends (family, state) command
respect because they are inherently ethical. (In modern
Shakespearean tragedy, the ends are not typically ethical or institutional, but the explosive energy with which the protagonists,
like raw forces of nature, pursue even evil ends commands awe.)
Comedy is distinguished from tragedy in that the ends pursued by
the different players do *not* command such awe. The ends fail to
arouse in the spectator even the temporary illusion that they are absolute. They are obviously finite, vain, or trivial.[104] What causes
laughter is the false pretense of attributing absolute importance to
such clearly vain ends. Molière in particular excelled in the comic
portrayal of such vain and ridiculous characters.
But Hegel is persuaded that the laughter provoked by the
modern comedy of Molière is not so pure as that provoked by
Aristophanes and Greek comedy.[105] In modern comedy the spectators laugh at protagonists who take themselves quite seriously,

who are not aware of the laughter they provoke, and who thus appear ridiculous. But the laughter caused by the spectacle of what is ridiculous is not unmixed with pain, and thus is impure. One cannot entirely enjoy the spectacle of someone making a fool of himself. One must also pity him. If he himself is not embarrassed, the spectator is embarrassed for him. Greek comedy allows a purer sort of laughter because the spectator laughs *with* the protagonist and not merely *at* him. [106] The modern comedy of Molière satisfies a desire to look down on others, and it thus may be considered essentially highbrow. Ancient comedy, by contrast, is lowbrow. It flourished among the simple people, who laid no claim to superior taste, insight, or culture, who treated even the weightiest claims lightly, and who were content to laugh *with* their equals rather than *at* their inferiors. The comic characters of Aristophanes do not take themselves seriously. They rise above all the finite ends which they pursue, for they know these ends from the start to be finite. In tragedy, knowledge of the limitation of finite ends is won, if at all, only at the end. Comedy takes its start where tragedy leaves off: for it, knowledge of the vanity of human pursuits is a point of departure, not of arrival. Despite its surface frivolity, comedy has a very serious purpose. In fact, because the vanity of finite ends is presupposed rather than discovered, comedy presupposes a deeper level of insight than tragedy. A ridiculous character appears unintelligent, but a truly comic figure, far from being ridiculous, shows great intelligence. A good clown, for example, has the intelligence to detach himself from all finite pursuits, to realize that the truth is nonfinite. Greek comedy was the inner self-critique and self-dissolution of the Greek religion which rested on the deification of finite gods. Comedy thus helped prepare the way for the Christian revelation of a truly infinite God. [107]

XIV   *Immortality of the Soul*

The passage of Greek tragedy into comedy signified the emancipation of the individual from the Greek Olympian religion. The individual could now laugh at everything which had previously appeared substantial and divine, and in his laughter he set himself up as the sole abiding center of events. [108] As the Greek city-state dissolved, the classical balance between the individual and the political community was upset in favor of the free individual. Free individual judgment laughed down the claim to absoluteness made by anything other than itself.

This triumph of the individual at the expense of the polis is seen on the religious level in the importance assumed by the concept of immortality in the postclassical Greek mystery religions. Whereas to Homer immortality had been a pale imitation of this life, essentially a misfortune, in the postclassical era, and as championed by Socrates, it became more clearly a consolation. The idea of immortality as such is not specifically Greek, and Hegel recognized that the Chinese and Egyptians had already affirmed it. What is new and specifically non-Oriental in the Greek idea of immortality is that eternal life comes for the first time to be clearly attributed to an *immaterial* soul. The Greek religion was not a nature religion, and thus the Greek gods were not primarily nature gods, but were instead distinctly human. But the Greeks did not merely adopt the age-old idea of what it is to be human and then apply it to the gods. They reformed the idea of what it is to be human. Their spiritualization of the gods presupposed a spiritual idea of man viewed as distinct from a natural object. In the postclassical Hellenistic era this spiritualization of the concept of man expressed itself in belief in immortality of the soul. A human being is not a natural object. But to be natural is to be decomposable, corruptible, hence mortal. A human being, who is nonnatural, therefore comes to be viewed as nondecomposable or immortal. The Greek idea of the immortality of the immaterial, supernatural soul has had a strong influence on the Christian notion of immortality. Today we may have serious reservations about the stock arguments for the soul's immortality. Hegel himself certainly had such reservations.[109] But this does not alter the fact that the emergence of belief in such immortality among the Greeks was nothing less than man's emerging consciousness of himself over against the natural world, endowed with a dignity placing himself above nature.[110] And the belief that man is not a merely natural being is true even if the belief in the immortality of individual souls is false. Politically this belief in the dignity of the individual human being passed over into the Roman world where it found expression in the gradual evolution toward a system of individual rights. It is to the emergence of this system of legal rights that our attention must now turn.

CHAPTER 7

Rome and its Law

I The Unity Of Graeco-Roman Civilization

T HE deepest value of Graeco-Roman civilization, from Greek mythology to the legal codes of Justinian, is too rich with overtones to be adequately expressed in a few words. It may variously be termed justice, moderation, harmony, balance, proportion, limitation, destiny, and necessity. It is fundamentally opposed to the grandiose, measureless splendor of Oriental despotism or Hebraic theology. It has its source in the basically aristocratic and nondespotic institutions of the ancient Greek world. These institutions aim at the preservation of a harmonious balance by assigning limits to the part played by every participant in political life. We may see a reflection of such institutions in the aristocratic society of Olympian gods. Classical Greek philosophy centers around the same basic value. Plato and Aristotle believe that the happiness of a society depends on a balance between classes, just as individual happiness depends on a harmonious development of the different parts of human nature. Virtue, for Aristotle, means the avoidance of extremes, the pursuit of a happy medium between excess and deficiency. Whereas the Hebrews held that divinity required the absence of all limitation, the Greeks, on the contrary, believed that perfection required limitation or definiteness. What was infinite or indefinite was unfinished and therefore imperfect. The Greek temple, with its proportion and moderate size, stands in characteristic contrast to the colossal architecture of the Orient. But the highest artistic expression of the Greek value system was attained in classical tragedy, which revealed the futility of overstepping the bounds of the roles assigned to individuals and institutions by destiny. The highest institutional expression of the same values, however, is to be found in the system of Roman justice and its quest

115

for a regular procedure for "assigning to each his due." Roman law
shows the influence of the Greek theater. The very term used by the
Romans to designate participants in legal proceedings—"persons"—is derived from classical Greek theater. Etymologically a
"person" is a theatrical mask. But in Roman usage an individual
became a "person" insofar as he played a role in the *legal* theater of
dramatic conflict and its just resolution.

The phrase "Graeco-Roman civilization" suggests the close
historical relation between the Greeks and Romans. Both peoples
were fundamentally aristocratic in their traditions. The early
Roman kings were not despots on the Oriental model, but were
charged to respect the rights of the family patriarch—*pater
familias*—to dominion over his wife, children, and slaves. And the
abolition of the monarchy in the sixth century B.C. reinforced the
aristocratic character of Roman society by increasing the power of
the patrician senatorial families. Gradually, however, the course of
history in the republic broadened political participation on an increasingly democratic basis as the plebs won limited rights of
representation.

II   *Roman Citizenship*

After the fall of the republic and the founding of the empire, the
political participation of all groups suffered a decline. Yet it would
be wrong to equate the Roman emperor with an Oriental despot.
Hegel sometimes seems to make this mistake.[1] His treatment of
Rome is, in general, inferior to that of Greece because he sees Rome
largely as the destroyer of the Greek city-state, which was his first
love. As a consequence, his attitude toward Rome was too negative.

The reason why the Roman emperor cannot be equated with an
Oriental despot is because, even though political participation in
legislation and meaningful elections disappeared under the empire,
the idea of citizenship did not disappear. If the imperial administration exercised a right to intervene in the domestic affairs of the
family it was not because all Romans were treated as children but
because all, including women, children, and slaves, were granted
certain rights of adults. The Romans remained citizens; they did not
fall into the condition of being mere subjects in the personal domain of the emperor. Citizenship is a specifically Graeco-Roman
idea. But it has two basic aspects: the right of participation in
political decision-making and the right to legal protection of one's
private interests (for example; property). We may thus say that

citizenship originally entails both political or *public* rights and *private* rights. Now, although public rights declined under the empire, private rights were, on the contrary, extended to ever broader groups. Originally under the republic the private right to initiate legal proceedings in the defense of one's interests was reserved to the *pater familias*. Such a right was denied to members of his family and household, as well as to foreigners. The Roman father held over his family a power of life and death which was legally limitless, despite the influence of public opinion. But the evolution of both the republic and the empire tended to place legal restrictions on this domestic despotism. Sons were emancipated from the power of their still living fathers by being granted the right to own property independently of the father. Wives were eventually granted similar rights. Further, debtors were granted certain safeguards against their creditors. And private rights were gradually extended to foreigners residing in Rome. Legal fictions were introduced by the administrators of legal procedure (praetors) permitting non-Romans to benefit from the same legal protection to which they would have been entitled if they had been Roman citizens. Beyond this measure, Roman citizenship was extended to an increasing number of non-Roman inhabitants of the empire. In 212 A.D. citizenship was extended to all inhabitants of the empire except slaves. But even slaves began to find protection under the law: many were emancipated, while others exercised the right to buy their liberty with accumulated savings *(peculum)*. Finally, the legal codes of Justinian specified that slavery, although a common human institution, was in contradiction to natural law.

III   *Roman Jurisprudence*

The decline of political rights may seem to us hard to reconcile with the extension of private rights in Rome. In the modern view, a principal guarantee that the state will respect the private rights of its citizens is to be found in the control which the citizenry exercises over the government by means of free elections. That private rights were, by and large, protected in the empire without any such control may seem surprising. What made the Roman system of extended private rights without public rights possible was, first, the requirements of the commercial revolution embracing the entire Mediterranean world and, second, the largely unchallenged authority of the Stoic tradition.

The commerical revolution reduced the power of Rome's agrarian aristocracy. The independent economic initiative of sons required their emancipation from fathers. And the interests of trade between Romans and non-Romans required the extension of legal rights to the latter. The final extension of citizenship to all inhabitants of the empire seems to have been, at least in part, motivated by fiscal reasons. However, the extensions of private rights was also promoted by the humanistic, Stoic cosmopolitanism and philosophy of natural law. Stoicism as a school of philosophy arose in Greece, although it was soon imported into Rome. But the Romans did not develop it theoretically as much as practically. Roman jurists, who championed the Greek philosophy against the provincialism of Rome's past, were not so much concerned to push Greek speculations farther than the Greeks as to realize Greek philosophical ideals institutionally. Both the public and the praetors responsible for administering the law in the far-flung empire relied on these jurists for legal guidance. In order to provide guidance to administrators in distant provinces, the jurisconsults undertook the task of codifying the body of Roman law in systematic digests. Thus was jurisprudence born as a science, borrowing much both from Stoic principles and Aristotelian methods of classification and definition.

The Roman empire is perhaps best understood as what we today call a technocracy. Technocracy means rule by experts. Rule is sanctioned by the appeal to expertise, to science, rather than by popular elections. More generally, technocracy is the rule of patriarchal intelligence without patriarchy. The kind of disciplined abstract intelligence which arose with the patriarchal revolution so develops into a rational and self-justifying scientific system that rule may be based on an appeal to "reason" and thus may dispense with the authoritarian appeal to patriarchal rights or the claims of superior force. In Rome the expertise in question was chiefly a legal expertise, jurisprudence, rather than the natural science expertise to which today's technocrats appeal. The technocrats of today could not be counted on as much as the Roman jurisconsults to protect rights. For today, unlike the Roman times, we recognize the authority of no *moral* intellectual tradition. The abdication of political responsibility by the citizenry is thus today more likely to lead to tyranny than in Rome.

Hegel convincingly argued, however, that the decay of political rights in the empire had negative consequences, even if it did not lead to despotism, for it resulted in an atomization and privatization of life.[2] Because citizens no longer participated in the political process they ceased to identify with the state and withdrew into exclusive pursuit of private interests. This tendency was apparent even in the early days of the empire. The Emperor Augustus was not very successful in his attempt to prevail upon the poet Horace to write hymns of praise to the imperial achievements.[3] Horace and many individuals like him enjoyed too much the leisure *(otium)* which came from political irresponsibility. Yet Hegel perhaps overstated his case in comparing the empire to a corpse whose death gives rise to a wormy life of the individual parts.[4]

IV   *Rome's Utilitarian Religion*

But despite his criticisms Hegel considered Rome's system of private rights to be a lasting contribution to Western civilization,[5] just as art had been the exemplary Greek contribution. The fact that he did not locate Rome's contribution, like Greece's, in the realm of art is significant. We saw in the previous chapter that Greek art is, for Hegel, of unsurpassable beauty because art to the Greeks was their religion. The Olympian religion is the "religion of beauty." It is often said that the Roman religion is the same as the Greek except that the names of the gods undergo a change: Zeus becomes Jupiter, and so on. But in Hegel's view the difference went much deeper. For him, the Roman religion was the "religion of utility,"[6] and the utilitarian Roman standpoint was basically incompatible with the Greek aesthetic perspective.

Even in the earliest stages of Roman history Hegel found a utilitarian, pragmatic approach to religion. The Roman gods could not be beautiful because the Romans *used* their gods as a means to worldly ends. Their sacrifices and feasts were not free and reverent worship, for they were aimed at fertility, military success, or the realization of other practical interests. Beauty can be experienced only by so detaching oneself from practical interests as to contemplate the godhead for itself and not as a mere means to an end. Since it is the "understanding" which, according to Hegel, abstracts, absolutizes, and pursues finite worldly aims, he was led to say that the Roman religion, which presents itself as a kind of substitute technology, was a religion of the understanding.[7] In this utilitarian aspect the Roman religion resembles the "religion of magic" considered in a previous chapter; the two differ largely in that the religion of magic is a nature religion, whereas the Roman religion succeeds in abstracting and differentiating its divinities from nature and natural objects. But, even so, the Roman gods, reduced to instruments, are reduced to mere things and thus robbed of true divinity. This tendency is illustrated by the Roman habit of worshipping pure abstractions of the understanding, such as Concord or Fortune.[8] The list of Roman deities is practically endless. The Romans imported gods from all over the empire, killing them by leveling them all as means to the same end of general welfare.[9] They prided themselves on being the most religious of peoples, but Hegel insisted that they were quite the opposite. Their religion was quite the contrary of turning oneself away from oneself and one's particular interests; and in this respect Roman piety was really godlessness.[10] It is true that the Romans were serious about their religion, but this seriousness—so different from the joyfulness and playfulness of Greek religion—was brought about by a manipulative approach to the gods. The Romans were serious because religious observances were part of their workaday activity.

The utilitarian character of Roman religion is well illustrated by the worship of Fortune. This cult has been thought to show the modesty of the Romans, who declined to attribute their worldly success to their own courage and endeavor, but for Hegel it rather showed their immodesty in deifying their temporal success.[11] The worship of Fortune also shows how the Roman religion is, in Hegel's view, essentially a state religion.[12] Fortune grew into an important divinity as the Roman state, in its relentless expansion, was especially favored by its graces. (The worship of Concord, consecrating the harmony of social classes in Rome, also illustrates Roman religion as a state religion.) The emperor eventually came to incarnate public Fortune, and this contributed to the rise of the religious cult and the deification of the emperor.[13] Another factor in the emergence of the emperor cult was the expansion of the empire to include Oriental peoples used to the idea of divine kingship and political despotism. Originally the meaning of emperor worship was probably different in Rome from what it was in the Oriental provinces. Caesar, in first proposing such deification, specified that it was to be inapplicable in Rome; but the course of the empire's history led to a process of increasing Orientalization.

V Israel and Rome: A Rendezvous With Destiny

The description of Roman religion as a "religion of the understanding" implies a similiarity to Judaism, to which Hegel applied the same description.[14] The Jews also pursued a practical aim in their religion, namely, the survival and welfare of Israel. As long as despotism was political rather than supernatural, religion could be a mystical escape from the finitude of practical pursuits. The acceptance of despotism by a population is motivated by the desire for security and welfare. In Judaism such acceptance was essentially a religious rather than a political act, and religion thereby became a practical pursuit. The difference between the Roman religion and Judaism is that the practical aim religiously pursued by the Romans was not limited to the welfare of a single chosen people, but was universalized under the empire into an aim of universal welfare embracing all peoples.[15] And, second, the aim of welfare as conceived by the Romans is far more pedestrian or mundane than the lofty ethical vision of the Hebrew prophetic tradition.[16]

But if the Roman religion, which Hegel uniformly treats subsequently to Judaism, is more advanced than Judaism, it is largely because of Roman law. There always was a close connection between law and religion in Rome. Just as religion in Rome was a pursuit of worldly interests, so the legal pursuit of worldly interests was shrouded in religion. Early Roman law was ritualistic, requiring the use of appropriate magic-like formulas kept in secrecy by the priestly class. But the great contribution made by Roman law was, in Hegel's view, to have recognized personal rights, although he thinks that the Romans conceived the person only as an abstract subject of property rights,[17] that is, only as a member of economic ("civil") society and thus not as a member of an ethically constituted family or political community. The family as an ethical institution in the modern world is based on love and not essentially, as in Rome, on the father's (proprietary) rights of dominion over members of his family.[18] As for the state, it failed to be an ethical institution in Rome because the bureaucratic imperial administration was too remote and unwieldy for the citizen to be able to identify with it.[19]

It is in his discussion of "abstract right" in the *Philosophy of Right* that Hegel seems to offer a systematic account of Roman law.[20] Yet there are considerable differences between this account and the historical law of ancient Rome. Since the sixteenth century modern legal theorists had popularized the myth that the surviving codes and digests of Roman law were remnants of a more highly developed rational system of law which had existed in classical Rome but which had later been lost. These "Romanists" sought to restore this original system, and in the process they produced a modern theory of "natural law" which differs considerably from the historical law of Rome. It is true that the basic terminology of modern European legal theory was drawn from Roman law: "person," "property," "contract," and so on. However, several fundamental concepts of modern natural law theory are foreign to Roman law. Central among these modern concepts are the idea of a presocial state of nature, the assumption of free asocial individuals living in the state of nature and yet rational enough to negotiate, the concept of a social contract constituting collective life on the basis of consent, and the idea of natural rights which the contract was supposed to protect. The Romans themselves never talked about "rights," although they did speak of permissible legal "actions." And for the Romans a "person" was a role, a legal mask, not the underlying subject, individual roletaker, or possessor of rights. Further, the Roman idea of a "contract" is based on some physical action, such as handing an object over to someone, rather than on anything as inward or covert as "consent." Moreover, Roman law knew nothing of the modern, individualistic fiction of a presocial state of nature. Finally, an obvious inconsistency between Roman law and modern natural law theory is that the former, unlike the latter, never rejected the institution of slavery.

Hegel realized that modern doctrines of natural law differed from the historical law of Rome, but he still seems to have thought that the modern theory remained in the Roman tradition, articulating the "spirit" of Roman law better than the Romans themselves, preoccupied with more practical problems, were able to do. Hegel's judgment on this question may be challenged.[21] On the other hand, it does seem clear that Roman law, in its historical evolution, tended, under the impact of both increasing commerce and the Stoic natural-law philosophy, toward the extension of private property rights to all individuals, including slaves. Further, it seems clear that the Romans initiated the task of scientifically systematizing the law, and in this respect also anticipated modern codes and natural-law systems.

The Romans distinguished three types of law: civil law, which was the law of a particular city; *jus gentium*, which consisted in practices common to different human societies; and natural law, which was based on man's universal biological or animal nature. In its historical evolution, Roman civil law tended to give way to *jus gentium* where the civil law (as in the case of its denial of commercial or private rights to foreigners) contradicted the general custom of civilized peoples. Finally, even *jus gentium* showed signs of ceding in authority to natural law where (as in the question of slavery) the two were thought to be in conflict. We thus see in Rome the incipient stages of a universal system of natural human rights. But providence would have it that such a system was also present (although more deeply buried) in Judaism, which affirmed that man was made in the image of God even while denying the individual proprietorship over his own body, which was thought to have been borrowed from God. But after Judaism came to be encompassed in the Graeco-Roman world, it is as if the incipient Roman system of human rights had triggered the discovery in Judaism of the meaning of man's "divine image." It is this discovery which, at the confluence of Rome and Israel, produced Christianity.

CHAPTER 8

Christianity's Hidden Meaning

I Judaism and the Graeco-Roman World

THE last chapters have dealt separately with Judaism and Graeco-Roman civilization. Historically, however, they did not remain in mutual isolation, and this despite the essentially Oriental or "Persian" origins of Judaism and the Western character of the Graeco-Roman world. After the political collapse of the Persian world, Judaism was a religion without a native civilization. And after the decline of the Olympian and Roman mythological religions, the Graeco-Roman world was a civilization without a native religion. Judaism was encompassed within Graeco-Roman civilization, and Graeco-Roman civilization felt the attraction of the Judaic religion. Throughout the Mediterranean world there arose "God-fearing" pagans who more or less embraced Judaism, and some, known as "proselytes," went so far as to be circumcised.

Of course, Judaism was not the only Oriental religion to enter into the void created by the decline of Graeco-Roman polytheism. The so-called mystery cults of Adonis, Osiris, and Mithra were also prominent. But Judaism enjoyed a special place in the Roman Empire. It was the only religion which was officially exempted from being incorporated into Rome's religious syncretism, and whose followers were exempted from participation in the state cult of the emperor. It must be admitted that Judaism and Graeco-Roman civilization remained superficially opposed. The latter evolved a humanistic system of justice which tended to abolish both political and domestic despotism. Because property rights were legally protected, the role played by the Roman emperor cannot, despite the imperial cult, be equated with that of an Oriental despot. And as rights tended to be extended to ever broader groups of individuals, including women, children, and ultimately even slaves, the domestic despotism of the *pater familias* was also gradually abolished. Judaism, on the other hand, tended to abolish political and domestic despotism without abolishing despotism in general and without developing a system of individual human rights, that is, by equalizing all men as children standing without rights before a transcendent divine despot. However, Hebraic religion and Graeco-Roman civilization did not remain merely juxtaposed, for in Christianity they became profoundly united.

II *Christianity's Judaic Heritage*

Christianity combines the supernatural, cosmic despotism of Judaism with the ethical humanism of Graeco-Roman civilization. The Judaic patriarchal God survives as the first member of the Christian trinity, as God the Father. At the same time, Graeco-Roman humanism is present in the idea that every human individual, no matter how degraded or evil, is worth saving in the eyes of God. It may appear that Christianity is an impossible composition of opposites, and in fact realization of this Judeo-Graeco-Roman combination required conception of the most stupendous theological drama that has ever existed. The Christian cosmic drama begins with Creation. God the Father created the world. The crowning work of His creation is man, who was made "in the image of God." But man sinned against the divine will by rebelling against his creaturely status and by claiming divine status for himself; and because of this sin of living up to the divine image *too well* and pretending to an autonomous creative power of his own man fell out of God's favor, was cast from the paradisical Garden of Eden, and was condemned to live by the sweat of his brow.

But God in his mercy did not forsake man. He opened to man a way of redemption by revealing His Law to Israel, his chosen people. Through Israel all nations would be blessed. God entered into a covenant with his people, promising prosperity in a land of milk and honey if only they would write His Law in their hearts and follow His commandments. But Israel repeatedly sinned, disobeying the Law by running after idols and bearing witness to false gods. God's prophets, sent to warn the people of the divine wrath to which it would be subject if they did not repent, went unheeded. Foreign nations were thus raised by God to punish Israel and to subdue it.

All this Christianity takes over from the Judaic revelation of God's mighty acts in history. But Christianity proceeds to draw the not unnatural conclusion that man is incapable of redeeming himself through heeding God's law. It is at this point that the second person or role of the trinity enters the stage. God's justice is implacable. On the other hand, it is impossible to restrict the mercy and love of God for man within definite bounds. Even in man's unacceptableness God finds it within Himself to accept man. Out of His infinite love He sends man his only begotten Son, Jesus Christ, to redeem man from his sins. Christ, the Son, is the Incarnation of the Father. Through the Son, the Father walked among men. But Christ did not come to abolish the Law but rather to fulfill it. Jesus radicalized the Mosaic Law into a law of love—a love so boundless as to embrace even one's enemies. It was certainly not the revelation of such a law which was designed to redeem man. On the contrary, the stringency of the demands made by the Law as revealed by Jesus could only throw man into even greater despair about his capacity to save himself. Christ could not have been the Redeemer if he had merely revealed the law of love. The redemption of man was rather effected through the Crucifixion. In an ultimate demonstration of the law of love in action, Christ sacrificed Himself on the Cross to pay for the sins of man, so that all who accept this sacrifice and abandon themselves to Christ's redemptive activity might be exempted from further punishment for sin and might be reborn in Christ and thus inherit with Christ the Kingdom of God. After suffering the agony of the Cross, Christ triumphed over death itself, rose from the dead, was glorified in Heaven beside the Father, and attained eternal life in his Church. It is here that the third member of the trinity, the Holy Spirit, enters. The Holy Spirit is the communion of the Son and the Father in the Kingdom of Heaven. To the extent that Christ's Church grows and that men are reborn in Christ, the Holy Spirit descends upon earth, incorporating it into the heavenly kingdom.

III *Christianity and the Middle-Road Hegelianism of Hegel*

Such in brief is the essential core of Christian *faith* which Hegel sought to transform into *knowledge*.[1] He considered himself a Christian, and Christianity was for him the "absolute religion,"[2] His whole mature philosophy may be considered an attempt at rational justification of Christian faith. He believed that the time had come for Christianity to put away the form of faith and assume the form of knowledge. The age-old conflict between faith and reason was to be resolved by preserving the content of faith on a rational basis.

Hegel's own position must be carefully distinguished from that of some of his followers. It has become standard practice since Hegel's death to say that the Hegelian school divided into right-wing and left-wing branches.[3] The left-wing Hegelianism of Ludwig Feuerbach and Karl Marx presents itself as an anti-Christian atheism,[4] while right-wing Hegelianism presents itself as a Christian theistic doctrine. In fact, however, neither of the extreme branches into which the Hegelian school divided is authentically Hegelian. So-called right-wing Hegelianism is a reaction by orthodox classical Christian theists who, lured by Hegel into deeper waters than they had anticipated, began searching for familiar ground by falsely reading traditional doctrines of personal immortality and creation *ex nihilo* into Hegel's writings. Left-wing Hegelianism shares with right-wing Hegelianism what, from the authentic Hegelian perspective, may be termed a false reduction of Christianity to classical theistic doctrines of creation *ex nihilo* and individual immortality. As a result it mistakes itself to be anti-Christian and thus falls short of the alliance of traditional Christian theological representations and radical philosophical comprehension characteristic of the authentic Hegelian middle.

The Hegelianism of Hegel himself is poised delicately between the two extremes.[5] Like the left wing, Hegel rejects traditional, dogmatic, literal-minded Christianity based on faith alone. But he nonetheless remains attached to the traditional forms of Christian worship and representation, and in this he resembles the right wing. Although he once wrote that "our universities are our churches,"[6] it was not his intention that Christianity should ever be totally secularized or demythologized. He would certainly not have looked with pleasure upon the disappearance of the Christian church as a separate institution in the modern world. His philosophy was a comprehension of a truth which, through institutional Christianity, already exists ritually and mythologically in the world. If the church disappeared, philosophy would lose contact with the world. Philosophical truth, which could no longer be presented as an interpretation of a truth already existing in the world, would become the esoteric preserve of an intellectual elite. However, Hegel remained attached to the traditional forms of Christianity only as the popular expression of truth. His real concern was to preserve traditional Christianity by translating its dogmas into the language of logical discourse and thus showing them to be rational. With Christianity the history of religions, he believed, came to an unsurpassable conclusion.

Any religion which claims to surpass Christianity, such as the Islamic one, really falls beneath its level, as Islam, in Hegel's view, theologically repeats the Judaic representation of God.[7] There can never again be a truly new religion. There can, from now on, only be further clarification and development of Christianity. The following paragraphs seek to explain and evaluate Hegel's rational justification of Christian belief.

IV   *Creation*

We begin with the doctrine of Creation. The doctrine is mythically presented in Genesis. God is said to have created the natural world out of nothing. Unlike some of his right-wing interpreters Hegel did not take this claim literally. But neither did he reject it as nonsense or pure falsehood. He purported to find a hidden truth behind it. That he did not accept the creation myth at face value is already suggested by his naturalistic account of the origin of the Judaic representation of God. We saw how, according to Hegel, the Judaic conception of God was formed in response to conditions of natural insecurity as illustrated by the biblical flood. Noah responded to the flood by forming the concept of an all-powerful God, in whose hands he proceeded to place himself. Implicit in this account of Hegel's is the admission that it was man who created the Judaic idea of God as an all-powerful Creator. But once this idea was formed the divine creation of nature was necessarily projected back into a past contemporaneous with nature's first existence. For it hardly would be consistent with the idea of an all-powerful Creator of all nature to suppose that nature existed prior to the existence of this Creator.

Hegel's nonacceptance of the creation myth literally interpreted is apparent from the fact that he held, contrary to that myth, that there *was* a time prior to God's creation of nature in which nature already existed.[8] Thus Hegel did not accept the doctrine of creation out of nothing. For him, to speak of such a creation was merely a way of magnifying the transcendence of God and of absolutizing God as an *all-powerful* Creator. In fact, the creation of nature was only the transformation of a pre-existing uncreated nature. This pre-existing, uncreated nature was nature as known by primitive man. We have already described its basic character in the section on the religion of magic. Uncreated original nature is the spiritualized nature experienced by the primitive animist. In the Garden of

Eden, before the invention of labor, man attributed spiritual autonomy and self-creativity to his natural environment. But this spiritualized nature of primitive man is not the nature whose creation is in question in the Old Testament. The created nature of Genesis is essentially different. It is a despiritualized nature.[9] The oneness of man and nature affirmed by primitive man embodies implicit truth and wisdom, but it is a wisdom of innocence, a truth unconscious of itself. For the truth of this oneness to be known, the disunion of man and nature must be set up and then transcended as error. The divorce of man from nature is the disappearance of primitive animism, and it is this divorce which is the historical reality hiding behind the Old Testament idea of the creation of nature. For the created nature of the Hebrews is, as we have seen, essentially marked by externality and otherness in relation to man or spirit. Strange as it may at first seem, we are forced to conclude that Adam and Eve in the Garden of Eden lived *before* the creation of nature. Creation, as we shall see, is a consequence rather than condition of the fall from Paradise.

The Judaic doctrine of creation is the theological representation of a momentous socio-economic revolution in the career of man and, indeed, of the universe: the patriarchal revolution. Economically, that revolution was marked by the domestication of animals and the introduction of agriculture, all made possible by the invention of labor and of the disciplined use of intelligence. Sociologically, the revolution placed the males who controlled the new means of production—herds and cultivated lands—in a position of dominance over wives, children, and servants within the patriarchal family. This revolution was, of course, not peculiar to the Hebrews. What is unique about the Hebrews is rather that in their religion the patriarchal standpoint achieved metaphysical expression, that is, was used to define the nature of ultimate reality, of the Absolute. In Judaism the Absolute itself is represented as a patriarch.[10] For Hegel religion in general was the self-awareness of the universe, of the Absolute. It is the essential nature of the Absolute, according to Hegel, to give to itself the appearance of being other than itself in order, by winning back this otherness, to realize itself. In the Judaic religion the Absolute is not represented as achieving self-realization. It is so represented only in the Christian doctrine of the Incarnation. But Judaism nonetheless initiates revelation of the true nature of the Absolute, and Judaic history is thus holy history. The Christian doctrine of the Incarnation, of the

oneness of God and nature, presupposes the Judaic doctrine of the
Creation, of the radical divorce of God and nature. The Creation of
an external, merely physical nature is an act of self-disincarnation,
establishing God as pure disembodied spirit, as pure thought, and
nature as despiritualized matter. And spirit had to disincarnate
itself, to abstract itself from nature as pure thought, in order,
through the Incarnation, to discover the error of the mind-matter
dualism and the truth of the oneness of mind and nature.

Hegel unquestionably altered the traditional interpretation of the
Creation doctrine. But it is important to see that he has not altered
it so much as to fall into atheism. It should be noted that he did not
hold that God was invented by the mind of man. God is not merely
a psychologically, socially, and economically conditioned idea.
Rather, Hegel held that it was the Hebraic *representation* of God as
an all-powerful Creator and patriarch which was invented. God,
Hegel maintained, really exists, being the Absolute, infinite and un-
restricted from without. The Hebraic Lord of the world is the Absolute as it manifested itself in the patriarchal religion of the Jews.
The Hebrew representation of God is modeled on the agrarian-
pastoral patriarch. In the actual world there are, of course, many
patriarchs, while for the Jews there is but one God. But it is the
secret wish of every patriarch to be omnipotent and thus to sub-
jugate all others. Noah's God is Noah's own repressed, secret ideal
self.[11] The Lord is what Noah himself would be if he were not so
finite and limited by an external environment which he could not
completely control. The Lord is not any natural patriarch, but the
secret dream of all natural patriarchs. The wish of every adult
patriarch is, if Freud is correct, to be as his father is imagined to be
by the child who still lives on in the adult's unconscious. In Judaism
the cosmos is modeled on one's own family, which when one was
young was the only world one knew; and in the family there is only
one patriarch, who is imagined by the child to be all-powerful. The
Hebraic God inherits the absolute status which the earthly father
loses when the child grows into a man. And since it is created in the
image of the earthly patriarch, the Hebraic representation of God is
one of a laboring God. Just as the natural patriarch wins his relatively dominant position through finite labor, so the Hebrew Lord wins
his absolutely dominant position through the labor of unlimited
creation *ex nihilo*. The dependence of the world on the God who
created it is a metaphysical projection of the pastoral-agrarian
dependence of property on the patriarchal owner. Because

ownership implies control, ultimately only dead matter can be truly owned because it alone can be completely controlled. The patriarchal theology of Judaism thus leads to a despiritualization of the natural world created by God. The worship of natural objects is idolatry in Judaism (and Islam), because it implies the autonomy and spiritual dignity of nature and thus constitutes a denial of nature's status as the property of God. To appropriate is to "thingify." And if ownership, as John Locke holds, derives from labor, God's labor in creating the world entitles him to proprietorship over it. The religion of the Old Testament would be incomprehensible, or at least completely foreign, in a society of food gatherers or hunters. The God of the Old Testament is a laborer, and the food gatherer has no sense of what we understand by labor and property. Since the ultimate source of creative labor is the applied intelligence of the patriarch, the patriarchal God of the Hebrews is, above all, characterized by the power of thought. Judaism absolutizes patriarchal intelligence, which is the Judaic definition of the Absolute.

V   *The Fall*

The crowning work of God's creation was man, made in the image of God Himself. But, for Judaism, man's likeness to God was his ruin rather than his glory. For it was the source of the Fall. The Fall of man was his revolt against his creaturely status.[12] It was his rise against God, his pretension to the status of being an independent Creator like God. Nature was reduced to a system of mere things by the Creation. But the Hebraic claim that nature is mere matter, devoid of spirit, is the greatest error conceivable about the nature of the material world.[13] In reality, nature and spirit, as primitive man implicitly knew in the Garden of Eden, are one. The Fall is simply the rise of the indomitable spirit of nature against the pretensions of a God who would reduce nature to being merely *created* and thus *noncreative*. (All human creativity, in the Hebraic view, is ultimately *borrowed* from God, the result of God's creative power working through man.) The Hebraic God's response to human self-assertion as an autonomous creator is much like that of a father who experiences his own child's growth toward autonomy and manhood as a painful "fall" of his own offspring, which refuses to remain faithful to its status as a product.

Genesis relates that the Fall was due to man's eating of the "tree of the knowledge of good and evil." By acquiring conscience man became like God and was punished by being banished from the Garden of Eden and forced to earn his living by labor. It is difficult not to find in the biblical account a veiled reference to the patriarchal revolution. Conscience is the result of internalizing the voice of patriarchal authority. Being like God means man's assumption of a patriarchal role for himself. Being cast from the Garden of Eden is abandonment of the life of a food gatherer and hunter. What Genesis calls the punishment for the Fall, namely labor, is really inherent in the Fall, essential to man's existence in the image of God. For what is God's own activity of creation but labor? Did not God rest on the seventh day? We must conclude, as already suggested, that the Fall was due to man's realizing *too well* the image of God. Of course, there remained a difference between human and divine labor. The human laborer is finite, while the divine laborer is omnipotent. But the similarity is also striking. We must infer that God did not inhabit the Garden of Eden, that the activity of creating the world was indeed the *Fall of God*. If labor is punishment for man, it is punishment for God as well. For labor, whether divine or human, inevitably *alienates* the laborer from the product of his labors. The very standpoint of the laborer divorces him from the possibility of communion with his natural environment. The world becomes object, the worker subject. Adoption of that standpoint is an act of self-disincarnation which establishes oneself as an ideal thinking subject over against the world as pure object. The creation of the world related in Genesis is, in fact, the creation of a radically new conception of the world, that is, the conception which essentially underlies the standpoint of labor. According to this conception, the world is essentially a field of raw materials, obstacles, instruments, and products, all relative to the project of labor. Judaism is the religion in which the ultimate nature of the world came to be, for the first time, defined in terms of what the world is *for labor*. The world is objective, nonsubjective, but essentially existing *for* a subject. But, to repeat, if the world is the product of labor, the worker as such cannot have any sense of his oneness with the world. One cannot have any vivid sense of the spiritual dignity of the hammer, wood, or nail while one is hammering the nail into the wood. Because the worker dominates the material with which he works, he cannot fully recognize himself in the product of his labor. For, as an agent of production, he is not produced.

VI *Christ*

As we pass on to the doctrine of the Incarnation, it will be well to remember what has just been said about God's own alienation from the world as Creator. It is commonly said that the purpose of the Incarnation is to achieve reconciliation between God and nature, specifically between God and man, but Hegel insists that this reconciliation responds to a need on God's part as well as to human need. In the Incarnation a *disincarnate* God ceases to relate to the world merely as its Creator and owner by assuming the standpoint of the natural creature. But we shall first consider the Incarnation as it is more usually considered, namely, from the human side of the man-God relationship. The Incarnation responded to Judaic man's increasing sense of helpless sinfulness in the ancient world. The increasing sense of sin reflects the increasing identification of the individual with the judgment passed upon him by God. In Freudian terms, the pre-Christian state of mind reflected the increasing strength and severity of the superego accompanying the progress of civilization and, hence, of repression. It is sometimes thought that the Roman world in which Christianity arose was particularly hard or brutal, and it must be admitted that Hegel's overly negative attitude toward Rome did not serve to correct this prejudice. But, if Freud is right, the pre-Christian need for salvation from sin bears witness rather to the *progress* of civilization in the Roman world than to a decline into some kind of dark age. The ethic of Jesus and its reception in the Roman world testify to a heightened moral sensitivity. It is surely wrong to suppose that people sought salvation and immortality in another world because the Roman world was somehow barbarian. Whereas the God of Wrath of the Old Testament, who threatens material misfortune, presupposes an absence of the punitive pangs of inner conscience, Jesus' contempt for merely external conformity to moral law testifies to a new inwardness, a heightened emphasis on purity of motive and heart. God knows one's most secret thoughts. No matter how impeccable one's outward conduct, there can be no freedom from guilt unless one's thoughts and inner impulses are equally impeccable. Christianity emerged as a religion of salvation, and it thus originally presupposed that the individual stood in need of a moral salvation which could not be effected by his own meager efforts.

Psychologically, Christianity presupposed an intensification of guilt feelings. That is why Christ is needed to atone for human sin through the Crucifixion. But the law of love, whose ultimate demonstration was the Crucifixion, is ambiguous in its effects. On the one hand, it places a far more stringent moral demand on us than Old Testament law, and to this extent its tendency is to heighten the awareness of sin. But, on the other hand, the same law of love, which commands us to detach ourselves from the standpoint of personal self-interest and to live for others as Christ lived for us, is, if we can but follow it, capable of releasing us from our guilt complex because it leads us to dissociate ourselves with the standpoint of private self-interest which is responsible for sin. Thus the law of love, which radically intensifies guilt as long as one accepts it without living up to it, offers equally radical release from guilt if one can succeed in living up to it. It was the pathos of the Crucifixion and Resurrection which was necessary to jolt men into actually surrendering themselves to the law of love, that is, to Christ. The meaning of the Crucifixion became clear only in the light of the Resurrection, for it then became clear that the Crucifixion was nothing less than the death of God, that Jesus was Christ, and that God had sacrificed Himself to atone for human sin, so that man would no longer have to do so. This living example of boundless love was the necessary stimulus for other men's participation in a similar love. Jesus said before the Crucifixion that he had to depart so that the Holy Spirit could descend on his disciples,[14] that is, so that they could be reborn in Christ. Christ's payment for human sin made it no longer necessary for men to pay, but it also made it possible for men, through resurrection in Christ, to overcome sin.

VII *The Holy Spirit*

The Crucifixion, following upon the Incarnation, may be seen as an act of disincarnation. But whereas the disincarnation of the Creation was a denial of Incarnation, the disincarnation of the Crucifixion is not a denial of Incarnation as such, but only a denial that God's Incarnation in a particular individual, the historical Jesus, is complete and definitive. The Crucifixion is a disincarnation which explicitly prepares the way for a new and higher Incarnation. For it annnounces the Resurrection, which is a reincarnation of God, a second coming. In the original Christian Incarnation God, out of infinite compassion for all men, incarnated Himself in but one individual, namely Jesus. In incarnating Himself in an individual of such lowly station He demonstrated His love for even the most lowly and forsaken of men. But the Incarnation in Jesus was exclusive and therefore incomplete. Jesus had to die in order for the work begun in this first Incarnation to be completed, in order for the rest of the world to be included in an infinite Incarnation. The Crucifixion was followed by the first Resurrection, a second Incarnation of Christ as he appeared to the Apostles, confirming his victory over the grave. There followed the Ascension, a new disincarnation, announcing the Second Coming, the final and ultimately infinite Incarnation of God in the natural world through the Holy Spirit. The Incarnation which preceded the Ascension was still, like the first Incarnation, that of an exclusive individual who appeared to the Apostles. But in the Incarnation of the Second Coming, following the Ascension, Christ is no longer a single individual, but is rather identical with the kingdom of heaven, the kingdom of God and the Holy Spirit.[15] Christ inherits the kingdom of heaven as God's only son, but by rebirth in Christ other men become capable of sharing in Christ's inheritance as the children of God. Yet we can inherit God's kingdom as His children only when we are no longer children in the sense of being immature, that is, only as adults. Our glorification in the kingdom through Christ signifies our rightful assumption of the image of God. Whereas in the Old Testament our assumption of the divine image signified the Fall, through Christ and the Incarnation existence in the divine image no longer indicates a Fall from paradise into the alienation of opposition to the world. As God the Creator incarnates Himself in His Creation through Christ, so we, in inheriting the kingdom of God, realize the divine image as creators capable of rest from the labors of creation, that is, of self-incarnation in the world we have created. Through this self-incarnation we realize ourselves in the world through noncreative, receptive, sensitive participation in the self-creativity of the universe. The work of incarnation is complete only when the mind-matter dualism is overcome and when the creative mind of man identifies with the entire material world as its own incarnation. To heal the patriarchal divorce between man and nature means to recover "paradise lost." This original paradise was founded on the primitive animism of the food gatherer and hunter. The new, recovered paradise does not mean that labor ceases to be the economic basis of life. It does not mean that the pastoral, agricultural, commercial, and industrial revolutions are reversed.

What it means is rather that the mind-matter dualism, which continues perpetually to be recreated on workdays,[16] is perpetually transcended on the day of rest through our rebirth in Christ, our share in God's kingdom and consequent self-incarnation in our world.

VIII   *The Historical Jesus*

Such is Hegel's mature understanding of Christianity. But his preoccupation with Christianity dates back to his student days as a Lutheran seminarian in Tübingen. The young Hegel was especially interested in the life of the historical Jesus. He attempted to understand Christianity and its destiny in the world by understanding the project and destiny of its founder. The conclusion which he reached about Jesus, however, was distinctly negative. Jesus rejected the principal ethical institutions of life *(Sittlichkeit)*.[17] These institutions, according to Hegel's mature account, are the family, economic society, and the state.[18] Jesus' rejection of the family is apparent in a number of biblical incidents. Jesus rerepudiated his own mother and family, and he bid his disciples to renounce their fathers and mothers.[19] Researchers have supposed that he did so in consequence of the opposition of his family to his mission. His family was, understandably, dismayed when he abandoned his workbench to announce the kingdom of God, and must have thought that he was crazy. Members of his family were converted only after the Crucifixion. Yet it must be said that Jesus' rejection of his family seems, if this account is correct, exaggerated and hardly justified in its severity. What is even worse is that it is possible to see in this rejection a violation of Jesus' own law of love, which commands one to resist one's opponents with love and not expressions of hate. Christian love, as championed by Jesus, is, because of its opposition to the ethical institutions of life, an abstract, subjective love which threatens, for this very reason, to turn into its opposite, that is, into hate and fanaticism.

Jesus' rejection of the other two major ethical institutions of life is equally apparent. His opposition to the values of economic society is evident in several places. He bids the rich youth to throw away all his wealth,[20] for what does it profit one to gain everything in this world and to lose all in the next? He says that it is more difficult for a rich man to enter the kingdom of heaven than for a camel to go through the eye of a needle.[21] And he tells his disciples to build their treasure in heaven, and urges them not to worry about their own economic welfare: "For consider the lilies of the field. . . ."[22]

Finally, regarding the state, Jesus advocates no more than passive obedience, saying that we should give unto Caesar what is Caesar's and that we should not refuse to pay taxes.[23] The only way to avoid transforming the Christian love practiced by Jesus into fanatical hate is, as in the case of Jesus' attitude toward the state, for man to endure stoically the rejected institutions of life as unavoidable burdens, as crosses to be borne in silence. Jesus' detachment from ethical institutions makes him what Hegel called a "beautiful soul," innocent and yet ultimately burdened by the guilt of innocence.[24] We have already noted that Christian love seeks to escape guilt by rejecting the worldly standpoint of private self-interest, especially as manifested in the egoism of the family and in the pursuit of economic gain. But such an escape from worldly involvement ultimately fails, in Hegel's view, to avoid guilt, for it leads to the guilt of inaction and irresponsibility.

IX *Jesus versus Christendom*

Hegel's Christianity was not that of the historical Jesus. Christianity, in his view, was not primarily the religion of Jesus. It was rather the religion of the Christian Church as it developed through history. When Hegel elaborated his justification of Christianity later in life, he never sought to ground it in the historical facts of Jesus' earthly career. Ultimately for Hegel, Christianity, in its modern Protestant form, became identical with Christendom, with Christian civilization as a whole. And Christian civilization has been noticeable for its infidelity to the ethic of the historical Jesus. But Hegel took this to be more a criticism of Jesus than of modern Christendom. The real meaning of Christianity, for the mature Hegel, was not to be found by interrogating the historical Jesus, but rather by grasping the ultimate development of Christianity in the modern secular world. Jesus was the seed, modern Christendom the full fruit.[25] Whereas the young Hegel tried to interpret the fruit in terms of the seed, the mature Hegel used the fruit to illuminate the seed. And one of the chief characteristics of modern Christendom is that it has overcome the antiinstitutional, antiethical, and antisecular bias of Jesus himself. Christian love in the modern world has made peace with the family, with economic society, and with the state. It has ceased to be escapist, abstract, and subjective. It has become realized in the secular world, and the secular ethical world has thereby become sanctified. Thus, in the Protestant Christianity defended by Hegel, marriage, gainful economic activity, and political participation are all unqualifiedly holy. This is in contrast to medieval Catholic Christianity, whose otherworldliness is closer to the Jesus of history. The monastic vows of chastity, poverty, and passive obedience imply that there is a state holier than marriage, earned prosperity, and good citizenship.[26] It remains to be seen whether, in the secularized Christianity of the modern world, it is the secular or the holy which wins out. In any case, it is clear that the Christianity espoused by Hegel is not chiefly motivated by a desire to escape sin, and that is perhaps why it is not a Christianity which repudiates the standpoints of domestic and economic egoism. Hegel's Christianity is not primarily motivated by the need for salvation from sin, and in this it differs markedly from early Christianity. The need for salvation presupposes a kind of slavery to the superego which is absent from the mature adult who has achieved ego autonomy. (This is not to say that the mature individual behaves immorally. Rather, when he behaves morally, his behavior is free and rational instead of compulsive.)

X   *The Philosophical Rise of Man to Divinity*

The gradual disappearance of guilt in the modern world, however, might seem to threaten the very existence of Christianity seen as a religion of salvation. What future can there be for Christianity, it may be thought, in a world in which fewer and fewer individuals experience an exaggerated need to be saved from sin? It is in response to this question that it is well to recall that the Incarnation responds to a need of God as well as man. God the Father is admittedly not haunted by a sense of sin. He is not the slave of a superego. Rather, exemplifying full and mature adulthood, the Father has so identified with the voice of conscience that He feels responsible only to the freely self-imposed obligations of his own autonomous ego. Yet although God the Creator is free of sin, He is still, as we saw, alienated from creation. The Creator desires reconciliation with the world he has created.[27] And Christianity has a future only to the extent that modern man, achieving the ego autonomy and free creativity of the Creator, needs the reconciliation of the Incarnation as much as man did when he was overwhelmed by guilty subjection to the superego. It is characteristic of Hegel's Christianity that it requires man to abandon the guilty standpoint of man as a sinner and to rise to the standpoint of God Himself. Hegelian Christianity is comprehended from the divine side of the divine-human relationship. It requires man to overcome the religious alienation which made him define himself as *other* than God,[28] and to inherit the kingdom of God. Yet Hegelian Christianity differs from the atheism of Feuerbach by accepting with greater seriousness the claim that man becomes God. For if man becomes God, God exists, and so atheism is ruled out. Man becomes God through becoming infinite, through an Incarnation in which he identifies himself participatively with the universe, and thus through a recovery of the prenatal Oceanic feeling of oneness with the world.

The Hegelian philosophy claims to be *the* Christian philosophy. It claims to comprehend rationally what in the Christian religion was at first only represented pictorially, mythically, and symbolically. The effect of the picture thinking of traditional Christianity has, Hegel thought, been to distort the Christian truth. Pictorial representation tends inevitably to juxtapose inseparable aspects of an organic whole as if they were mutually exclusive and could exist apart from one another. Only the pure, imageless thought of philosophical comprehension is capable of assimilating an organic whole of internally related aspects without fragmenting or atomizing it. The effect of pictorial representation within Christian theology, he thinks, has been to impose artificial separations between essentially related aspects of the God-man totality. Picture thinking falsifies the very essence of Christian truth by making God essentially other than, and transcendent to, man. Thus traditional Christianity speaks of the Incarnation as being due to God's gratuitous and totally selfless love for what is other and externally related to Himself, that is, for man. Out of infinite mercy and love for man, God sacrificed Himself. The philosophical standpoint of rational comprehension *(Vernunft)*, however, cancels the separation which representation tends to establish between God and man. Whereas for representation *(Vorstellung)* God is transcendent to, and essentially independent of man, philosophy ceases to comprehend the God-man relation on the model of mutually external, spatially adjacent images. Philosophy comprehends God as what Hegel calls the "good infinite," by which he means the infinite which succeeds in being truly infinite because it includes the finite and human within it instead of, like the God of pictorial representation, excluding the finite and thus becoming itself finite or limited.[29]

As a consequence of the difference between philosophical comprehension and pictorial representation, the former interprets as *divine self-love* what the latter takes to be God's selfless love for man.[30] For philosophy, God's love for man turns out not to be love for something external to Himself. The Hegelian philosopher thus takes the Creation and Incarnation to be the speculative drama of God's own self-alienation in nature (Creation) and self-realization through Christian civilization and culture in the Holy Spirit. In man's divorce from nature, following upon the patriarchal revolution, the Absolute, or universe, itself is self-divorced or self-alienated in man. For man, we are reminded, belongs to the universe. And by means of the Christian Incarnation of God in creation and—what is essentially connected with it—of man (realizing the divine image) in nature, the universe itself achieves self-awareness and self-realization.

Thus philosophy comprehends selfless divine love for man as self-love, as the Absolute's own striving for self-realization in self-awareness. Hegel's comprehension of the divine love which for traditional religious representation is selfless agrees neatly with his negative judgment of Jesus' repudiation of the standpoints of domestic and economic self-interest. When philosophy recognizes that God Himself does not really live merely for others, man is no longer required to live merely for others either. Hence the way is open for a reconciliation between Christian ethics and the classical Aristotelian ethics of self-realization and happiness.

XI   *The Christian Trinity and the Dialectic*

Just how Hegelianism claims to be the philosophical self-comprehension of Christianity becomes clearer if we realize that the basic concepts of Hegel's famous dialectic articulate the content of the Christian trinity. The dialectic is commonly summarized as a three-stage process of thesis, antithesis, and synthesis. It is a process of position, counterposition (opposition), and composition. On the level of Christian theology, God the Creator is the thesis, the created world is the antithesis, while the Incarnation of God in the world appears as the synthesis. The Hegelian system of philosophy follows a parallel three-stage development: the "logic," the "philosophy of nature" and the "philosophy of Spirit." Hegel's logic is the philosophical comprehension of God the Father or Creator. The philosophy of nature seeks to comprehend the created world, while the philosophy of Spirit treats the reconciliation between God and the world, that is, it treats the Incarnation.

The terminology of thesis, antithesis, and synthesis has been frequently criticized as a parody on the genuine Helegian dialectic.[31] What can truthfully be said is that it is an oversimplification if presented as an adequate analysis of the dialectic. But, seen as a first approximation, the common characterization of the dialectic certainly does no harm, and in fact, because it is widely current, it serves as a convenient jumping-off point for more analytic expositions. On a somewhat more analytic level, we should understand by the term "thesis" the *abstraction* and *absolutization* as a complete whole of some partial aspect of an organic whole of internally (essentially) related aspects.[32] Thus the logic abstracts the sphere of pure imageless abstract thought and absolutizes it as a complete whole in itself. But, in fact, the sphere of pure thought is not a complete and independent whole, since it is essentially relative to the natural, sensory world from which it abstracts itself. The patriarchal revolution leads to the abstraction and absolutization of the pure thinking subject over against the material world. Hegel's "deduction" of the natural world from the logical realm of pure thought is really not as mysterious or impossible as many commentators have supposed. The deduction is possible because nature is the original whole out of which abstract thought abstracts itself. Thus the abstract thought of the logic presupposes nature as its own basis. Thought establishes itself by distinguishing itself from nature, which it implicitly presupposes as its other. Thought is thus internally related to nature as the child is internally related to a parent. And just as it is possible to deduce from the fact that a child exists the fact that a parent also exists, so it is possible to deduce from the fact that thought exists the second fact that nature also exists.

In the Judaic religion, the pure thinking subject is identified as God. Hegel's logic articulates the inner nature of this thinking subject. Thus Hegel says that his *Logic* articulates the nature of God as He exists eternally in Himself prior to the Creation of the world.[33] Hegel's comprehension of the Judaic God, of course, goes considerably beyond what the Hebrews themselves considered comprehensible. Hegel claims to penetrate and dissipate the mystery of God the Father. God the Father is abstract thought. It is abstract thought, that is, patriarchal intelligence, which is the basis of patriarchal power both over nature and over men. And it is abstract thought which, by absolutizing the thinker apart from the objective world, creates the patriarchal subject-object, God-world dualism. But it is also abstract thought which, driven by its own inner nature, eventually overcomes both itself and the subject-object dualism which it initially establishes. For abstract thinking discovers the contradiction of taking to be absolute what is essentially nonabsolute or relative, and by this discovery abstract thought transforms itself into what Hegel calls *concrete thought*. Abstract thought, which begins by absolutizing a self which is relative to an *other*, is negated by the other which it (by absolutizing itself exclusively) negates. The negated other, because it is really essential to the self, refuses to go away. Finally, overcoming its self-caused negation by the other, abstract thought abandons its absolutization of a finite, relative, and abstract self, and it absolutizes instead an expanded, infinite self conceived as overreaching and encompassing its other. And, in so doing, it becomes concrete thought. This overreaching of the other which previously negated thought from without is known in the terminology of Hegelianism as "negation of the negation,"[34] that is, negation of thought's negation of the other, and hence of the other's negation of thought. This overreaching is at once what is known as the stage of "synthesis" in the Hegelian dialectic. It is a synthesis of the initial abstract self and its other. The Christian Incarnation is nothing other than such a synthesis. It is the negation of the negation, the dialectical overreaching accomplished by abstract patriarchal thought. God the Father is negated by nature as His other. The ultimate form taken by the Incarnation, that is, Christ resurrected as the Holy Spirit, is the Father's act of overreaching and encompassing creation. The world is regenerated as something no longer devoid of spirit. The Father overcomes the unrealized abstraction of pure thought and, through union with Christ, becomes all in all.

The chief reason why Hegel's Christian comprehension of the Hebrew Creator goes beyond the Hebrews' own comprehension is that Hegel understands the Son and Holy Spirit to be contained by anticipation within the Creator or Father. The logic of pure thought, which is the articulation of the Hebrew God, is itself trinitarian. It is divided by Hegel into three main sections: "Being," "Essence," and "Concept" (*Begriff*). The sphere of Being is the most abstract sphere of thought. It is here in the sphere of undifferentiated immediacy that thought begins. The sphere of Essence is that of differentiation, opposition, or mediation. If Being is the realm of quiet self-identity, Essence is that of restless otherness. It is the sphere of Essence which anticipates the Creation and the consequent dualism of God (Creator) and world (creation). The concept of essentiality is correlative to that of accidentality.

God the Creator, we may say, is the essential reality of the world, while the world is an accidental manifestation of that essential inner reality. The third section of Hegel's *Logic* is that of Concept (*Begriff*). This is the sphere of the overreaching of opposition, of differentiated immediacy. It is this sphere which anticipates Spirit, the third member of the Christian trinity. It is the concrete thinking which becomes fully articulate in this section of the *Logic* which makes the realization of spirit, of the synthesis of thought and nature, possible.

Because of the logic's anticipation of the Creation and Incarnation in spirit it becomes possible to speak of a "preworldly trinity" to match and make possible the "worldly trinity" of God the Father's temporal incursion into real history in the Incarnation.[35] The Hegelian philosophy thus recovers an important dimension of Pauline Christianity. For St. Paul insisted that Christ existed before the Incarnation.[36] Christ existed united with the Father in the divine Logos before he became flesh in the Incarnation.[37] The preexistence of Christ in the divine Logos (that is, in the Father prior to creation) is, within the Hegelian philosophy, nothing other than the third division of the logic, the logic of the Concept and conrete thinking.

XII   *The Necessary Recurrence of Alienation*

Socioeconomically, the perpetually renewed realization of the Holy Spirit presupposes maintenance of essentially patriarchal conditions, that is, of labor as the economic basis of life. Patriarchal intelligence must retain its dominant position even if it is no longer the exclusive possession of the patriarchal class and is generalized, for example, to women as well as men. Women's liberation means the achievement and use by women of what was originally patriarchal and hence male intelligence. The Holy Spirit could not be realized if human society were to lapse into prepatriarchal conditions. The quiet communion with nature which the food gatherer enjoys contains no awareness that God is essentially the transcendence of alienation from nature. As a creative laborer or producer man brings about the necessary alienation without which reconciliation with creation cannot be known to be the truth.

Reconciliation is achieved through infinite self-incarnation in nature by the worker who rests from his labors. This self-incarnation is a communion and identification with nature. And it is, of course, also a communion with one's fellow men, who are a part of nature. It is a nonwillful, sensitive, empathetic participation in the self-creativity or self-will of nature, and it is capable of reconstituting one's own creative will. Through this identification with nature, the worker, resting from his labors, overcomes labor's inescapable sense of being limited by nature and wins confirmation of his infinite oneness with the cosmic Absolute. But this self-aware empathetic self-incarnation in nature is reserved for Sundays, and subject-object dualism is perpetually reasserted on weekdays in order to be overcome on Sundays.[38]

Philosophically, participatory identification with the cosmos has, in our own century, taken the form of the panpsychist cosmology of Alfred North Whitehead as developed by Charles Hartshorne.[39] Panpsychism defends the thesis that the apparently merely physical world is, in fact, shot through and through with mind or spirit, and so is fundamentally of a like nature with man himself. Although Hegel did not use the term "panpsychism," he adopted the basic panpsychist thesis of the natural philosophy of his one-time collaborator Schelling.[40] Even inorganic nature is shot through with spirit or feeling, although it is only on the organic, and indeed human, level that the cosmic spirit finally realizes itself through the infinite self-awareness of the Christian Incarnation. But it is perhaps only to be expected that panpsychism will never become the commonsense view of the world. For, despite theoretical arguments on its behalf,[41] the mind-matter dualism denied by panpsychism is perpetually being reasserted on weekdays. Panpsychism, as the theoretical expression of the doctrine of the Incarnation of mind in the cosmos, has practical import only on the Sundays of the human spirit.

XIII *Immortality*

Since Hegel's death, the question concerning his reconstruction of Christianity which has been most heatedly discussed has been whether it is a correct interpretation of the Christian religion. Many have held, like Sören Kierkegaard, that Hegelianism is heresy from the true Christian standpoint. Hegel has, in the first place, been accused of denying immortality. And if eternal life is understood as personal, individual immortality, the infinite extension into the future of one's individual stream of sensory consciousness, it is clear that Hegel did deny it.[42] The "need for salvation" is sometimes understood as a desire for blissful immortality in this sense. But fixation on such individual immortality may be a last stronghold of the very egoism from which true salvation delivers one. Egoism, Hegel admits, has its place in economic and family life, and we have seen that he does not wish to repudiate either sphere. Christian love as practiced by Jesus, through repudiating the egoism of the world, really ended up reinforcing it by freeing it of religious control. Christian love as understood by Hegel is elastic enough to embrace the world. It succeeds, moreover, in transfiguring the egoism of the world by embracing it and relating it to what is higher than itself. But although egoism has its place in secular ethical life, its place is not in religion. Ethical life (*Sittlichkeit*) is the sphere of external action in the world, and such action requires fixation on narrow personal goals and interests. Religion is the sphere of inner contemplation of one's oneness with the cosmic Absolute, and thus requires abandonment of the egoism appropriate in ethical life. The doctrine of individual immortality is not misguided for asserting egoism, but rather for promoting egoistic claims at the wrong place, in the higher sphere of religion. Egoism in religion makes it impossible to achieve the essential purpose of religion, which is to have participative experience of one's oneness with the Absolute. True salvation does not lie in individual immortality. It lies rather in a reconciliation with the institutional life of man and, more broadly, with nature as a whole, a reconciliation which extinguishes the desire for the false salvation of individual immortality. Eternal life means Sunday abandonment of the workaday standpoint of labor, a standpoint which is essentially temporal because it situates one between the obstacle course of a *present* environment and the *future* of an unrealized project. Eternal life means finding oneself by surrendering oneself to the "eternal now," that is, embracing the world in its presence instead of seeking to transform it.

The desire for individual immortality reflects fixation at the level of what we might call "aesthetic spirit," that is, sensory spirit. Death for the individual means the cessation of sensation, and the person who does not want to die as an individual is one who is identified with the stream of his sensation. But one who goes beyond the level of individual spirit to attain that of "objective" or intersubjective spirit, and who identifies with the on-going total institutional life of man and cosmic life of nature in which the individual but temporarily participates, no longer desires the infinite extension of his stream of sensory consciousness. What he desires is rather the extension of this institutional and cosmic life. Those versions of Christianity which promise immortality to the individual person presuppose a fixation at the level of aesthetic spirit. They presuppose the atrophy of objective spirit and the emergence of private individuals incapable of identifying with a cosmic or even human social whole.

XIV *Pantheism*

A second heresy of which Hegel has been accused is pantheism, the identification of God with the world. Despite Hegel's denial that he was a "pantheist"[43] there seems to be one clear sense of the term in which his philosophy is pantheistic. For he denies the self-sufficient otherness or transcendence of God and insists that God needs the world for the sake of His own self-realization.[44] Hegel's denial of the transcendence of God is clear from his insistence that the infinite includes the finite, from his identification of the Christian Holy Spirit with the "spirit" (*Geist*) of his own philosophy (the union of nature and thought), and from his denial of creation *ex nihilo*. And if one's credentials as a "theist" are made to depend on one's fidelity to the creation *ex nihilo* doctrine and God's consequent transcendence of the world, it cannot even be denied that Hegel is an "atheist." But surely the more important question about Hegelianism concerns the truth of its basic claims rather than its conformity to Christian orthodoxy. Orthodoxy is difficult to pin down, for Christianity has been given numerous interpretations by its followers over the centuries. What can be said of Hegelianism is that it certainly constitutes one possible interpretation. The Hegelian philosophy is deeply immersed in the Christian writings and tradition. If it should turn out that its basic claims are false or meaningless, the insistence that it is a correct interpretation of Christianity would have, in a Christian civilization, a largely negative purpose. But if it should turn out that these claims are warranted, there would be a temptation, not necessarily dishonest, to prefer Hegelianism to alternate interpretations of Christianity for acceptance in a Christian civilization.

CHAPTER 9

God, Art, and Revolution in the Modern World

I The Myth of the Twilight of Christianity

A distinguishing feature of modern Christendom, as we have seen, is its abandonment of Jesus' negative attitude toward the secular domestic, economic, and political world. Protestantism is the form taken by Christianity as it reconciled itself with the secular ethical world. Catholicism has remained more constantly apart from the world, and thus has maintained its identity more uniformly and successfully than mainstream Protestant Christianity. Through a process of secularization Protestant churches have lost much of the distinction which comes from holding out to the world something other than a mirror image of its own self. Many Protestants have wondered what the point of a church is which simply repeats the liberal social ideologies with which the existing political world is already impregnated. Modern Protestant Christianity thus looks very much like what Stephen Crites believes is the "twilight of Christendom."[1]

Hegel, who received his education in the tradition of the eighteenth-century Enlightenment, was already well aware of the seeming decline of Christianity in the modern world. To many, religion seemed either superstition or a sinister plot of priests and princes to keep the masses downtrodden by the illusory hope of consolation in the afterlife. In any case, Christianity seemed inherently medieval and thus nonmodern. Most people, confronting the apparent decline of Christianity, are led to make a choice between the modern world and the Christian tradition. They either abandon Christianity in order to embrace the secular world or repudiate the world in order to hold on to Christianity. What sets Hegel apart is his philosophy of what Sören Kierkegaard called the "both-and."[2] For Hegel, the choice between *either* the world *or* Christianity does

147

not exist. It is possible and indeed necessary, in his view, to embrace *both* the world *and* Christianity. It is my purpose here to show how this seemingly spectacular feat is accomplished.

A noted commentator on Hegel's philosophy of religion has voiced the opinion, incorrectly if the thesis propounded in this chapter is right, that so realistic a philosopher as Hegel, were he alive today, would surely not be a Hegelian.[3] What this opinion suggests is that in the century of atomic weapons and genocide, of Hiroshima and Auschwitz, the Hegelian belief that the modern secular world is the realization of the Christian kingdom of God would be incredible even to Hegel. In reply, however, it could be argued that of all religions Christianity is the one which is able to allow for suffering and diabolical evil. For it is the religion in which God Himself is crucified. It is possible to believe that no day goes by on which Christ is not being crucified a thousand times somewhere in the world. Yet such a reply would be insufficient. For the kingdom of God presupposes that the Crucifixion has essentially been relegated to the past. It presupposes the resurrection and glorification of Christ. It is true that Hegel speaks of the present as a "cross" to be borne. But it can be borne only because it is possible to see a "rose" in it, and to see "the rose in the cross of the present"[4] is to see present suffering from the glorious standpoint of implicit triumph over it. And so the basic question returns with ever greater force: where, in the world in which we live, is to be seen the glory of Christ reigning in the kingdom of heaven?

The general Hegelian answer may be summarized as follows: the kingdom of God has already broken through to real existence on earth, but it has by no means been completely constructed. Reactionary diabolical forces (for example, Nazi genocide) have not yet been completely routed. And the heavenly kingdom itself has thus far failed to organize itself on the basis of stable and orderly institutions; hence much of the anarchy of the world. But what is just as bad is that the kingdom of God has not yet attained awareness of its real identity. For it is none other than the world revolution for human rights whose onset occurred in Hegel's own time and which continues even today to seek a satisfactory issue. This revolution has in its own immediate self-understanding taken place *against* Christianity, against the Middle Ages, against heaven. In the Hegelian view it has not comprehended itself. It is really not a revolution against the Christian heaven, but rather against the *transcendence* or otherworldliness of heaven, that is, against the traditional conception of heaven. For it is nothing less than the realization of heaven on earth. The revolution thinks it is making a clean slate with the Christian past. In fact, it is representing and giving realization to the deepest Christian aspiration. For Christianity is the ultimate source of the revolution for universal human rights which is sweeping the world. Christianity promises all human beings, without regard to race, religious background, nationality, or social class, the right to inherit God's kingdom through Christ. But inheritance of God's kingdom means man's rightful assumption of the image of God. And since God is a creator, inheritance of the kingdom means the universal human right to creative labor. But since God rested on the seventh day and, indeed, eventually incarnated Himself in his creation, man also has a natural right to rest from his labors and incarnate himself compassionately and participatively in the world which he has claimed to create. Ultimately, inheritance of the kingdom of God means the death of God as a Lord standing above man, but this is not simply the death of God, because man himself, by discovering both the glory and the misery of creative labor, becomes one with the world through his participation in the Incarnation: thus man himself rises to divinity.

In order to explain this view more fully, it will prove useful to follow the historical emergence of the kingdom of heaven out of medieval Christian civilization. Hegel shows how the Christian doctrine of universal human rights first became a part of our cultural heritage in modern architecture, painting, music, and literature and then, beginning with the French Revolution, embarked on the process of its institutional realization in the world. Accordingly, we shall first discuss in some detail Hegel's theory of Christian art and then consider his political philosophy and philosophy of modern history. It is only by pursuing such a historical method that it is possible to see how Hegel can be both a conservative Christian and a modern revolutionary. He was a conservative because he wished to preserve the deepest values of the Christian tradition; he was a liberal because he discovered the deepest of these values to be universal freedom and hence equality; and he was a revolutionary because he was not content to embrace the values embodied in Christian culture without joining in the search for the means of their stable institutionalization.

II   *The Death of Art*

We saw that the symbolic art of the Orient sought to discover a still unknown meaning.[5] This search came to a successful conclusion in the classical art of Greece, which revealed the spirit of a divinely ideal individuality.[6] But the romantic art of the Christian world is no longer concerned to reveal ideal individuality. Art here implicitly realizes that the truly divine cannot be revealed in the ideal individuality of the Greek gods. For such individuality, despite its ideality, shares in the finitude of all individual existence, whereas the one true God must be infinite and free of external limitation. But it might be thought that Christian art would, for the same reason, renounce the attempt to reveal any form of individual existence. It would seem that the romantic art of Christianity has no alternative to the vain quest for a sensory realization of the one infinite and thus ultimately supersensible God. And in fact much Christian art has taken the life, death, and glorification of Christ as its theme, even while recognizing that it was a theme which no collection of works of art could begin to exhaust. To the Christian mind, a work of art is never an original disclosure of the truth. It is not originally from a painting of Jesus that the Christian discovers the meaning of the Christian revelation.[7] Whereas the Greek statue is itself an original religious revelation, Christian art presupposes that the revelation has already taken place through the life and death of Christ, and in the witness of Christ's Church. Christian art is a *reminder* of a truth which it cannot itself reveal.

But the art of Christian civilization is by no means exclusively devoted to explicitly religious themes. Indeed, in art as in other spheres of modern life, we find an increasingly powerful trend of secularization.[8] Alongside religious art we find the ever-growing body of art which takes as its theme even the seemingly most trivial individual detail of profane life. Modern art seems to take a special delight in the choice of insignificant themes: individuals of neither classical beauty or pose nor of any obvious Christian religious identity, prosaic objects of everyday life, and so on. But this secularization process is, in Hegel's view, only apparently an emancipation from religion. The artistic portrayal of unaccomplished and even repulsive individuals finds its Christian justification in the fact that in God's eyes every human being is worthy of salvation.[9] This applies even to the artist himself. The justification for much modern art, which we are tempted to dismiss as nonart, lies in the fact that the artist himself thereby makes a claim on our attention and recognition which is grounded in the belief that he too is a child of God.[10] A classical or explicitly religious artist effaces himself before the obvious beauty or inherent significance of his theme. But an artist who gives us apparently meaningless themes calls attention to himself. If the theme is trivial, the artist's right to select the theme, to call it to our attention and express himself in its execution is significant. The nominal theme is here only a pretext. The true content of apparently meaningless art is the selection and artistic treatment of the nominal content. The true content is the concrete, subjective individuality of the artist himself.

The general evolution of art in the Christian world from explicitly religious themes to works apparently empty of content does not really point to the process of de-Christianization and invading nihilism which so many have claimed to see. It reflects, on the contrary, a deepening realization and appropriation of Christian truth. The traditional artist who selects explicitly religious themes alienates himself in the product of his art. He perpetuates the Hebrew view that God is other than oneself. The greater the cathedral, the poorer the architect who has put everything he has into its design and construction. On the other hand, the artist who selects trivial themes realizes himself in his art. His works are to be seen as the expression of his unique subjectivity more than the evocation of eternal and universal truth. But to use art as a vehicle for self-expression is a negation of the universal and eternal truth of Christianity only in appearance. For Christianity affirms the universal right of all human beings, however endowed or unendowed by nature, to share in divine creativity. In the Christian view everyone has the right to win recognition as a creative genius. Thus the ultimate development of romantic Christian art would be a world in which art is no longer, as it was in the Renaissance, reserved for the exalted few. In the kingdom of heaven everyone can win recognition as an artist. Thus the evolution of Christian art toward banality is inescapable. But what art loses in exaltation it gains in universality.

Yet the increasing banality of art in the modern world has a deeper ground than the universalization of artistic creation. The abandonment of explicitly religious themes is indeed partly to be explained by the realization that art is not capable of grasping the truth. If the above analysis is correct, the adoption of trivial or prosaic themes does not mean that art has ceased to be Christian, but it does mean that men have lost confidence in the capacity of art to express universal truth adequately. One of the most constant themes of Hegel's philosophy is that truth can be adequately grasped only in the form of pure thought, that is, philosophy. And the consequence is what Hegel has notoriously called the "dissolution of art."[11] It was the feeling that through art man could extend his knowledge of reality which, in the past, made man rivet his attention to it. Today we live in a postartistic era, not because art has disappeared but because it has ceased to serve the metaphysical-religious function of revealing truth which it served so clearly in classical Greece. At its best, art has become the means of expressing individual genius; at its worst mere diversion or distraction, now purely decorative, now serving a purely aesthetic function in stimulating the play of the senses, or of abstract geometrical form. No doubt art will continue to exist. The great art works of the past will be preserved and reenacted. They are precious documents of bygone stages in the upward struggle of man for truth and freedom. But it is unlikely that such works will ever again be produced. Man now finds fact more awe-inspiring than fiction, historical reality more captivating than art,[12] rigorous conceptual grasp of the Absolute more satisfying than either the dumb symbolization of the Absolute, the hopeless quest for an adequate aesthetic expression of it, or the adequate aesthetic expression of a superficial content.

And yet Hegel does not deny that art will continue to play a subsidiary role in modern culture. Man remains an aesthetic, sensory creature as well as a rational being.[13] Our conceptual comprehension of reality is not always in gear. Enjoyment of the great art of the past heightens our affective involvement with metaphysical-religious truth. The history of art is a record of human striving for knowledge. Now that this knowledge has been attained, this history cannot affect us existentially as it did before. We know the truth independently of the artistic precipitates of past striving. But we may continue to attend performances of *Antigone*, not in order to comprehend reality, but to celebrate the artistic heroes who made our comprehension possible, and to revivify our present comprehension by reenacting transcended stages in the history of its emergence.

But what is perhaps most surprising is that the same Christian civilization which, in Hegel's view, spells the death of art has produced some of the greatest art the world has seen: the Gothic cathedrals, the sculpture of Michelangelo, the painting of the Italian and Dutch masters, the music of Mozart and Beethoven, the poetry of Shakespeare and Goethe. It was not Hegel's intention to say that this Christian art was simply inferior to classical Greek masterpieces. If the purpose of art is to reveal truth in sensory form, Christian art is, no doubt, inferior *as art* because, unlike Greek art, it rests on the premise that the truth cannot be aesthetically revealed. But precisely for this reason Christian romantic art is deeper and closer to the truth than Greek art.[14]

III   *Romantic Architecture*

We have seen that, for Hegel, architecture is an essentially Oriental art form. This does not mean that there is no classical Greek or Christian romantic architecture, but rather that it is in the Orient, more particularly in Egypt and Mesopotamia, that architecture enjoyed a central place among art forms.[15] The very fact that the architecture of these ancient civilizations has defied the ravages of time indicates something of the importance attached to this art form in the Orient. Given the primitive construction methods of the time, the giganticism of the ancient structures—for example, the pyramids—required the mobilization of unprecedented masses of labor and made architectural construction the chief unifying, collective activity of the ancient peoples.[16] The colossal character of the pyramids extends far beyond the limits of functional necessity. They stand as monuments to the peoples who devoted their lives to their construction. In Greek architecture we have quite the opposite quality: simplicity, freedom from ostentation, subordination to the functional purpose at hand.[17] Romantic architecture combines features of both symbolic ("independent") and classical ("dependent," functional) architecture.[18] The most characteristic example of romantic architecture is, in Hegel's estimation, the Gothic cathedral.[19] On the one hand, it has a functional purpose, since it is designed to contain a congregation of believers. But, on the other hand, the complexity and ornateness of its form connot be justified as a means to this functional end. Nonetheless, there is a connection between the functional end and the non-functional elaboration of form. Form is more than an instrument of function, but what it is beyond being such an instrument is a *reminder* of the functional purpose. The cathedral serves to contain the congregation in worship, but its form, soaring weightlessly to the heavens beyond all earthly bonds, serves as a reminder of the same detachment from finite aims which marks the Christian worship of which the cathedral is an instrument. The exterior of the cathedral, like the ringing of its bells, is a call issued to the believer to turn away from his finite worldly concerns and withdraw into the inner self—there to seek reconciliation with God. Thus form, even where it no longer serves a function in any direct sense, still serves one indirectly by preparing and moving us to use the cathedral for the purpose for which it was intended.[20]

It may be said generally that the design of a functional structure is romantic when it seeks to give the observer an anticipatory illusion of actually realizing the purpose for which the structure is intended. Thus a romantic automobile design may incorporate a long, low look and even wings in order to give the viewer a foretaste of the speed and power which may be his once he gets behind the wheel. Forsaking the understatement and eloquent silence of classical design, romantic design addresses a personal appeal to the viewer. Thus the individual viewer of romantic design feels solicited by the architect or designer. The romantically designed car has been made as much to interest the viewer as a prospective driver as to satisfy the actual driver. Romantic architecture arouses the viewer's dissatisfaction with the limitations of his present situation and moves him to wish emancipation from such limitation. That is perhaps why it is Christian. For Christianity is a religion which seeks salvation of every individual. The Greek temple exudes an aristocratic attitude of indifference to the viewer. Such a temple exists for the sake of the god whom it houses. But a medieval cathedral exists for the conversion of the whole outside world which sees it. In the modern commercial world, commercial art has inherited this feature of church design. Modern economic society makes everyone feel important. It stimulates demand by continually bombarding everyone, regardless of income, with romantic appeals to various sorts of self-transcendence. It bears the imprint of Christianity by holding out the promise of freedom from limitation to all.

IV *Painting*

But despite the achievements of romantic architecture it was clear to Hegel that architecture was not the art form best adapted to the Christian genius. Romantic architecture alludes to, and even stimulates, the striving of individual Christian subjectivity, but it does not succeed as well as other art forms in *revealing* such subjectivity. (Moreover, much modern architecture seems to have little aesthetic function at all. The pressure of cost tends to force architecture out of the artistic competition altogether, and romantic architecture, due to its ornateness and illusory weightlessness, has particularly suffered.) Since the essential medium of architecture consists in heavy masses of matter, the Gothic effect of weightlessness, adapted to the evocation of immateriality, goes against the natural tendency of architecture.[21] It is true that the industrial revolution, by multiplying nonarchitectural artefacts and vehicles, has opened up new frontiers for romantic design outside the realm of architecture. Still, the aesthetic expression of human subjectivity requires a type of art more naturally suited to itself than the non-human forms of architecture and design.

Sculpture offers greater possibilities for Christian art, for the natural form of sculpture is the human body which, precisely because it is human, is suffused with spirit. However the spirit more easily expressed in sculpture is the substantial, abiding, ideal spirit of a Greek god, not the individual, fleeting, subjective spirit of a unique and real human being. Hegel admits that the genius of Michelangelo permitted him to defy the normal limitations of sculpture and create statues of a truly romantic-Christian character,[22] but most romantic artists have preferred to give themselves better odds by sticking to painting, music, or poetry. For these are, in Hegel's view, the three inherently romantic arts.

The entire cycle of arts which Hegel gives us goes from the least to the most spiritual, from architecture through successively sculpture, painting, and music to poetry.[23] As spiritual expressiveness increases, spatiality decreases.[24] Thus while architecture and sculpture are three-dimensional, painting is two-dimensional and thus less spatial. Music is spatially dimensionless. (Hegel is not denying the difference we detect between monophonic and stereophonic recordings. He is referring to visual and tactile space, not to aural space.) Like poetry—but unlike architecture, sculpture, or painting—music is a performing and not a visual art. But Hegel's classification of the arts needs to be supplemented by at least a few words about dance. Surprisingly, Hegel offers no detailed examination of dance comparable to his examination of the other arts, although he does refer to it as a synthesis of sculpture and music.[25] Dance has the distinction of being, far more obviously than drama or opera, both a visual and a performing art. Dance is sculpture come to life, animated with rhythm, grace, and movement. Generally, we may infer that just as civilization evolves from the Orient to the Christian West, the art forms evolve from the visual to the performing arts, from frozen matter to the animation of spirit. The performing arts are more capable of revealing individual, living spirit, first of all because the performers—dancers, singers, and actors—are living human beings. The unique place of dance in the cycle of art forms situates it as a meeting ground between East and West, space and time, sculpture and music.

The one visual nonperforming art which is capable of revealing living individual spirit is, according to Hegel, painting, and that is why it came into its own only in the Christian era, particularly in the Middle Ages and the sixteenth and seventeenth centuries.[26] A main reason why painting is more suited to the task of expressing living subjectivity than sculpture is the greater importance assumed in it by the countenance and, in particular, by the look of the eyes.[27] A statue is meant to be viewable from a great variety of angles. No single viewpoint is singled out by the artist as *the* viewpoint intended by him. But the revelation of the individual soul depends on seeing the countenance and look from a single privileged and fleeting angle and viewing point. It follows that sculpture is not naturally suited to the revelation of the individual soul so important to Christian theology. If sculpture is at all capable of giving such a revelation, it is only after much study and experimentation in which the spectator tries viewing the statue from a variety of standpoints. The advantage of painting is that it saves the viewer such exertion. The painter, unlike the sculptor, preselects for the viewer a single angle of vision as *the* angle from which to see the depicted figure.[28] For a painting can be properly viewed only by taking a position directly in front of it. The problem with viewing a statue is that there is no single frontal view.

The above difference between sculpture and painting is due to the fact that a painting is only two-dimensional, its spatiality being reduced to a single surface. A statue, being three-dimensional, supplies an endless series of possible two-dimensional surface views. And since no spectator can possibly exhaust the series, the statue exists objectively on its own and is essentially indifferent to the spectator. A painting, on the other hand, is much more intimately related to the viewer.[29] The artist, by forseeing a particular angle for viewing the depicted figure or scene, paints for the viewer. Whereas the classical statue acquires an independent reality and, so to speak, exists for itself in aristocratic and cold aloofness from the spectator, the figures depicted in paintings exist only for the viewer. Leonardo's Mona Lisa, unlike the David of Michelangelo, is not a real figure. She is but a single momentarily revealing appearance of one, but the revealing moment has, through the magic of painting, been captured and preserved for the viewer. The painting, as a mere appearance, resembles a hallucination. A good painting causes the illusion of a real figure, but the error is quickly corrected when it is realized that the real existence of the figure cannot be confirmed by viewing it from different angles. The Mona Lisa exists, alas, only in the mind of the beholder. But the viewer feels correctly that the painter is addressing himself to him; he thus ceases to be a detached spectator and becomes personally engaged as the recipient of a communication. Painting is, therefore, a much warmer art form than sculpture. It thus becomes clear why it is a romantic art form. It resembles romantic (as opposed to classical) architecture in soliciting a response from the viewer, and in thus heightening the viewer's self-awareness. We also see why painting is a more typically Christian art form. The revelation of the recesses of the individual soul of the figure and the self-consciousness which such a revelation calls forth in the viewer are expressions of a civilization sensitive to hypocrisy and insincerity, given to soul-searching and marked by a high degree of psychological sophistication.

Thus far we have been speaking of painting as if its thematic content were, like that of sculpture, the human form, painting being distinguished from sculpture chiefly in its greater attention to individual subjectivity. It is, of course, true that most explicitly religious painting from the Middle Ages and Renaissance treats the human form, although it does so more individually than ideally. For Christ, the Holy Family, the Apostles and the Saints were living individuals, not purely ideal creations of art. However, it is equally apparent that modern painting has expanded to include a much wider range of thematic material in which the human form is absent: still-life, landscape, and the purely geometrical forms of abstract art. But this expansion of thematic content does not belie the claim that painting is concerned to express individual human subjectivity. What has happened is that painters, by going beyond the attempt to express the subjectivity of portrayed figures, have undertaken to express their own subjectivity.[30] They have done this by exercising the right to eliminate completely the human form from their paintings and to express themselves in the selection, arrangement, and treatment of ostensibly nonhuman forms. Thus, when a painter communes empathetically with his natural environment, nature echoing the inspiration of his own soul, he may express himself by painting this echo in the form of a landscape.[31] The human form carries with it ethical and religious significance. Its elimination from painting accordingly indicates an evolution toward ostensibly less significant subject matter. But the more the subject matter is apparently insignificant, the greater the opportunity for the painter to express the personal idiosyncrasy of his own genius by the selection, highlighting, and treatment of an inherently trivial or even meaningless theme. We thus see in the long-term evolution of painting a good example of the general evolution of Christian art from self-alienation in the portrayal of a subjectivity which transcends the artist to self-realization achieved through the artist's claim to the right to express himself in his work.

The limitation of painting to a single surface requires the outline of figures and objects to be made by the use of lighting, shading, and color rather than by the three-dimensional molding of sculpture. Thus, whereas lighting effects and color are unessential, and sometimes even distracting, in sculpture, they are absolutely necessary to painting: "At one point a color stops and another begins, and by this means one has everything."[32] Whereas sculpture depends on chance lighting effects from an external source, the painter builds into his work specific desired lighting effects.[33] These effects form an essential part, not of the depicted figures or objects, but of the momentary subjective appearances of objects which painting is concerned to preserve for us. And color plays an additional role in presenting objects in their living individuality.

V *Music*

But just as painting is a spiritually deeper art form than sculpture, so music and poetry penetrate more deeply than painting. Sculpture, which eventually abandons isolated figures for groups of dramatically related ones, shows a tendency to evolve toward painting.[35] For it is painting which typically relates figures not only to the viewer but to one another in the "composition" of a group. Early painting, which tends to portray figures in statuesque isolation, shows traces of its evolution out of sculpture.[36] Painting did not come into its own until it freed itself from sculpture to paint figures and objects intimately attuned to their settings. But painting shows, in its turn, a tendency to evolve toward music.[37] The history of painting, we have noted, shows an evolution away from preoccupation with ethically or religiously significant thematic content. It tends toward a preoccupation with the artistic treatment of the subject more than with the subject itself. But "artistic treatment" in painting means the creative use of colors. As the subject matter recedes into the background, the main emphasis comes to be placed on the harmony, contrast, tension, and reciprocal attack and retreat of different colors. The symbolism of pure colors also receives attention, and the dance of reflections is highlighted. Hegel, who lived before impressionism and modern abstract art, could not know how well the actual evolution of painting has confirmed his intuitions. But the important inference which he made from this evolution was that painting thereby tended to approach music. For it is music—pure music—which abandons all explicit reference to specific subject matter in order to focus on a play of contrasts, tensions, and harmonies. But the inner emotional life of the human soul is also one of contrasts, tensions, releases of tension, and harmony. Music thus resonates and resounds with the pure emotional life of the soul, and it thereby engages the soul's sympathetic participation.[38] But although music expresses the life of emotion, it is by no means a self-abandonment to emotion and the means of its natural release. The purpose of music is not to satisfy human longing but rather to present it for contemplation. Music, the most purely emotional art form, is at once as intellectual and mathematical as architecture.[39]

The capacity of music for providing a sensory echo of the imageless emotional life of the soul far exceeds even that of modern painting. Painting labors under the disadvantage of having to express the interplay of sadness, longing, gaiety, anger, and calm frozen in the image of a single moment. The painter has to present a temporal process nontemporally and spatially. If painting reduces the full spatiality of sculpture to the two-dimensional space of a single surface, music completely dispenses with visual space to expand in the temporal realm whch is the soul's own natural element.[40] But precisely because of the temporal character of music, it lacks the permanence of architecture, sculpture, or painting. Music is essentially fleeting, and this marks it as a predominantly performing art.[41] Its works, in order to survive, must be reenacted by living musicians. Both because of the need for interpretation by a living performer and because of its purely temporal character, music's capacity for expressing individual subjectivity exceeds that of the plastic arts considered thus far. Although music certainly existed in pre-Christian civilization, it is only in the Christian world, in a civilization marked by Christian inwardness, that music assumes a central place among the arts. Hegel apologized for knowing less about music and its technicalities than about the other arts.[42] Yet his insight about the essential modernity of music appears confirmed in the explosion of the recording industry in our century. But from the Hegelian standpoint it would have to be kept in mind that the new technology has developed at least in part because of a preexisting affinity between our Western civilization and music. The affinity and taste for music is not to be explained as due merely to the new possibilities of technology. It is true, however, that the recording industry has severed the link between the living performer and his audience which Hegel took to be essential to the very survival of music. If music were no longer performed but merely heard from recordings made in an ever more distant past, it would surely lose much of its capacity for engaging the hearer in a sympathetic response. Music would become more an object of detached contemplation. It would gain in classicism and lose its essential romanticism. The enjoyment of music depends on the sympathetic response of the hearer to the musician. The living presence of the performer heightens this response.

We have been speaking chiefly of pure music, in which all explicit reference to significant content disappears. The disappearance of such reference, which marks the transition from painting to music, means that music in its essential nature is the sort of art in which the musician or composer expresses himself, and is not the sort, like sculpture or painting (in its early stages), in which the artist effaces himself before the overpowering content which his art is intended to reveal. Beginning with music, and to an even greater extent in modern lyric poetry, art becomes a revelation of the subjective experience of things rather than (as in sculpture or epic poetry) of the things themselves. Painting is a revelation of individual subjectivity from the outside, from its physiognomy or its sympathetic echoes in nature. In music, individual subjectivity begins to express itself from within.[43] Yet in order to be classed as art this subjectivity must not be so idiosyncratic as to be totally private and incommunicable. It must be capable of calling forth a sympathetic response from the hearer and thus must not be entirely devoid of universality.

But music, of course, does not always come in pure form. It is sometimes accompanied by lyrics.[44] Pure music then gives way to song, as the inner emotion sympathetically aroused by the musician seeks release in the verbal expression of poetry. Poetry is the highest of the arts because it is the most capable of expressing the inner life of the soul. Music arouses this life, but fails to give it the explicit outward expression which can be provided by the representations of poetic imagery.[45] (Where sculpture expresses contents in the outwardness of real perceptual space, poetry expresses them in a less outward outwardness, namely, in the inner world of the outward representations of the imagination.) But as an accompaniment to music, poetry, especially if it contains deep or subtle reflections, is apt to detract from rather than enhance the music.[46] The spontaneous flight of pure emotion is apt to be broken and inhibited by reflection. Thus if there is any lyric accompaniment to music at all, it is preferable from the musical standpoint for it to be repetitive, vapid, and devoid of deep reflections. On the other hand, if the lyrics do call attention to themselves by an intrinsic significance of their own, it is rather the music which is a subordinate accompaniment to the text than the other way around. For the boundary separating music from poetry has been crossed.

VI   *Romantic Literature*

We have already discussed poetry in the chapter on Greece. In Greece lyric poetry played a comparatively minor role, chiefly functioning as a transitional stage between epic and classical tragedy. But in the romantic world of Christian art lyric poetry sets the tone for all poetry. Just as music shares a natural affinity with the romantic temper of the modern world, so the poetic genre which is inherently more musical than either epic or drama, namely, lyric poetry, acquires a dominant position throughout modern literature. This, of course, does not mean that modern literature consists predominantly of lyric poems. But it does mean that this literature favors a lyrical treatment even within the provinces of epic and drama.[47] Why this is so becomes clearer once we recall that lyric poetry is, among the basic poetic genres, the one most suited to the self-expression of the individual soul. Epic poetry is chiefly concerned with revealing the total collective life of a nation. Drama is more concerned with action and conflict between characters. It is in the effusions of lyric poetry that the individual soul withdraws within itself from the objective world of institutions and the dramatic confrontations of social life to unburden itself of its inner feelings.[48] It is perhaps not surprising that the Greek spirit is more closely attuned to epic, for epic is far closer to sculpture than lyric. In the epic, the individual loses itself in the independent world of things and events. In the lyric, the poet recollects himself and turns within to explore his subjective response to things. But a great poet does not express purely private sentiments which cannot be experienced by others. For poetry is a form of communication, and thus the sentiments must become intersubjective and must not remain privately subjective.[49]

Lyric poetry has a cathartic function in the discharge of sentiment and pent-up emotion. In drama feeling is discharged in action; in lyric poetry it finds release in words which represent as well as express it. But Hegel specifies that lyric poetry does not so much deliver the individual *from* sentiment as it frees him *in* sentiment;[50] that is, it preserves the sentiment even in the individual's deliverance from its tyranny. Domination by blind passion results from the soul being so overwhelmed by sentiment as to be unconsciously one with it. Lyric poetry, by leading the individual to awareness of the passion, frees him from enslavement to it. By becoming aware of the passion one is led to distinguish oneself from it.

Lyric poetry exists in all phases of a nation's life, but it is especially typical of the postheroic and postepic stage in which political life has become so institutionalized and routinized that the individual may take it for granted and detach himself from it to explore the inner world of personal sentiment.[51] Lyric poetry is particularly characteristic of the modern world in which it serves as a means of romantic revolt by the individual against what Hegel calls the "prose" of circumstances and everyday life.[52] In the modern world a lyric poem tends chiefly to be an ode of self-expression. This is in contrast to the Orient, where lyric poetry tends in the direction of a hymn of praise in which the poet heaps superlatives of adulation upon a deity, prince, loved one, or metaphysical absolute apart from himself.[53] For in the Orient the individual has not yet discovered individual autonomy. Individual subjectivity does not (as in the West) rest content with itself. It has not yet found its focus and center in itself. It does not celebrate itself but rather its release in objectivity. The very idea of Oriental lyricism might sound like a contradiction in terms, and the subjectivism of lyric might appear inconsistent with the Oriental absorption of subjectivity in objectivity, were it not for the fact that in the Orient lyricism is a quest for such absorption. It is only in the Christian West that lyricism has come to be an end in itself, and that the attempt is made to absorb the objective world into individual subjectivity.

The dominance of lyricism in modern literature may be seen in many ways, but perhaps the clearest way is to contrast classical Greek tragedy with the essentially Christian romantic tragedy of Shakespeare.[54] The heroes of Greek tragedy are normally individuals who are passionately identified with substantial ethical principles, as illustrated by Antigone's identification with the code of family ethics or Creon's identification with the state. A Shakespearean hero is, by contrast, rarely identified with anything beyond himself. Hamlet is so lost in lyrical soliloquy and soul-searching that he seems incapable of the dramatic action demanded by the situation.[55] But it is characteristic of Shakespeare that even evil characters, such as Macbeth, Iago, or Richard III, individuals absorbed in their own quest for power and purely personal aggrandizement, can attain heroic stature.[56] Such awesome individuals, at the command of extraordinary energy, fascinate us as they proclaim their right to unchecked self-assertion. The modern Christian world is pursued by the thought that society is evil and that even the criminal has his rights against the oppressiveness of society.

Adolf Hitler is for us the archexample of the modern Shakespearean antihero of romantic tragedy. The romantic hero tends to free himself from all ethical tradition. Iago and Hitler are uprooted products of a society alienated from traditional ethical values. Writers such as Emile Fackenheim have surmised that the Hitler phenomenon is the undoing of Hegelianism and its world-historical optimism.[57] But Hegel himself was no stranger to the German anti-Enlightenment culture of nationalism and anti-Semitism which eventually came to flower in the Third Reich. In Hegel's time, this culture was but a subculture, but it was represented in his own immediate environment by the student associations (*Burschenschaften*) of the day.[58] Hegel understood the phenomenon as a perverse deformation of the Christian belief in the infinite value of *every* human soul. The basic lesson of Shakespearean tragedy is that the value of stridently antisocial individualism is not infinite. The claims of the individual personality to self-expression are, however great, not absolute and must be reconciled with respect of universal human rights, of the equal claims of other individuals. But Hitler shows how art has been overtaken by reality, how fact has stolen the thunder of fiction. Developments of modern technology and the mass media have permitted the fiction and romance of an earlier age to be realized on the stage of history. It is doubtful that even Shakespeare could approach the power and profundity of the tragic rise and fall of the Third Reich.

VII   Hegel: Philosopher of the French Revolution

The one great theme of modern romantic literature has been the Christian-inspired principle of the universal human right of the individual to self-expression and self-realization. It is this principle which has been growing to self-conscious articulation in the development of Christian art from architecture through painting and music to literature. The death of art is philosophically conditioned, as we saw, by the fact that the truth has now left even poetry behind to express itself in the form of logical discourse, its own proper medium. But the death of art may be understood to be socially conditioned as well. It may be seen as a consequence of the fact that art succeeded so well in culturally enshrining the Christian principle that, going beyond "enculturation," the task of institutionalizing it in existing society could no longer be postponed. It is this world-historical, millenial task which was first undertaken in the American and French Revolutions.

Two scholars in particular, Alexandre Kojève and Joachim Ritter, have accustomed us to the view that Hegel is not primarily the "official philosopher of the Prussian Restoration" for which generations, following Rudolf Haym, have taken him.[59] The Haym thesis, as a way of taking leave of Hegel by pigeonholing him in the early nineteenth century, simply will not do. (Nor will it do to chain him to the more spacious but still stuffy "bourgeois" world of the nineteenth century. If anything is clear from the central theme of Hegel's philosophy of world history, it is that the demands of universal freedom in the modern world are more imperious than those of any particular class to represent these demands.) The view held by Kojève and Ritter is that Hegel was, to the last, rather the philosopher of the French Revolution. He presumably acquiesced in the role of official Prussian philosopher because he believed the Prussia of the post-Napoleonic era to represent the continuing and ultimately invincible cause of the French Revolution. This judgment of Hegel's may appear mistaken in the light of developments in Prussia after Hegel's death, but it should be remembered that Hegel rallied to Prussia in an era in which its government had instituted liberal reforms in order to mobilize the nation in the war against French imperialism, and in which the Prussian king had even promised his people a constitution guaranteeing greater political participation. After the White Terror and the Bourbon Restoration in France it is perhaps not surprising that Hegel no longer saw the homeland of the Revolution as its present standard-bearer. And his last published writing (1831), on the Reform Bill in England, explains why he could not assign Britain this role: Britain was, he thought, still a largely medieval state in which public law had not yet been freed from a confusing system of private historical rights and privileges. [60]

But it is necessary to go beyond a simple identification of Hegel with the French Revolution. First, if Hegel is the philosopher of the French Revolution, he is also the philosopher of the American Revolution. For both revolutions were grounded in the Enlightenment philosophy of universal human rights. If it is true that the American Revolution started out as an attempt to win merely the rights of Englishmen for the American colonists, it was quickly led, in severing itself from Britain, to justify itself in the court of world opinion by incarnating the principle of universal natural rights in the Declaration of Independence. If Hegel was more preoccupied with the French Declaration of the Rights of Man, it was because he lived in an era in which Europe was still the center of world history, and because as a European he felt the immediate impact of the revolution occurring in a neighboring country. But the course of world history since Hegel's time has both revealed the American Revolution to be equal in impact with the French Revolution and, more importantly, to be essentially allied with the revolutionary cause in France. In fact, both revolutions are the initial stages of a single world revolution, indeed of *the* revolution of the modern world.

The second way in which Ritter's position requires supplementation becomes apparent if we consider the question as to *when* the French Revolution is supposed to have ended. The point which needs to be made is that the question is unanswerable. It is unanswerable because the Revolution *is not over*. Since it is a revolution in the name of universal human rights and not merely the rights of Frenchmen, it could not be contained within one country. It eventuated under Napoleon in the attempt to construct a universal or world state. Hegel was identified over many years with the Napoleonic project. Shortly before the battle of Waterloo, turning a deaf ear to the newly arisen German nationalism, he wrote to a close friend that if he saw any chance of Napoleon carrying the day he, G. W. F. Hegel, would not hesitate to sling a rifle over his shoulder and join him.[61] (He was not so indiscreet in his published writings.)

Even French historians frequently criticize Napoleon for his overweaning ambition, for placing his personal goals of empire and dynasty above the national interests of France. Like Hitler after him, he could not be content with any finite attainment. He seemed to need ever new proofs of his omnipotence. But the comparison with Hitler should not make us forget that Napoleon was, to the last, even despite himself, the soldier of the Revolution, whereas Hitler inherited the tradition of the romantic, nationalistic, anti-Enlightenment Restoration in an era when, in the aftermath of World War I, the disappearance of the Hohenzollern and Hapsburg dynasties deprived the romantic reaction of its aristocratic and traditionalistic anchoring. If Napoleon stood for something beyond the national interests of France, it was in part because the universalism of France's own Revolution carried France beyond itself and indeed pointed in the direction of a world state. For only such a state could protect and enforce the rights of *man*.

VIII   *Economics and World Revolution*

Hegel wrote that man must leave the state of nature in order to give human rights real existence;[62] and elsewhere he agreed that states exist in a state of nature relative to one another.[63] This would seem to be an implicit recognition of the necessity of dismantling the nation-state system. Implicit recognition of the same necessity is also present in his admission that modern economic ("civil") society, by its tendency to create a world economy in which all peoples are interdependent, undermines the economic basis of national independence and sovereignty.[64] Ultimately, the right to buy and sell freely, to work and produce where one wishes, poses a threat to the national economic independence which is the condition of real national sovereignty. The principles of the French Revolution are the political formulation of principles implicitly at work in modern economic society.[65] The economic dynamism of the modern world breaks down historical barriers between peoples based on religion, nationality, or social class. The economic basis of political freedom is freedom of trade. The Arab boycott of Jewish firms illustrates the kind of violation of human rights—the right to be treated as a human being and not chiefly as Jew or Gentile—which is condemned to disappear by the pressure of economic progress. Hegel anticipated the Marxist-Leninist thesis about imperialism being the destiny of capitalism by holding that overproduction in the industrial countries and the resulting class division between affluent industrialists and proletarian poverty would lead to colonialism and thus the creation of a world economy. Looking even further, he saw that the prosperity of the Western world would eventually require the liberation of the non-Western world from colonial dependence. Modern economic society, by the increasing division and specialization of labor, tends to overproduction and is led to extend itself over the entire globe in order to find new markets, cheap raw materials, new fields of investment, and an outlet for surplus laborers through colonialization. The extension of world trade and the international division of labor tend to create a universal "civil society."[66]

Hegel did not believe that the laws of civil society were eternal like the laws of physics. He believed that the rise of modern economic society was a historically conditioned and, indeed, Christian, liberation of man from traditional religious, ethnic, and social barriers, creating a society composed merely of human beings in their common condition as consumers and producers.[67] The result is that historical differences between human beings tend to be canceled. But he also believed that the state had a responsibility to intervene in economic society and modify the laws of its operation insofar as the promotion of what he himself called "welfare" required it. Thus he recognized human rights other than those which alone would be automatically protected by the unimpeded operation of the laws of supply and demand inherent in the modern economy: in particular, the right to work, and to those essential social services and necessities of life deemed necessary to "welfare."[68] Hegel, while by no means totally denying the rights of laissez-faire competition and free trade, accordingly presents himself as the theoretician of the modern welfare state. His position is that modern economic society, which has itself made an immense contribution to emancipation from feudal and other traditional obstacles to the recognition of universal human rights, is to be controlled and regulated by the state insofar as it itself becomes such an obstacle. But the state is justified in impeding the natural working of free trade only to the extent that such interference is necessary for the protection of welfare. A tariff or other special governmental support to a national industry or population group threatened by international competition may, in the short run, be justified. But in the long run the universal human right to welfare can be promoted and protected only by the progress of world trade and the accompanying increase of wealth. Restrictions on free trade purely for the sake of national independence which fail to serve universal human welfare (for example, certain policies of Gaullist France) find no support from Hegel, who firmly rejected the ideal of a "closed commercial state" advocated by his contemporary Fichte.[69]

Nevertheless Hegel was no utopian. In particular, he relished every chance to ridicule those who opposed the claims of an unrealizable ideal to the existing world. The idea of a world state enforcing international justice he dismissed in his time as a pure "ought" incapable of imminent realization,[70] and with few exceptions he declined to speculate about the future. Yet his grasp of the inherent trends of modern economics led him to one of these exceptions. Although he accepted the existing nation-state system, he also recognized that the long-term evolution of civil society is such as to destroy the economic independence on which national sovereignty rests.

The conclusion to which we are driven is that the world political revolution initiated in America and France under the double influence of the Enlightenment philosophy of human rights and the expansion of modern economic society is not yet over. On more than one occasion Hegel bemoaned the fact that the revolution in France, which he always supported in principle, had yet failed to produce a stable order to replace the one it destroyed.[71] In saying this he was implicitly admitting that the institutional order described in his own *Philosophy of Right*—an order centering on the idea of corporate representation according to one's profession rather than mass-democratic representation as exists in the United States[72]—was not solidly entrenched and was to be taken as a tentative proposal, as Hegel's own contribution to the ongoing search for an institutional order consistent with the revolutionary principles. The task of finding an adequate means of institutionalizing human rights was one which, he said, would have to be passed on to future generations.[73]

Today we are still burdened with this task. The conflict between Communism and bourgeois capitalism is, just like the conflicts internal to each of these two camps, essentially one between the heirs of the French Revolution over the question as to who is the *rightful* heir. The two World Wars may, in world-historical perspective, be seen as stages in a single revolutionary war, for they opposed forces identified with the revolutionary cause of human rights—France, the

United States, Great Britain, and ultimately the Soviet Union and China—to the forces of the romantic, nationalistic, racist and antirational reaction—Germany, Austro-Hungary, Japan. It is noteworthy that after World War II the victors reaffirmed the Declaration of the Rights of Man in the Preamble to the Charter of the United Nations. This may largely be a matter of lip service. Yet history shows that it is dangerous for governments to pay lip service to ideals which they do not intend to take seriously. These simple facts were too easily lost sight of in the passion excited by the Cold War. The so-called "New Conservativism" of the postwar era in the United States imported much of the romantic-restoration antirevolutionary ideology from Europe. The enemy, which a century and a half before had been the revolution in France, became Communism. But Americans should remember that the Soviets, unlike the Nazis but like themselves, can at least be embarrassed by the charge that they are violating human rights. The main point which follows from all this which is important in the present context is that Hegel, if he is the philospher of the French Revolution, is not only the philosopher of the American Revolution. He is, more than that, the philospher of the modern world.

IX   *The American Counterculture of the 1960s*

In order to confirm the continuation of the revolution in our own time and country, we need but look at the so-called American counterculture of the 1960s. There are two basic ways in which the cause of human rights can be advanced. One way is to so institute the power of the state as to protect rights through legal coercion and the threat of punishment. But rights do not exist to be protected until they have first been claimed. The counterculture saw individuals of various backgrounds claim human rights of an unprecedented scope. Hippies claimed the right to unremunerative self-expression and creativity in the face of a depersonalizing technocratic society. Individuals felt unrecognized in their status as human beings by a society bent on reducing them to proverbial cogs in the machine. The black power movement claimed the protection of the Constitution in the face of institutionalized violation of human rights. The women's liberation movement brought home the fact that the cause of human rights required a considerable loosening of the patriarchal family's age-old grip on human society. The American counterculture, it may be said, is over. But this is no truer than the claim that the French

Revolution is over. There has indeed been a lull, a reaffirmation of a more authoritarian philosophy of government, a benign neglect of radical black demands, a resurgence of the work ethic, boredom with the rhetoric of some feminists, a weariness with pornography, a reaction against antitechnological environmentalism. But the permanent gains of the counterculture are nonetheless undeniable. The *status quo ante* cannot be restored, and the revolutionary potential of the countercultural legends and tradition which has been established has not yet been exhausted. Future gains will build on those already attained.

One reason why the dialectic of "revolution and restoration" has been enacted in America well over a century after its enactment in France is that the United States, despite the Declaration of Independence and its assertion of human rights, was so protected from the pressures of modern economic society by its open frontier and isolation from Europe that a modern "state" in the Hegelian sense was not previously felt to be required to protect rights. In the crisis of the world depression of the 1930s or of war, the United States saw the beginnings of a strong state, but the increasing role of central government in the 1960s and 1970s, an era marked by no extreme world economic or military crisis, made a strong central state for the first time a normal, nonexceptional state of affairs. It is thus possible to see in the counterculture and its relative collapse America's discovery of the modern Hegelian welfare state, a type of state which has already long existed in Western Europe. But certainly another reason for the reenactment of the dialectic of revolution and restoration in America so long after the Revolution in France is that the later revolution was never over and cannot be over until the full extent of human rights has been both subjectively discovered and claimed by the people and objectively recognized and protected by the state. No restoration of state power can be final until all popular demands for human rights have been politically satisfied.[74]

X *Christianity and World Revolution*

However, the Revolution with which Hegel is identified is more than simply the revolution of the modern world. For it is also, in Hegel's view, nothing less than the realization of the kingdom of heaven on earth.[75] This is the ultimate basis of Hegel's distinctive union of revolutionism and conservatism. One problem posed by his view of the Revolution as the kingdom of heaven breaking through to earth is, of course, that the Revolution in France was formally or expressly anti-Christian. Hegel's position, then, must be that the Revolution has not comprehended itself. In identifying Christianity as part of the *ancien regime*, in seeing the Christian religion as fixated upon the idea of an eternally transcendent heaven, the Revolution mistakenly saw itself as an emancipation from Christianity. But in fact, Hegel holds, the Revolution is secretly, unknowingly, allied with Christianity.[76] For it is the Christian religion which is the ultimate source of the principle of universal human rights for which the Revolution seeks adequate institutional realization.

This view may sound suspicious. Certainly, it may be thought, there is more to Christianity than the modern secular system of rights. The question can be asked as to whether Christianity was really necessary to the emergence of this system of rights. Could not such a system have evolved from trends in the Graeco-Roman world such as Stoicism? Some would even ask whether human rights are even necessary to Christianity.

The last question is more easily answered. Christ, according to his Church, was sent to save men of all races, nationalities, and social classes. A system of human rights is necessary to Christianity because after Christ every man can rightfully claim to be an object of God's solicitude and love. Everyone has the right, if he will but claim it, to inherit through Christ the kingdom of God. To inherit the kingdom is for men to realize their divine image by partaking of the divine life. But God is a Creator who, resting from the labors of creation, goes on to incarnate Himself participatively and compassionately in the created world. Everyone, claiming his inheritance as a child of God, thus has a right to creative labor, and to re-creative rest through participatory and empathetic self-incarnation in the world. Everyone has a rightful claim to try himself out at creating his world, and to re-create himself by sympathetic participation in the self-creativity of this world (for example, by listening to music or communing with a natural landscape). It is a right to discover both the glory and misery of creation. The glory of creating a world is that of being a lord and despot, but the rights of despotism are granted only over nature and not over other human beings, that is, only insofar as they are compatible with the right of everyone to a similar despotism. In the preceding chapters on world history we have had numerous occasions to talk of despotism: so-called Oriental despotism, theological despotism, and the aristocratic despotism of Graeco-Roman patriarchs. The reference to despotism in connection with Christiani-

ty serves to assign the Christian religion its world-historical
significance: Christianity universalizes the despotism which the
Orient limited to one, and which in the Graeco-Roman world was the
privilege of some. But there is also reason to speak of the misery of
lordship, since it establishes an alienation between the self and the
world, creator and creation, which only the self-realizing Incarnation
of the creator in creation can overcome. In pursuing the apparently
secular aim of guaranteeing the right to *work* and *welfare,* the revolution of the modern world is silently setting about the realization of
the Christian kingdom of God.

Christianity is the religion in which the human claim to divine
status is no longer seen as a challenge to God or the gods. The modern
world is the beginning of the Christian heaven on earth because it is a
world in which the power of creation, which Judaism denied to man
and restricted to God, begins to be claimed as a human right, first in
the Renaissance by an occasional "genius," and finally by all men.
For the revolutionary demand is that all human beings should be
Renaissance men. But the rights to creation and re-creative self-
incarnation in the world, more prosaically the right to work and to
welfare, are the sole rights guaranteed to man through his divine inheritance. The seemingly endless list of human rights—the right of
free trade, of a minimum wage, of public education, health care,
protection against unfair discrimination, and so on—are in fact but
an exploration of the full meaning of the universal right to "work"
and to "welfare."

That all the sublimity of the Hegelian philosophy should even-
tuate in something as prosaic and pedestrian as the modern welfare
state may strike one as anticlimactic. Yet the nontotalitarian welfare
state can be seen as something pedestrian and everyday only if it is
taken for granted. The effect of the Hegelian philosophy of history
should be to show that this form of the state, which even today is not
securely established, is a world-historical achievement and thus not
to be taken for granted. And this is to show the everyday world to be
in itself extraordinary. It is to sanctify something secular. It is also to
show why politics is the religion of the modern world.

But we can say more than that the modern secular state is essential
to the kingdom of God and thus to Christianity. For it is also true that
Christianity was necessary to the emergence of the modern system of
human rights. Graeco-Roman Stoicism could not have fathered it by
itself. The reason is that Christianity, unlike Graeco-Roman civilization but like Hebraism, recognizes the dignity of labor, for God
Himself is a laborer. Stoicism, an essentially aristocratic doctrine,

could not have fathered the system of rights which actually has made its appearance in the world. It is unlikely that Stoicism by itself could have established any right other than a wholly inner right to freedom of thought. But that is a right which, once it was claimed, was inalienable, and which thus required little in the way of protection (at least until the invention of brainwashing and other methods of mind control). Hegel said of Stoicism that it amounted to the freedom of thought, and thus was only the thought of freedom.[77] A Stoic could be free even in chains. Quite the opposite of Stoic escapism, impassiveness, and detachment from the world, the compassion arising from the Christian's self-incarnation in the world leads him on to the revolutionary struggle for rights.

One of the most common criticisms of Hegel over the years has been that he deified the state.[78] It is true that he speaks of the state as the advance or way of God on earth.[79] But everything depends on how such phrases are interpreted. Deification of the state is usually thought to mean that we should bow down to the state and worship it. But to impose this interpretation is to have what for Hegel is an all too Hebraic notion of God. Hegel is not saying that we should serve the state as our master. For he does not primarily conceive God as master or Lord. He is rather saying that the modern state is the incipient realization of the kingdom of the spirit, that is, of the infinite Incarnation of the Lord in the world. In a sense, Hegel is the first truly Christian philosopher of the whole classical tradition of Western thought. The previous great philosophers of the Western tradition betrayed a Hebraic bias by claiming to demonstrate philosophically the existence of only God the Father-Creator, the first "Hebraic" member of the Christian trinity. The Son and Holy Spirit were left to faith. Hegelianism presents itself as a rational demonstration not merely of the Father but, more importantly, of the Son and Spirit. St. Paul in Athens restricted himself to preaching the Hebrew doctrine of the Creator, and the subsequent history of Western philosophy suggests that he was right to think that the Christian doctrine of the Incarnation could only be assimilated after the Creation doctrine had been absorbed. In Hegel Western philosophy became earnest about the Incarnation. But it was an earnestness meant only to give the world the measure of its own implicit earnestness. It is because the Spirit already exists in the world that its philosophical proclamation becomes possible.

CHAPTER 10

Hegel in the History of Philosophy

THIS volume has sought to reach those not specializing in philosophy by avoiding lengthy discussion of Hegel's relation to other philosophers. A few basic reflections addressed to students of philosophy and its history are relegated to this final chapter.

It has frequently been noted with some amazement that Kant, whose philosophy sought to show the impossibility of metaphysical knowledge of supersensible realities—of God, the soul, and things subsisting *in themselves,* as opposed to how they exist *for us* in our experience—called forth in the person of Hegel perhaps the most unabashed explosion of speculative metaphysics in the entire tradition of Western thought.

It is true that Hegel, while taking Kant's "transcendental ego" as the original model for his absolute spirit, rejected the skeptical Kantian view that there are known limits to human knowledge: to know a limit as a limit, Hegel maintains, is to pass over it and know what does the limiting as well as what is limited.[1] Thus ultimate reality for Hegel is knowable and, indeed, known to be spirit.

We should not be too quick, however, to assume that Hegel affirmed knowledge of things-in-themselves existing apart from human experience. To suppose the existence of such things-in-themselves is to admit metaphysical pluralism: reality is construed as an aggregate of essentially independent substantial entities. Yet little seems more characteristic of Hegelianism as usually interpreted than the monistic claim that reality is a single undivided substance, an all-encompassing organic whole of essentially related aspects. To know the aspect is to know all reality, the whole itself, for the aspect is what it is through its relations with the whole.

The common pluralistic view that reality is an aggregate of essentially independent things and successive events Hegel takes, with Spinoza, to be a product of abstract thinking: different aspects of the whole are abstracted and falsely isolated from one another in thought.[2]

One would expect that anyone taking this view of Hegel's would deny to nature any existence in itself essentially independent of our experience of it. But in fact—and this is what I am tempted to call Hegel's most fundamental philosophical incoherence—he does *not* deny this. Like Schelling, and in opposition to Fichte, he insists that nature, far from being a mere object of our knowledge existing only for our consciousness, exists in and for itself with a life of its own. It is self-productive, not merely a product posited by our conscious activity. It is in itself spirit and not merely matter, "subject" and no mere "object."

Yet how can there be no things-in-themselves if nature exists in itself with a life of its own? One way in which, it might be suggested, the independent in-itself-ness of nature is possible without the assertion of things-in-themselves is if the independent life of nature can be interpreted as a mere postulate of practical reason without any theoretical validity. A German scholar, Wolfgang Wieland, argues persuasively that this is how Schelling and, by implication, Hegel interpreted it.[3] Although the dualistic Kantian opposition of the theoretical and the practical would be uncharacteristic of Schelling and Hegel, the suggestion is worth considering.

Let it for once be granted that the one unconditional imperative to which every spiritual being is subject is that of self-realization, and more particularly that man knows he ought to realize himself. But as long as nature is merely object, merely the *other* of spirit, merely dead matter, alienation is inevitable and complete self-realization impossible. The human spirit can realize itself completely only by identifying with nature, and this it can do only if nature itself is of a basically spiritual character.

However, it can be shown, I think, that postulates of practical reason are *also* truths of theoretical reason, and thus that the commonly made point that some claim is a postulate of practical reason and thus *not* a truth of theoretical reason is groundless. "Ought" implies "can"; what ought be done must be possible to do. It logically follows that whatever is a necessary condition of the possibility of what *ought* to be done is just as much actually the case as conditions of the possibility of what *is*. If the spiritual inwardness of nature conditions the possibility of self-realization, it is a condition which accordingly must obtain as a theoretical truth. This may be termed the "moral argument for panpsychism."

It is also a moral argument for things-in-themselves, for nature, on the panpsychist reading, is shot through with spiritual things-in-themselves existing for themselves regardless of whether we experience them or not (for example, with Whiteheadian actual occasions interpreted as centers of *feeling*). If self-realization is to be possible, the inwardness of nature must not be denied by being affirmed to be a *mere* postulate.

However, the moral argument for panpsychism and things-in-themselves suffers from the same weakness as all similarly constructed moral arguments. It falsely supposes that what ought to be is more surely known than what can be, and that we are thus in a position to discover what can be on the basis of assured knowledge of what ought to be. If "ought" implies "can," it is equally true that "cannot" implies "ought not." And what can, or cannot, be is in fact more surely known than what ought, or ought not, to be. Rather than inferring "can" from "ought" we are well advised to investigate the bounds of possibility before seriously attempting to determine the reaches of obligation.

I conclude that the spiritual inwardness of nature can be *neither* a postulate of practical reason to the exclusion of being a truth of theoretical reason *nor* a truth of theoretical reason established by its function as a postulate of practical reason. Panpsychism and things-in-themselves, which are required if the Hegelian oneness of man and nature is possible, must thus be theoretically established, and must be established on grounds other than the moral argument. It is in vain that dictates are handed down to nature from the moral point of view. In conformity with Hegel's largely Aristotelian critique of Kantian morality, what ought to be must rather be seen as growing out of the essential potentialities of what is.

To make the objective inwardness of nature a mere postulate nullifies the "objective idealism" which Schelling claimed to oppose to Fichte's "subjective idealism." There is a contradiction in wishing to hold *both* that nature does not merely exist for consciousness *and* that its in-itselfness is a mere postulate of consciousness. The independence of nature from the Fichtean ego would seem to come down to a postulated independence of postulation! Schelling's Spinozistic insistence on the all-encompassing nature of a single undivided substance mystically open to direct intuition by human consciousness also leads back to subjective idealism: despite, or rather precisely because of, its pantheistic submersion of consciousness in the All, such insistence precludes recognition of the self-creative autonomy of a natural world knowable only by inference and not by direct acquaintance.

A coherent Hegelianism requires a consistent and complete move from subjective (phenomenalistic) to objective (realistic) idealism. It requires a clear option for Leibniz over Spinoza, pluralism over monism. An authentic objective idealism must construe the cosmos as a community of independent, self-productive spiritual things-in-themselves. Hegel began his philosophical career in Jena under the auspices of Schelling's Spinozism. His declaration of philosophical independence from Schelling, dating from publication of the *Phenomenology,* amounted to a repudiation of the Spinozistic definition of the Absolute as merely substance. Substance without the flux of accidents, he came to see, is nothing at all; it is the famous Schellingian night in which all cows are black. Yet Hegel's break with Schellingian Spinozism, though clearly embarked upon, was not so clearly consummated. It is the cosmology of Whitehead and Hartshorne, in which the flux of accidents becomes a dance of real events and *no mere Spinozistic play of abstractions,* which is the most vigorous contemporary strain of objective idealism, and which offers the most promising basis for the reconstruction of Hegelianism consistent with the natural science of the current century.

Recapitulation

The Hegelian philosophy examined in the previous chapters may be recapitulated something like this. In the *patriarchal revolution* man *abstracted* and *absolutized* himself as *subject* over nature as *object*. Taking his own power of abstract thought to be absolute, he negated nature as unessential to him. But because the thinking subject is in fact essentially related to the natural world from which it abstracts itself and to which it opposes itself, nature refuses to suffer negation passively and reacts against the subject who would thus negate it. The thinking subject's *negation* of nature, its objective *other*, thus calls forth its own *self-negation*, that is, the negation of itself by the negated other.

The patriarchal pastoral-agricultural revolution began with the domestic despotism of the patriarchal family, but in the historical era evolved into the *political despotism* of the Far Orient. In the *theological despotism* of Judaism the *Absolute* itself came to be defined as a patriarchal despot. Thus in Judaism the patriarchal revolution achieved religious and metaphysical self-consciousness. But Judaic man was capable of defining the Absolute as a despot only by projecting the divine despot beyond man and making him supernatural. In Graeco-Roman humanism, however, patriarchal rights ceased to be the exclusive possession of a single individual political despot or God and began to be generalized to broader groups of individuals (citizens).

In the pre-Christian Judeo-Roman consciousness there arose an awareness of the self-contradictoriness of taking the transcendent patriarchal God (thinking subject) to be absolute. In the Christian Incarnation, the thinking subject—whose religious absolutization in Judaism brought on its self-negation—was negated as a transcendent Absolute, and the Absolute came to be redefined in essential relation to the natural world (*negation of the negation*). It is this oneness of the divine subject with the objective world which Christian civilization strove to realize aesthetically in the medieval world, and both institutionally and philosophically in the modern world.

Following the natural, unselfconscious despotism of China we found in India how the natural despot discovers the misery of despotism and incarnates himself in all nature. Following the supernatural, reflective despotism of Judaism we found in Christianity how the supernatural Despot incarnates Himself in nature. Judeo-Christian history repeats on a higher, reflective level what the Orient accomplishes on the natural level. The Indian mystic renounces lordship to attain oneness with the natural world of which he is a part. The Judeo-Christian God renounces lordship to attain oneness with a natural world to which He stood opposed. The alienation of the Judeo-Christian God (and of Western man stepping outside nature, which becomes an object dominated by a non-natural subject) exceeds that of Oriental man. So much the greater is the consequent self-realization. In the Orient a part of nature alienated from the whole incarnates itself in the whole. In Christianity a negation of nature standing outside nature incarnates itself in nature. The Indian self-incarnation of the part of nature in the whole is pantheistic and naturalistic. The Christian Incarnation is humanistic and ethical. The incarnation of Indian religion in the cosmos means identification with a self-contradictory infinite substance independent of determinate finite accidents. The Christian Incarnation means identification with an infinite spirit essentially manifested in determinate ethical institutions and cultural forms. In the Orient we have a religious transcendence of political despotism. In the West a political transcendence of theological despotism.

Notes and References

Preface

1. Karl Barth, *Protestant Theology in the Nineteenth Century* (Valley Forge, 1973), pp. 384, 390.
2. Bertrand Russell, *Our Knowledge of the External World* (Chicago, 1914), chap. 1.

Chapter One

1. Joachim Ritter, *Hegel und die Französische Revolution*, (Cologne, 1957).
2. *Phenomenology of Mind*, trans. J. Baillie (London, 1931), p. 598.
3. A good and detailed English account of Hegel's early intellectual development can be found in H. S. Harris, *Hegel's Development: Toward the Sunlight, 1770 - 1801* (London, 1972).
4. "Über einige charakteristische Unterschiede der alten Dichter (von den neueren)," in *Dokumente zu Hegels Entwicklung*, ed. by Johannes Hoffmeister (Stuttgart, 1936), pp. 48 - 51.
5. Friedrich Schiller, "Über naive und sentimentalische Dichtung," in *Sämtliche Werke*, ed. Jost Perfahl (Stuttgart: 1968), Vol. 5, pp. 433 - 517.
6. "Fragmente über Volksreligion und Christentum," in *Theologische Jugendschriften*, ed. by Hermann Nohl (Tübingen, 1907), pp. 3 - 29.
7. *Hegel in Berichten seiner Zeitgenossen* (Hamburg, 1970), pp. 13 - 14.
8. *Theologische Jugendschriften*, pp. 73 - 136.
9. *Early Theological Writings*, trans. T. M. Knox (Chicago, 1948), pp. 205 - 301; *Theologische Jugendschriften*, pp. 261 - 342.
10. Raymond Plant, *Hegel* (London, 1973), pp. 56 - 71.
11. *Early Theological Writings*, pp. 182 - 89; *Theologische Jugendschriften*, pp. 243 - 48.
12. *Philosophy of Right*, trans. T. M. Knox (London, 1952), p. 12; *Sämtliche Werke*, ed. by Hermann Glockner (Stuttgart, 1927) VII, 35.
13. *Briefe von und an Hegel* (Hamburg, 1952), I, 59.
14. *Werke*, I, 44 - 49.
15. I have given a more detailed account of the dialectic in: "On the Reducibility of Dialectical to Standard Logic," *The Personalist* 56 (1975), 414 - 30.
16. *Werke*, I, 122 - 44.

17. The sole exposition by Hegel of his entire system is contained in his *Encyclopaedia of Philosophical Sciences* (1st ed., 1817; 2d ed., 1827). The *Encyclopaedia* is available in English in three volumes: *Logic of Hegel*, trans. W. Wallace (London, 1975); *Philosophy of Nature*, trans. A. V. Miller (London, 1970); *Philosophy of Mind*, trans. A. V. Miller (London, 1971).

18. *Briefe von und an Hegel*, II, 51.

19. *Ibid.*, III, 323

20. A good book on the Hegelian background of post-Hegelian philosophy is Richard Bernstein, *Praxis and Action* (Philadelphia, 1971).

Chapter Two

1. *Briefe von und an Hegel*, I, 161.

2. Hegel did claim for his sytem a completeness which has been claimed for no previous sytem of philosophy. But he did not go so far as to identify Reality with this system. He did not—as many critics have suggested—take the Absolute to be contained in his head. The system remains, like all thought products, abstract and thus in some sense incomplete. To be sure, the system seeks concreteness, but by this very fact it remains abstract, opening onto the true Absolute, onto the total natural, institutional, and cultural universe. For Hegel's admission of the abstract character of his own philosophy, see *ibid.*, II, 100 - 101. What, then, is the kind of completeness claimed for the system? It is a completeness of standpoints. We shall see that Christianity is for Hegel the "absolute" religion. The Hegelian philosophy, as the Christian religion rationally comprehended, thus presents itself as the absolute and unsurpassable standpoint. What remains is only to achieve satisfactory institutional realization of that standpoint in the world. The standpoint of the absolute philosophy remains but a *cultural* standpoint until it is adequately realized on the institutional level. Yet Hegel's philosophy undeniably takes itself as the self-comprehension of what to some extent already exists in the modern world, in modern economic society and the modern state, although Hegel was forced to conclude that these modern institutions were still unstable. See his *Philosophy of History* (New York, 1956), pp. 451 - 52; *Werke*, XI, 562-63. The Hegelian philosophy is thus a self-comprehension of what already exists only in the form of unstable and inadequate institutions. It accordingly presents itself as a call for continuation of a political revolution already begun but not yet completed. But there will be no further religious revolutions. See Chapter 9 of this study.

3. "Spirit knowing itself is in religion primarily and immediately its own self-consciousness" (*Phenomenology of Mind*, p. 687; *Werke*, II, 519).

4. *Philosophy of Religion* (London, 1895), I, 18 - 23; *Werke*, XV, 36 - 41. *Logic of Hegel*, p. 3; *Werke*, VIII, 41.

5. *Philosophy of History*, pp. 50 - 53; *Werke*, XI, 84 - 88.

6. *Philosophy of Religion*, I, 4 - 5. *Werke*, XV, 22 - 23.

7. *Werke*, III, 304 - 5.
8. *Science of Logic*, trans. A. V. Miller (London, 1969), pp. 77 - 78; *Werke*, IV; 83.

Chapter Three

1. *Philosophy of Religion*, I, 2; *Werke*, XV, 20.
2. This is the attitude characteristic of the workaday world. See *ibid.*, I, 7; *Werke*, XV, 24.
3. Sigmund Freud, *Civilization and Its Discontents* (New York, 1962), chap. 1.
4. *Phenomenology of Mind*, p. 133; *Werke*, II, 69.
5. *Philosophy of Mind* (London, 1971), pp. 304 - 13; *Werke*, X, 460 - 74.
6. *Science of Logic*, p. 28; *Werke*, IV, 17.
7. *Philosophy of Religion*, I, 290 - 316; *Werke*, XV, 299 - 324.
8. *Ibid.*, pp. 286 - 90; *Werke*, XV, 295 - 99.
9. *Ibid.*, pp. 273 - 75; *Werke*, XV, 282 - 84.
10. *Ibid.*, pp. 278 - 79; *Werke*, XV, 287 - 88.
11. *Ibid.*, p. 276; *Werke*, XV, 285.
12. *Ibid.*, p. 133; *Werke*, XV, 145.
13. *Ibid.*, p. 299; *Werke*, XV, 307.
14. *Ibid.*, 290 - 98; *Werke*, XV, 299 - 306.
15. *Ibid.*, p. 264; *Werke*, XV, 273 - 74.
16. *Ibid.*, p. 300; *Werke*, XV, 308.
17. This absence of "free adoration" is illustrated by the irreverent use and discard of fetishes. See *ibid.*, p. 309; *Werke*, XV, 316.
18. *Ibid.*, III, 55; *Werke*, XVI, 267.
19. *Ibid.*, I, 291; *Werke*, XV, 299 - 300.
20. *Ibid.*, pp. 291 - 92; *Werke*, XV, 300.
21. *Ibid.*, p. 301; *Werke*, XV, 309.
22. *Ibid.*, pp. 302 - 3; *Werke*, XV, 310 - 11.
23. *Ibid.*, pp. 310, 336; *Werke*, XV, 317, 342 - 43.
24. *Ibid.*, pp. 309 - 16; *Werke*, XV, 316 - 24.
25. Friedrich Engels, *Ludwig Feuerbach and the Outcome of Classical German Philosophy* (New York: 1941), chap. 4.
26. *Philosophy of History*, p. 116; *Werke*, XI, 164.
27. *Ibid.*, p. 112; *Werke*, XI, 159.
28. *Ibid.*, p. 116; *Werke*, XI, 164.
29. *Ibid.*, pp. 257 - 58; *Werke*, XI, 336.
30. *Ibid.*, p. 103; *Werke*, XI, 149 - 50.
31. World history for Hegel can, in fact, not return to China because it reaches an "absolute end" in European civilization. This civilization produced a system of universal human rights which, in spreading around the globe, terminates world history understood as a succession of dominant national spirits. See Chapter 9.

32. *Ibid.*, pp. 18 - 19; *Werke*, XI, 45 - 46.
33. *Ibid.*, p. 123; *Werke*, XI, 172.
34. *Ibid.*, pp. 130 - 31; *Werke*, XI, 181 - 82. The principal exception is the right of family inheritance.
35. *Philosophy of Religion*, I, 336 - 37; *Werke*, XV, 342 - 43.
36. *Philosophy of History*, p. 132; *Werke*, XI, 183 - 84.
37. *Ibid.*, p. 121; *Werke*, XI, 170.
38. *Philosophy of Religion*, I, 336, 338 - 39; *Werke*, XV, 342, 344 - 45.
39. *Ibid.*, pp. 346 - 47; *Werke*, XV, 352.
40. *Philosophy of History*, p. 136; *Werke*, XI, 188.
41. *Ibid.*, p. 122; *Werke*, XI, 171.
42. *Ibid.*, p. 128; *Werke*, XI, 179.
43. *Ibid.*, p. 129; *Werke*, XI, 180.
44. *Ibid.*, p. 131; *Werke*, XI, 182.
45. *Ibid.*, p. 137; *Werke*, XI, 189.
46. *Philosophy of Mind* pp. 215 - 18; *Werke*, X, 347 - 52.
47. *Philosophy of History*, p. 126; *Werke*, XI, 176.
48. See p. 180.
49. *Philosophy of History*, pp. 142 - 43; *Werke*, XI, 196 - 97.
50. Edgar Snow, *Red Star Over China* (New York, 1968), pp. 130 - 33.

Chapter Four

1. *Philosophy of History*, pp. 112 - 13; *Werke*, XI, 159 - 61.
2. *Ibid.*, pp. 113, 161; *Werke*, XI, 160 - 61, 219.
3. *Ibid.*, p. 165; *Werke*, XI, 224.
4. *Ibid.*, p. 152; *Werke*, XI, 208 - 9.
5. But it is precisely because the Indians achieve a mystical liberation from the finite that they, of all Oriental peoples, are outwardly the most content with despotism. See *ibid.*, p. 161; *Werke*, XI, 219 - 20.
6. *Ibid.*, p. 167; *Werke*, XI, 226.
7. *Philosophy of Religion*, II, 48; *Werke*, XV, 400.
8. Reinhard Leuze, *Die ausserchristlichen Religionen bei Hegel* (Göttingen, 1975), pp. 61 - 62.
9. *Philosophy of Religion*, II, 1; *Werke*, XV, 355.
10. *Philosophy of History*, p. 139; *Werke*, XI, 191 - 92.
11. *Ibid.*, pp. 161 - 63; *Werke*, XI, 220 - 21.
12. Leuze, pp. 69 - 70.
13. *Philosophy of History*, p. 140; *Werke*, XI, 192 - 93.
14. *Phenomenology of Mind*, pp. 234 - 40; *Werke*, II, 153 - 58.
15. *Philosophy of History*, p. 150; *Werke*, XI, 205 - 6.
16. *Ibid.*, p. 139; *Werke*, XI, 191 - 92.
17. *Ibid.*, p. 139; *Werke*, XI, 192.
18. *Logic of Hegel*, pp. 274 - 75; *Werke*, VIII, 339.
19. *Briefe von und an Hegel*, I, 38 - 40; my translation.
20. *Phenomenology of Mind*, pp. 80, 85 - 86; *Werke*, II 22, 27 - 28.

21. Aristotle, *"Categories"* and *"De Interpretatione"*, trans. J. K. Ackrill, (London, 1963), pp. 4, 5 (2a11 and 1a20).

22. *Ibid.*, p. 11 (4a10).

23. Spinoza, *Ethics*, ed. J. Gutmann (New York, 1949), pp. 41 - 52.

24. *Logic of Hegel*, p. 239; *Werke*, VIII, 298.

25. *Ibid.*, pp. 276 - 77; *Werke*, VIII 341 - 42.

26. *Philosophy of Religion*, II, 1-11; *Werke*, XV, 355 - 64.

27. *Philosophy of History*, p. 157; *Werke*, XI, 214 - 15.

28. *Ibid.*, pp. 141, 155; *Werke*, XI, 193 - 94, 211 - 12.

29. *Ibid.*, p. 158; *Werke*, XI, 216.

30. *Ibid.*, p. 155; *Werke*, XI, 212. The German text distinguishes between "Brahm" and "Brahma."

31. Leuze, pp. 82 - 87.

32. *Philosophy of Religion*, II, 24; *Werke*, XV, 376 - 77.

33. *Ibid.*, p. 24; *Werke*, XV, 376.

34. *Ibid.*, p. 9; *Werke*, XV, 362.

35. *Ibid.*, pp. 2 - 5; *Werke*, XV, 356 - 58.

36. Helmuth von Glasenapp, *Das Indienbild deutscher Denker* (Stuttgart, 1960), p. 54.

37. *Philosophy of Religion*, II, 51; *Werke*, XV, 403. The reference to Schleiermacher remains, it is true, implicit.

38. *Ibid.*, p. 48; *Werke*, XV, 400.

39. *Ibid.*, p. 48; *Werke*, XV, 400.

40. A simple example of such paradoxes is the one about the impossibility of motion between any two points: such motion would require the moving object to exist in an infinite number of intermediary positions, which is impossible in any finite amount of time. On Whiteheadian grounds the reply is that motion is an illusion which does not require occupation of an infinite number of positions.

41. *Phenomenology of Mind*, pp. 80 - 86; *Werke*, II, 14 - 20.

42. I have elaborated on connections between Hegel's dialectic and psychoanalysis in "Hegel and Freud: A Comparison," *Philosophy and Phenomenological Research* 36, no. 4 (June, 1976), 506 - 22.

43. Charles Taylor, *Hegel* (London, 1975), chap. 20.

44. Charles Hartshorne, "Panpsychism," in *A History of Philosophical Systems* ed. V. Ferm (New York, 1950), pp. 442 - 453.

45. *Briefe von und an Hegel*, II, 85 - 86.

46. William James, *A Pluralistic Universe* (New York, 1909)

47. John M. E. McTaggart, *Studies in Hegelian Cosmology* (London, 1918).

48. *Philosophy of Nature* (London, 1970), pp. 273 - 78ff; *Werke*, IX, 449 - 56. Note that if higher life exists on other planets, the universe may have more than one spiritual center, that is, there may be more than one "earth."

49. Alfred North Whitehead, *Process and Reality* (New York, 1960), p. 11.

50. *Ibid.*, pp. 10 - 11.
51. *Science of Logic*, p. 557; *Werke*, IV, 698.
52. *Logic of Hegel*, pp. 267 - 74; *Werke*, VIII, 330 - 38.
53. *Ibid.*, p. 274; *Werke*, VIII, 338. See also *Science of Logic*, pp. 555 - 56; *Werke*, IV, 698 - 700. The question can still be raised, however, as to whether Hegel meant quite the same thing as Whitehead in insisting on the substantiality of the accidents. See Chapter 10.
54. *Logic of Hegel*, pp. 267 - 74; *Werke*, VIII, 330 - 38.
55. von Glasenapp, pp. 39 - 60.
56. *Logic of Hegel*, p. 275; *Werke*, VIII, 339

Chapter Five

1. *Philosophy of History*, p. 173; *Werke*, Vol. XI, 233.
2. *Ibid.*, p. 187; *Werke*, XI, 251.
3. *Ibid.*, p. 187; *Werke*, XI, 250.
4. *Ibid.*, p. 173; *Werke*, XI, 233.
5. *Ibid.*, p. 176; *Werke*, XI, 237.
6. *Ibid.*, p. 173; *Werke*, XI, 233 - 34.
7. *Ibid.*, pp. 174 - 75; *Werke*, XI, 234 - 35.
8. *Ibid.*, p. 175; *Werke*, XI, 235. See also, *Philosophy of Religion*, II, 74ff; *Werke*, XV, 425 - 26.
9. *Philosophy of History*, p. 175; *Werke*, XI, 235 - 36.
10. *Ibid.*, p. 178; *Werke*, XI, 240.
11. *Ibid.*, pp. 113 - 14; *Werke*, XI, 160 - 61.
12. *Ibid.*, p. 195; *Werke*, XI, 260. *Philosophy of Religion*, Vol. 2, pp. 122 - 30, 166 - 70; *Werke*, XVI, 3 - 10, 42 - 46.
13. *Philosophy of Religion*, p. 74; *Werke*, XV, 425.
14. *Ibid.*, p. 73; *Werke*, XV, 425.
15. *Ibid.*, pp. 86 - 88; *Werke*, XV, 437 - 39.
16. *Ibid.*, pp. 82 - 85, 101; *Werke*, XV, 434 - 37, 451 - 52. *Philosophy of History*, pp. 193 - 94; *Werke*, XI, 257 - 60.
17. *Philosophy of Religion*, II, 108; *Werke*, XV, 458.
18. *Aesthetics*, trans. T. M. Knox (London: Oxford University Press, 1975), I, 347 - 61; *Werke*, XII, 463 - 85.
19. *Philosophy of History*, p. 137; *Werke*, XI, 190.
20. *Aesthetics*, I, 332 - 47; *Werke*, XII, 445 - 63.
21. *Ibid.*, pp. 323 - 61; *Werke*, XII, 433 - 81.
22. *Ibid.*, pp. 378 - 421, *Werke*, XII, 502 - 56.
23. *Philosophy of Religion*, II, 93; *Werke*, XV, 444. *Aesthetics*, I, 360 - 61; *Werke*, XII, 479 - 81.
24. *Aesthetics* pp. 360 - 61; *Werke*, XII, 480 - 81.
25. One of the most widespread objections to Hegelianism is precisely that Hegel identified the Absolute with his own philosophical system. The objection is made by Marxists who have claimed that Hegel stands on his

head, by existentialists who have accused Hegel of an "essentialism," which dissolves individual existence into concepts, and by Bertrand Russell who revolted against what he took to be the Hegelian reduction of reality to something "thin and logical." A principal source for this criticism appears to be the Berlin lectures of Schelling, begun in 1841. But the objection rests on a misconception. In view of the historical success of Schelling's criticism, the point bears repeating. The Absolute, for Hegel, is not the system. The system, it is true, seeks the Absolute. It seeks ever greater concreteness. But for this very reason it remains abstract; that is, it opens onto the Absolute which is the total natural, institutional, and cultural universe. For an admission by Hegel of the abstract character of even concrete philosophical thought, see *Briefe von und an Hegel*, II, 100 - 1.

26. Leuze, pp. 124 - 25.

27. *Ibid.*, pp. 117 - 20.

28. Jean-Louis Vieillard-Baron, "La 'religion de la nature,' étude de quelques pages de la 'Phénoménologie de l'Esprit' de Hegel," *Revue de métaphysique et de morale* 61 (1971), 323 - 43.

29. *Philosophy of Religion*, II, 102; *Werke*, XV, 454.

30. *Ibid.*, I, 337; *Werke*, XV, 343.

31. *Ibid.*, II, 102; *Werke*, XV, 454.

32. *Ibid.*, p. 85; *Werke*, XV, 437.

33. *Ibid.*, pp. 120 - 21; *Werke*, XV, 470 - 71.

34. *Theologische Jugendschriften*, pp. 214 - 31.

35. Jean-Paul Sartre, *Being and Nothingness* (New York, 1956), pp. 557 - 75.

36. *Early Theological Writings*, pp. 182 - 88; *Theologische Jugendschriften*, pp. 243 - 48.

37. *Ibid.*, p. 185; *Theologische Jugendschriften*, p. 245.

38. *Ibid.*, p. 184; *Theologische Jugendschriften*, pp. 244 - 45.

39. Thomas Hobbes, *Leviathan*, ed. by Michael Oakeshott (New York, 1962), chap. 17.

40. *Philosophy of History*, pp. 197 - 98; see also pp. 113 - 14 on "Persian" monarchy understood in a sense inclusive of the Hebrews; *Werke*, XI, 263 - 64, 160 - 61.

41. *Philosophy of Religion*, II, 180 - 89; *Werke*, XVI, 54 - 62.

42. John Locke, *Of Civil Government* (Chicago, 1955), chap. 5.

43. *Philosophy of History*, pp. 195 - 96; *Werke*, XI, 111 - 13.

44. *Philosophy of Religion*, II, 186 - 87; *Werke*, XVI, 60 - 61.

45. *Ibid.*, pp. 122 - 69; *Werke*, XVI, 3 - 46.

46. That is, "individual" as opposed to "universal" spirit; it is also called "finite mind." See *Philosophy of Mind*, pp. 18 - 24; *Werke*, X, 35 - 46.

47. *Early Theological Writings*, p. 196; *Theologische Jugendschriften*, p. 254.

48. Immanuel Kant, *Critique of Judgment*, trans. J. C. Meredith (London, 1952), bk. 2, paragraphs 23 - 29.

49. *Aesthetics*, I, 371 - 77; *Werke*, XII, 494 - 501.

50. Johann Wolfgang von Goethe, *West-östlicher Divan*, ed. H-J Weitz (Wiesbaden, 1971).

51. *Philosophy of Religion*, II, 206; *Werke*, XVI, 78 - 79.

52. Judaism originally began on a prepolitical pastoral basis. Hegel says that Judaism is in principle incompatible with the state. See *Philosophy of History*, p. 197; *Werke*, XI, 262 - 63. Trust in God may be an alternative to the faith in the public works revolution which is the basis of the Oriental despotic state.

53. *Logic of Hegel*, p. 210; *Werke*, VIII, 265.

54. *Philosophy of Mind*, p. 60; *Werke*, VIII, 102.

55. *Early Theological Writings*, p. 140; *Theologische Jugendschriften*, p. 209.

56. *Ibid.*, pp. 317 - 19; *Theologische Jugendschriften*, pp. 350 - 51.

57. Immanuel Kant, *Critique of Practical Reason*, trans. L. W. Beck (New York, 1956), bk. 1, chap. 1.

58. *Theologische Jugendschriften*, pp. 385, 388.

59. "Differenz des Fichteschen und Schellingschen Systems der Philosophie," in *Werke*, I, 122 - 44.

60. *Briefe von und an Hegel*, pp. 38 - 40.

61. Raymond Plant argues persuasively that Hegel's conclusion about the impossibility of resurrecting the classical Greek spirit was due to the influence of the British economist Sir James Steuart. See Raymond Plant, *Hegel*, pp. 64 - 75.

62. *Philosophy of Religion*, II, 322 - 23; *Werke*, XVI, 187 - 88.

63. *Ibid.*, III, 1; *Werke*, XVI, 218.

64. *Ibid.*, II, 184; *Werke*, XVI, 58.

Chapter Six

1. *Early Theological Writings*, pp. 182 - 85; *Theologische Jugendschriften*, pp. 243 - 45.

2. Hobbes, *Leviathan;* chap. 13 and Locke, *Of Civil Government*, chap. 2.

3. *Early Theological Writings*, p. 184; *Theologische Jugendschriften*, pp. 244 - 45.

4. *Philosophy of History*, pp. 18 - 19; *Werke*, XI, 46.

5. *Ibid.*, pp. 250 - 56. *Werke*, XI; 327 - 34.

6. *Aesthetics*, I, 436 - 38; 509 - 11; *Werke*, XIII, 15 - 17, 109 - 13.

7. *Philosophy of History*, p. 253; *Werke*, XI, 330 - 31. *Philosophy of Right*, pp. 103 - 4; *Werke*, VII, 223 - 24.

8. *Philosophy of History*, p. 251; *Werke*, XI, 328. Charles-Louis de Secondat Baron de Montesquieu, *Spirit of the Laws*, trans. T. Nugent, (New York, 1949), chaps. 3, 4.

9. Jean-Jacques Rousseau, *Emile*, ed. by François Richard, (Paris, 1964 pp. 354 - 55.

10. Immanuel Kant, *The Moral Law, or Kant's Groundwork of the Metaphysics of Morals*, trans. H. J. Paton (London, 1948).

11. *Philosophy of History*, p. 261; *Werke*, XI, 340.

12. *Ibid.*, pp. 254 - 55; *Werke*, XI, 332 - 33.

13. *Philosophy of Right*, p. 221; *Werke*, VII, 453 - 54.

14. Dominique Janicaud, *Hegel et le destin de la Grèce* (Paris, 1975), p. 188.

15. Maurice Merleau-Ponty, *Humanisme et Terreur* (Paris, 1947), p. 190; my translation. See, however, chap. 12, pp. 185 - 89.

16. *Philosophy of History*, pp. 267 - 71; *Werke*, XI, 348 - 52.

17. "To draw philosophy out of the solitude into which it has wandered—to do such work as this we may hope we are called by the higher spirit of our time" (*History of Philosophy* [London, 1892], I, xii - xiii; *Werke*, XVII, 21.)

18. *Aesthetics*, I, 436; *Werke*, XIII, 15.

19. *Philosophy of Religion*, II, 224; *Werke*, XVI, 95 - 96.

20. *Aesthetics*, I, 272; *Werke*, XII, 366.

21. *Ibid.*, pp. 502 - 3; *Werke*, XIII, 100 - 2.

22. *Ibid.*, pp. 436 - 38; *Werke*, XIII, 15 - 17.

23. *Philosophy of History*, p. 250; *Werke*, XI, 326 - 27.

24. Ludwig Feuerbach, *The Essence of Christianity*, trans. M. Evans (New York, 1957).

25. *Early Theological Writings*, pp. 184 - 85; *Theologische Jugendschriften*, p. 245.

26. *Aesthetics*, I, 453 - 56; *Werke*, XIII, 37 - 41.

27. *Ibid.*, II, 708; *Werke*, XIII, 362.

28. *Ibid.*, I, 436; *Werke*, XIII, 13.

29. *Ibid.*, pp. 431 - 36; *Werke*, XIII, 8 - 15.

30. *Ibid.*, pp. 41 - 55; *Werke*, XII, 71 - 89.

31. *Ibid.*, pp. 502 - 11; *Werke*, XIII, 100 - 13.

32. *Ibid.*, II, 713; *Werke*, XIII, 369 - 70.

33. *Ibid.*, pp. 643 - 44; *Werke*, XIII, 282 - 83.

34. *Ibid.*, pp. 631 - 32; *Werke*, XIII, 267 - 68.

35. *Ibid.*, pp. 635 - 59; *Werke*, XIII, 272 - 302.

36. *Ibid.*, p. 642; *Werke*, XIII, 281.

37. *Ibid.*, p. 637; *Werke*, XIII, 275.

38. *Ibid.*, pp. 638 - 39; *Werke*, XIII, 276 - 78.

39. *Ibid.*, pp. 726 - 27; *Werke*, XIII, 385 - 86.

40. *Ibid.*, pp. 665 - 76; *Werke*, XIII, 309 - 22.

41. *Ibid.*, I, 477 - 486; *Werke*, XIII, 67 - 79.

42. *Ibid.*, II, 725; *Werke*, XIII, 383.

43. *Philosophy of History*, p. 237; *Werke*, XI, 312 - 13.

44. *Philosophy of Religion*, Vol. 2, p. 254; *Werke*, XVI, 123 - 24.

45. *Aesthetics*, Vol. 2, pp. 779 - 84; *Werke*, XIII, 451 - 57.

46. *Ibid.*, p. 1162; *Werke*, XIV, 484 - 85.

47. *Ibid.*, pp. 1162 - 63; *Werke*, XIV, 484 - 86.

48. *Ibid.*, pp. 475 - 76; *Werke*, XIII, 381 - 82.

49. Johann Joachim Winkelmann, *Gedanken uber die Nachahmung der griechischen Werke in der Malerei und Bildauerkunst* (Stuttgart, 1969), p. 4.

50. *Phenomenology of Mind*, p. 713; *Werke*, II, 538.

51. *Ibid.*, p. 715; *Werke*, II, 540 - 41.

52. *Ibid.*, p. 717; *Werke*, II, 541.

53. *Philosophy of Religion*, II, 267 - 69; *Werke*, XVI, 136 - 38.

54. *Phenomenology*, p. 725; *Werke*, II, 548.

55. *Philosophy of Religion*, II, 280 - 83; *Werke*, XVI, 148 - 51. *Philosophy of History*, p. 247; *Werke*, XI, 223 - 24.

56. *Phenomenology*, p. 729; *Werke*, II, 552.

57. *Ibid.*, p. 728 - 30; *Werke*, II, 551 - 53.

58. *Ibid.*, p. 731; *Werke*, II, 553.

59. *Aesthetics*, II, 1037 - 39; *Werke*, XIV, 321 - 25.

60. *Ibid.*, p. 1098; *Werke*, XIV, 403.

61. *Ibid.*, p. 1072; *Werke*, XIV, 368.

62. *Ibid.*, p. 1056; *Werke*, XIV, 347.

63. *Ibid.*, pp. 1048 - 49; *Werke*, XIV, 337 - 38.

64. *Ibid.*, pp. 1043 - 44; *Werke*, XIV, 330 - 32.

65. *Ibid.*, p. 1045; *Werke*, XIV, 332.

66. *Ibid.*, p. 1044; *Werke*, XIV, 331 - 32.

67. *Ibid.*, pp. 1052 - 55; *Werke*, XIV, 342 - 43.

68. *Ibid.*, pp. 972 - 78; *Werke*, XIV, 237 - 46.

69. *Ibid.*, pp. 1051 - 52; *Werke*, XIV, 341 - 42.

70. *Ibid.*, pp. 1062 - 77; *Werke*, XIV, 355 - 75.

71. *Ibid.*, p. 1048; *Werke*, XIV, 336 - 37.

72. *Ibid.*, p. 1053; *Werke*, XIV, 343.

73. *Ibid.*, pp. 1053 - 54; *Werke*, XIV, 343 - 44.

74. *Ibid.*, p. 1061; *Werke*, XIV, 354 - 55.

75. *Ibid.*, p. 1057; *Werke*, XIV, 348.

76. *Ibid.*, pp. 1064 - 65; *Werke*, XIV, 357 - 59.

77. Josiah Royce, *Lectures of Modern Idealism* (New Haven, 1964), pp. 147 - 56.

78. *Aesthtics*, II, 1060 - 61; *Werke*, XIV, 352 - 53.

79. *Ibid.*, pp. 1053, 1105; *Werke*, XIV, 344, 410 - 11.

80. *Ibid.*, p. 1086; *Werke*, XIV, 386 - 87.

81. *Ibid.*, pp. 1067 - 68; *Werke*, XIV, 361 - 62.

82. *Ibid.*, p. 1070; *Werke*, XIV, 366.

83. *Ibid.*, pp. 1050, 1087; *Werke*, XIV, 339; pp. 388 - 89.

84. *Ibid.*, p. 1049; *Werke*, XIV, 338.

85. *Ibid.*, p. 1050; *Werke*, XIV, 339.

86. *Ibid.*, pp. 1046 - 47; *Werke*, XIV, 334 - 35.

87. *Ibid.*, p. 1047; *Werke*, XIV, 335.

88. *Ibid.*, pp. 1061 - 62; *Werke*, XIV, 354 - 55.

89. *Ibid.*, p. 1062; *Werke*, XIV, 355.
90. *Ibid.*, p. 1109; *Werke*, XIV, 416 - 17.
91. *Ibid.*, p. 1092; *Werke*, XIV, 395.
92. *Ibid.*, p. 1062; *Werke*, XIV, 355.
93. *Ibid.*, pp. 1123 - 24; *Werke*, XIV, 434 - 35.
94. *Ibid.*, pp. 1129 - 30; *Werke*, XIV, 443.
95. *Ibid.*, p. 1206; *Werke*, XIV, 523 - 24.
96. *Ibid.*, pp. 1159 - 67; *Werke*, XIV, 480 - 492.
97. *Ibid.*, I, 464; *Werke*, XIV, 51.
98. Anne Paolucci, "Bradley and Hegel on Shakespeare," *Comparative Literature* 16, no. 3 (1964), 211 - 25.
99. *Aesthetics*, II, 1219 - 20; *Werke*, XIV, 557 - 58.
100. *Schriften zur Politik und Rechtsphilosophie*, ed. G. Lasson (Leipzig, 1913), p. 380; my translation.
101. *Aesthetics*, II, 1219; *Werke*, XIV, 557 - 58.
102. *Ibid.*, pp. 1206 - 7; *Werke*, XIV, 542 - 43.
103. *Ibid.*, p. 1220; *Werke*, XIV, 559.
104. *Ibid.*, p. 1220; *Werke*, XIV, 559.
105. *Ibid.*, pp. 1234 - 35; *Werke*, XIV, 577 - 79.
106. *Ibid.*, p. 1233; *Werke*, XIV, 576 - 77.
107. *Ibid.*, p. 1236; *Werke*, XIV, 579 - 80.
108. *Ibid.*, pp. 1220 - 21; *Werke*, XIV, 559 - 60.
109. See chap. 8, pp. 156 - 58.
110. *Aesthetics*, I, 355; *Werke*, XII, 473 - 74.

Chapter Seven

1. *Philosophy of Religion*, II, 308, 322; *Werke*, XVI, 174, 186 - 87. Yet elsewhere Hegel distinguishes between Oriental despotism and the Roman Empire. See *Philosophy of History*, pp. 105 - 8; *Werke*, 151 - 55.
2. *Philosophy of History*, pp. 316 - 17; *Werke*, XI, 407 - 8.
3. *Ibid.*, p. 315; *Werke*, XI, 405.
4. *Ibid.*, p. 317; *Werke*, XI, 407.
5. *Ibid.*, pp. 314, 316 - 17; *Werke*, XI, 404, 407. *Philosophy of Religion*, II, 316; *Werke*, XVI, 181. *Philosophy of Right*, pp. 122, 221 - 22; *Werke*, VII, 260, 454.
6. *Philosophy of Religion*, II, 288; *Werke*, XVI, 156.
7. *Ibid.*, p. 288; *Werke*, XVI, 156.
8. *Ibid.*, pp. 301 - 3; *Werke*, 167 - 69.
9. *Ibid.*, pp. 309, 322; *Werke*, 175, 186 - 87.
10. *Ibid.*, pp. 304 - 5; *Werke*, XVI, 170 - 71.
11. *Ibid.*, pp. 307 - 8; *Werke*, XVI, 173 - 74.
12. *Ibid.*, pp. 296, 298; *Werke*, XVI, 163, 165.
13. *Ibid.*, p. 308; *Werke*, XVI, 174.
14. *Ibid.*, p. 294; *Werke*, XVI, 161

15. *Ibid.*, p. 294; *Werke*, XVI, 161.
16. *Ibid.*, pp. 294 - 95; *Werke*, XVI, 161 - 62.
17. *Philosophy of History*, pp. 316 - 17; *Werke*, XI, 407 - 8.
18. *Philosophy of Right*, pp. 17 - 20, 41, 121 - 22, 124, 221 - 22; *Werke*, VII, 44 - 50, 97, 253.
19. *Early Theological Writings*, pp. 156 - 57; *Theologische Jugendschriften*, p. 223.
20. *Philosophy of History*, p. 303; *Werke*, XI, 391. *Philosophy of Right*, pp. 37 - 74; *Werke*, II, 88 - 163.
21. See Michel Villey, "Das Römische Recht in Hegels Rechtsphilosophie," in *Materialien zu Hegels Rechtsphilosophie*, ed. by Manfred Riedel, (Frankfurt, 1975), II, 131 - 51.

Chapter Eight

1. *Briefe von und an Hegel*, II, 326 - 27.
2. *Philosophy of Religion*, II, 327; *Werke*, XVI, 191.
3. Carl Ludwig Michelet, *Geschichte der letzten Systeme der Philosophie in Deutschland* (Berlin, 1838), pt. 2, pp. 637ff.
4. Ludwig Feuerbach, *The Essence of Christianity*, trans. by George Eliot (New York, 1957).
5. Karl Friedrich Göschel, *Aphorismen über Nichtwissen und absolutes Wissen in Verhältnisse zur christlichen Glaubenserkenntnis* (Berlin, 1829).
6. This thesis, which was put forward by Carl Ludwig Michelet shortly after Hegel's death, is developed in Emil L. Fackenheim's *The Religious Dimension in Hegel's Thought* (Bloomington, 1967), chap. 4.
7. *Philosophy of History*, p. 356; *Werke*, XI, 454.
8. On the one hand, Hegel defines created nature in terms of otherness and externality in relation to spirit. See *Philosophy of Nature*, pp. 13 - 14; *Werke*, IX, 49. On the other hand, he admits that there was once a primitive unity of spirit and nature (*ibid.*, pp. 8 - 9.). These two facts together imply that Hegel admits the existence of an ensouled nature prior to the despiritualized nature articulated in the philosophy of nature and "created" by God (the logical "Idea").
9. *Philosophy of Religion*, III, 1; *Werke*, XVI, 218.
10. This is implicit in Hegel's insistence that Judaism represents God merely as "the Lord." See *Logic of Hegel*, p. 210; *Werke*, VIII, 265. See also *Philosophy of Religion*, II, 196 - 97; *Werke*, XVI, 69 - 70 on the "patriarchal" character of Judaism.
11. *Early Theological Writings*, pp. 182 - 83; *Theologische Jugendschriften*, pp. 243 - 44.
12. *Philosophy of Religion*, III, 52 - 54, *Werke*, XVI, 264 - 65.
13. *Ibid.*, II, 322 - 23; *Werke*, XVI, 187 - 88.
14. *Ibid.*, III, 97; *Werke*, XVI, 305.

15. *Ibid.*, III, 97, 100 - 51; *Werke*, XVI, 305, 308 - 56.

16. *Philosophy of Religion*, I, 7; *Werke*, XV, 24.

17. Hegel possibly exaggerates Jesus' opposition to Judaic ritual law, not distinguishing sufficiently between the position of Jesus and that of the Gentile mission of Saint Paul. See *Early Theological Writings*, pp. 202 - 52; *Theologische Jugendschriften*, pp. 261 - 301. His early views continue to be reflected in his lectures on the philosophy of religion: *Philosophy of Religion*, III, 80 - 83; *Werke*, XVI, 289 - 92.

18. *Philosophy of Right*, p. 110; *Werke*, VII, 236 - 37.

19. *Early Theological Writings*, p. 236; *Theologische Jugendschriften*, p. 286. See also *Philosophy of Religion*, III, 80; *Werke*, XVI, 289. Hegel's position is based on bibilical citations such as *Luke* 11:27 - 28 and 14:26.

20. Matt. 19:21.

21. Matt. 10:24 - 25.

22. Matt. 6:19 - 34.

23. Luke 20:20

24. *Early Theological Writings*, pp. 232ff; *Theologische Jugendschriften*, pp. 283ff.

25. This is clearly brought out in Stephen Crites, *In the Twilight of Christendom: Hegel versus Kierkegaard on Faith and History* (Chambersburg, Penn., 1972), chap. 2.

26. *Philosophy of History*, p. 380; *Werke*, XI, 483 - 84.

27. *Philosophy of Religion*, III, 1; *Werke*, XVI, 218.

28. "The simple unity, identity, and abstract affirmation of the infinite [apart from the finite] is, in itself, no truth. . . . Nor does the standpoint of the finite represent any more that which is true. On the contrary, it must annul itself, and it is only in this act of negation that we have what is true. The finite is therefore an essential moment of the infinite in the nature of God, and thus it may be said that it is God Himself who renders Himself finite. . . .God is infinite; I am finite; these are false, bad expressions. . . . It is equally true that God exists as finite and the Ego as infinite. . . . God is movement towards the finite, and owing to this He is, as it were, the lifting up of the finite to Himself" (*Philosophy of Religion*, I, 198 - 200; *Werke*, XV, 208 - 10.)

29. *Logic of Hegel*, pp. 174 - 77; *Werke*, VIII, 222 - 25.

30. Fackenheim makes this point, and yet correctly insists that the standpoint of faith, representation, and religious alienation, that is, of God's otherness and transcendence, is not totally displaced by that of philosophical comprehension pp. 204 - 6, 218 - 19). For what would philosophy have to comprehend if its content did not already exist in the world independently of it in the form of religious representation?

31. See Gustav Emil Müller, "The Hegel Legend of 'Thesis-Antithesis-Synthesis,' " *Journal of the History of Ideas* 19 (1958), 411 - 14.

32. The following difficult passage on the dialectic should be read in conjunction with chap. 1, pp. 8 - 9. For a fuller analytic account of the

dialectic, see my "On the Reducibility of Dialectical to Standard Logic," *The Personalist* 56 (1975), 414 - 31.

33. *Philosophy of Religion*, III, 1; *Werke*, XVI, 218.

34. *Logic of Hegel*, p. 176; *Werke*, VIII, 224.

35. The terminology is Fackenheim's (see pp. 149ff).

36. Col. 1:16.

37. John 1:1.

38. *Philosophy of Religion*, I, 7; *Werke*, XV, 24.

39. See Hartshorne, "Panpsychism."

40. *Differenz des Fichte'schen und Schelling'schen Systems der Philosophie (1801)*, in *Werke*, I, 122 - 44.

41. I attempt to provide such arguments in "The Mind-Body Problem: A Non-Materialistic Identity Thesis," *Idealistic Studies* 2 (1972), 229 - 48. See also "Panpsychism: A Reconstruction of the Genetic Argument," *Idealistic Studies*, forthcoming.

42. Heinrich Heine, who was a student of Hegel's, reports that Hegel replied in the following terms to his expression of surprise on hearing his teacher deny a transcendent heaven: "So you still want a tip for having taken care of your sick mother and not having poisoned your brother?" (*Hegel in Berichten seiner Zeitgenossen*, ed. Günther Nicolin (Hamburg, 1970), p. 234; my translation.)

43. See pp. 45 - 50.

44. "God without the world is not God" (*Philosophy of Religion*, I, 200; *Werke*, XV, 210.)

Chapter Nine

1. Stephen Crites.

2. Sören Kierkegaard, *Concluding Unscientific Postscript*, trans. W. Lowrie (Princeton, 1941).

3. Fackenheim, p. 24. See also Emil Fackenheim, "Would Hegel Today Be a Hegelian?" *Dialogue* 9 (1970), 222 - 26.

4. *Philosophy of Right*, p. 12; *Werke*, VII, 35.

5. See pp. 70 - 71.

6. See pp. 97 - 98.

7. *Aesthetics*, I, 535; *Werke*, XIII, 143 - 44.

8. *Ibid.*, pp. 552 - 53; *Werke*, XIII, 165 - 67. See also, *ibid.*, pp. 573 - 75; *Werke*, XIII, 191 - 93.

9. *Ibid.*, pp. 521 - 22; *Werke*, XIII, 125 - 27.

10. *Ibid.*, II, 836 - 37; *Werke*, XIV, 59 - 60.

11. *Ibid.*, pp. 1236 - 37; *Werke*, XIV, 579 - 81.

12. *Ibid.*, p. 1236; *Werke*, XIV, 580 - 81.

13. *Ibid.*, p. 1128; *Werke*, XIV, 441.

14. *Ibid.*, I, 520 - 21; *Werke*, XIII, 124 - 25.

15. *Ibid.*, II, 636; *Werke*, XIII, 274.

16. *Ibid.*, pp. 638 - 40; *Werke*, XIII, 276 - 79.
17. *Ibid.*, pp. 661 - 62; *Werke*, XIII, 304 - 5.
18. *Ibid.*, pp. 684 - 85; *Werke*, XIII, 332 - 33.
19. *Ibid.*, pp. 684 - 98; *Werke*, XIII, 332 - 50.
20. *Ibid.*, pp. 685 - 87; *Werke*, XIII, 334 - 36.
21. *Ibid.*, p. 696; *Werke*, XIII, 347 - 48.
22. *Ibid.*, p. 790; *Werke*, XIII, 463 - 64.
23. *Ibid.*, I, 83 - 90; *Werke*, XII, 124 - 32.
24. *Ibid.*, pp. 85 - 88; *Werke*, XII, 125 - 30.
25. Dance adds to lyric (that is, musical) poetry a "plastic" (that is, sculptural) element (*ibid.*, II, 1151; *Werke*, XIV, 471). Hegel explains that it is precisely because dance is a hybrid that it receives no separate thematic treatment (*Ibid.*, II, 627 - 28; *Werke*, XIII, 261 - 62).
26. *Ibid.*, II, 799 - 800; *Werke*, XIV, 12 - 13.
27. *Ibid.*, p. 797; *Werke*, XIV, 9.
28. *Ibid.*, pp. 797, 805 - 6; *Werke*, 9 - 10, 19 - 21.
29. *Ibid.*, pp. 797 - 98; *Werke*, XIV, 9 - 11.
30. *Ibid.*, pp. 831 - 37; *Werke*, XIV, 52 - 60.
31. *Ibid.*, pp. 831 - 32; *Werke*, XIV, 53 - 54.
32. *Ibid.*, p. 810; *Werke*, XIV, 26.
33. *Ibid.*, pp. 808 - 9; *Werke*, XIV, 23 - 25.
34. *Ibid.*, pp. 838 - 39; *Werke*, XIV, 61 - 63.
35. *Ibid.*, pp. 765 - 71; *Werke*, XIV, 435 - 41.
36. *Ibid.*, pp. 851 - 53; *Werke*, XIV, 77 - 81.
37. *Ibid.*, p. 853; *Werke*, XIV, 81.
38. *Ibid.*, p. 902; *Werke*, XIV; 143 - 44.
39. *Ibid.*, p. 894; *Werke*, XIV, 132 - 33.
40. *Ibid.*, pp. 889 - 90, 907; *Werke*, XIV, 126 - 28, 150.
41. *Ibid.*, p. 955; *Werke*, XIV, 215.
42. *Ibid.*, p. 893; *Werke*, XIV, 131.
43. *Ibid.*, p. 960; *Werke*, XIV, 221 - 22.
44. *Ibid.*, p. 891; *Werke*, XIV, 220 - 22.
45. *Ibid.*, pp. 899 - 900; *Werke*, XIV, 139 - 41.
46. *Ibid.*, p. 900; *Werke*, XIV, 141.
47. *Ibid.*, pp. 1152 - 53; *Werke*, XIV, 472 - 74.
48. *Ibid.*, p. 1111; *Werke*, XIV, 419 - 20.
49. *Ibid.*, pp. 1111 - 12; *Werke*, XIV, 420.
50. *Ibid.*, p. 1112; *Werke*, XIV, 420.
51. *Ibid.*, pp. 1122 - 23; *Werke*, XIV, 433 - 35.
52. *Ibid.*, p. 1123; *Werke*, XIV, 434 - 35.
53. *Ibid.*, pp. 1147 - 49; *Werke*, XIV, 466 - 69.
54. *Ibid.*, I, 557 - 86; *Werke*, XIII, 172 - 207. *Ibid.*, II, 1205 - 8; *Werke*, XIV, 540 - 44.
55. *Ibid.*, I, 583 - 85; *Werke*, XIII, 204 - 5. *Ibid.*, II, 1225 - 26; *Werke*, XIV, 556.

56. *Ibid.*, I, 577 - 78; *Werke*, XIII, 196 - 98.

57. Fackenheim, pp. 235 - 36.

58. Jacques d'Hondt, *Hegel en son Temps* (Paris, 1968.), pp. 147 - 70.

59. See Alexandre Kojève, *Introduction to the Reading of Hegel* (New York, 1969); Joachim Ritter; Rudolf Haym, *Hegel und seine Zeit*, Hildesheim, 1962).

60. "Über die englische Reformbill," in *Werke*, XI, 471 - 518.

61. *Briefe von und an Hegel*, II, 50 - 51.

62. *Philosophische Propädeutik*, in *Werke*, III, 70 - 71.

63. *Philosophy of Right*, p. 213; *Werke*, VII, 442.

64. *Ibid.*, pp. 151 - 52; *Werke*, VII, 320.

65. Ritter, pp. 31 - 46.

66. *Philosophy of Right*, pp. 149 - 52, 278; *Werke*, VII, 318 - 23.

67. *Ibid.*, p. 126; *Werke*, VII, 270 - 71. Hegel's position here, to which Karl Marx also subscribed, contrasts with that of Adam Smith, for whom the laws of the free market were eternal.

68. *Ibid.*, pp. 145 - 46, 150, 275 - 76, 277; *Werke*, VII, 310 - 11, 316.

69. Johann Gottlieb Fichte, *Der geschlossene Handelsstaat* (1800), in *Werke* (Berlin, 1971), vol. 3, pp. 387 - 513.

70. *Philosophy of Right*, p. 134; *Werke*, VII, 286.

71. In 1819, following a witch-hunt for "demagogues," Hegel wrote to a colleague: "I am about fifty years old, and I have spent thirty of these fifty years in this ever unrestful era of hope and fear. I had hoped that we might for once be done with it. Now I must admit that it is with us as always; indeed, it seems in one's darker hours that it is getting increasingly worse" (*Briefe von und an Hegel*, II, 219; my translation). For brief accounts by close associates on his similar reaction to the July Revolution of 1830, see *Hegel in Berichten seiner Zeitgenossen*, pp. 415, 527 - 28.

72. *Philosophy of Right*, pp. 152 - 55; *Werke*, VII, 323 - 28.

73. *Philosophy of History*, p. 452; *Werke*, XI, 563.

74. See my "Technological Society and Its Counterculture: A Hegelian Analysis," *Inquiry* 18 (1975), 195 - 212. This article took the counterculture to be a subjective revolt, that is, a chiefly *cultural* revolt with little effect on *institutions*. The counterculture appears this way insofar as it is analyzed in abstraction from its total historical context. The key to seeing its *objective* world-historical significance lies in seeing it in this context as a continuation—but hardly a completion—of the revolution which began in the eighteenth century.

75. *Phenomenology of Mind*, p. 598; *Werke*, II, 448.

76. *Ibid.*, pp. 549 - 98; *Werke*, II, 406 - 48.

77. *Ibid.*, p. 245; *Werke*, II, 161.

78. Karl Popper, *The Open Society and Its Enemies* (Princeton, 1963), vol. 2., pp. 27 - 80.

79. *Philosophy of Right*, p. 279; *Werke*, VII, 336.

Chapter Ten

1. *Logic of Hegel*, pp. 172 - 73; *Werke*, VIII, 218 - 21.
2. *Werke*, I, 336 - 45.
3. Wolfgang Wieland, "Die Anfänge der Philosophie Schellings und die Frage nach der Natur," in *Materialien zu Schellings philosophischen Anfängen*, ed. M. Frank and G. Kurz (Frankfurt am Main, 1975), pp. 237 - 79.

Selected Bibliography

PRIMARY SOURCES

1. Collected editions

Sämtliche Werke. Edited by Hermann Glockner. 26 vols. Stuttgart: Frommann, 1927 -.

Historisch-kritische Gesamtausgabe. 4 vols. Hamburg: Felix Meiner, 1968 -. Currently being edited by the staff of the Hegel-Archiv, Bochum, West Germany. The final number of volumes is still unknown. It will be decades before all the volumes of the new Felix Meiner edition have appeared. The publisher has been trying to bring out a critical edition of Hegel's works since the 1920s, and several volumes have appeared since 1913 under the editorship of Georg Lasson and, later, Johannes Hoffmeister. These efforts, however, were never brought to completion, and they will be superseded by the Hegel-Archiv edition. Both the Glockner edition and the Hegel-Archiv edition will probably remain in print, the older one because it presents Hegel's works in the form in which they have exercised their great historical influence for well over a century, the Hegel-Archiv edition because it presents manuscripts which either have never been published or have appeared only in mutilated form. The Glockner edition is little more than a reprint of the 1832 - 1845 edition published shortly after Hegel's death by his students and friends, although it is supplemented by a useful four-volume *Hegel-Lexikon.*

Werke. 20 vols. Edited by Eva Moldenhauer and Karl Marcus Michel. Frankfurt: Suhrkamp, 1970 -. This relatively inexpensive paperback edition is, like the one by Glockner, based on the 1832 - 1845 edition, except for Volume 1 which contains early "theological" writings by Hegel unpublished until this century.

2. Collections of posthumous writings

Theologische Jugendschriften. Edited by H. Nohl. Tübingen: Mohr, 1907.

Dokumente zu Hegels Entwicklung. Edited by J. Hoffmeister. Stuttgart: Frommann, 1936.

Der junge Hegel in Stuttgart, Aufsätze und Tagebuchaufzeichnungen 1785 - 1788. Edited by F. Nicolin. Marbach, 1970.

Briefe von und an Hegel. Edited by J. Hoffmeister. 4 vols. Hamburg: Felix Meiner, 1952 - 1960.

Philosophie des Rechtes. Edited by K-H Itling. 6 vols. Stuttgart:

Frommann, 1973 -. Hegel's lectures on the philosophy of law arranged by the year in which they were given.
3. English translations
For a bibliography of English translations see Daniel Breazeale, "English Translations of Fichte, Schelling, and Hegel: an Annotated Bibliography," *Idealistic Studies* 6, no. 3 (September, 1976), 279 - 97. The following lists currently available English translations.
"The Tübingen Essay of 1793." Translated by H. S. Harris. In *Hegel's Development*, by H. S. Harris, pp. 483-507. London: Oxford University Press, 1972.
"The Berne Plan of 1794." In *Hegel's Development*, pp. 508 - 10.
"The Positivity of the Christian Religion." In *Hegel's Early Theological Writings*, translated by T. M. Knox and Richard Kroner, pp. 67 - 181. Chicago: University of Chicago Press, 1948.
"The Earliest System Programme of German Idealism." In *Hegel's Development*, pp. 510 - 12.
"The Frankfurt Sketch on 'Faith and Being.' " In *Hegel's Development*, pp. 512 - 15.
"On the Recent Domestic Affairs of Württemberg, Especially on the Inadequacy of the Municipal Constitution." In *Hegel's Political Writings*, translated by T. M. Knox, pp. 243 - 45. London: Oxford University Press, 1964.
"Love." In *Early Theological Writings*, pp. 302 - 8.
"The Spirit of Christianity and its Fate." In *Early Theological Writings*, pp. 182 - 301.
"Fragment of a System." In *Early Theological Writings*, pp. 309 - 19.
"The German Constitution." In *Hegel's Political Writings*, pp. 143 - 242.
The Difference Between Fichte's and Schelling's System of Philosophy. Translated by W. Cerf and H. S. Harris. Albany: State University of New York Press, 1977.
Faith and Knowledge. Translated by W. Cerf and H. S. Harris. Albany: State University of New York Press, 1977.
Natural Law. Translated by T. M. Knox. Philadelphia: University of Pennsylvania Press, 1975.
The Phenomenology of Mind. Translated by J. B. Baille. London: Allen and Unwin, 1931. Retranslated as *Phenomenology of Spirit.* Translated by A. V. Miller, with introduction and commentary by J. N. Findlay. London: Oxford University Press, 1977.
Hegel's Science of Logic. Translated by A. V. Miller. London: Allen and Unwin, 1969.
"The Proceedings of the Estates Assembly in the Kingdom of Württemberg, 1814 - 1816." In *Hegel's Political Writings*, pp. 246 - 92.
Hegel's Philosophy of Right. Translated by T. M. Knox. London: Oxford University Press, 1942.

The Logic of Hegel. Translated by William Wallace. London: Oxford University Press, 1892.

Hegel's Philosophy of Nature. Translated by A. V. Miller. London: Oxford University Press, 1970.

Hegel's Philosophy of Mind. Translated by W. Wallace and A. V. Miller. London: Oxford University Press, 1971.

"The English Reform Bill." In *Hegel's Political Writings*, pp. 295 - 330.

Hegel's Aesthetics: Lectures on Fine Art. Translated by T. M. Knox. London: Oxford University Press, 1975.

Lectures on the Philosophy of Religion, Together with a Work on the Proofs of the Existence of God. Translated by E. B. Speirs and J. B. Sanderson. London: Kegan Paul, Trench, Trubner & Co., 1895.

Lectures on the Philosophy of History. Translated by J. Sibree. New York: Dover, 1956.

Lectures on the Philosophy of World History, Introduction: Reason in History. Translated by H. B. Nisbet. London: Cambridge University Press, 1975.

Hegel's Philosophy of Subjective Spirit. Translated with commentary by M. J. Petry. Dordrecht: Reidel, 1977. 3 vols.

4. Anthologies

Hegel: The Essential Writings. Edited by F. G. Weiss. New York: Harper and Row, 1974.

Hegel on Tragedy. Edited by Anne Paolucci and Henry Paolucci. New York: Harper and Row, 1975.

SECONDARY SOURCES

1. Bibliography

STEINHAUER, KURT, S.J. *Hegel: An International Bibliography.* Munich: Verlag Dokumentation, 1977. A multilingual bibliography of secondary sources containing 12,000 entries.

2. Biography

BEYER, WILHELM. *Zwischen Phänomenologie und Logik, Hegel als Redakteur der Bamberger Zeitung.* Cologne: Pahl-Rugenstein, 1974. Treats Hegel's stint (1807 - 1808) as a journalist from a Marxist perspective.

GULYGA, ARSEN. *Georg Wilhelm Friedrich Hegel.* Frankfurt am Main: Roderberg, 1974. Originally written in Russian by a Soviet philosopher.

HARRIS, H. S. *Hegel's Development: Toward the Sunlight, 1770 - 1801.* London: Oxford University Press, 1972. An original synthesis of much recent research by an excellent scholar.

HAYM, RUDOLF. *Hegel und seine Zeit.* 1857. Reprint. Hildesheim: Georg Olms, 1962. A key source of the common view of Hegel as the philosopher of the Prussian state and the Restoration.

D'HONDT, JACQUES. *Hegel et son temps*. Paris: Editions Sociales, 1968. Documents Hegel's liberalism in the Berlin period.

LUKACS, GEORG. *Der junge Hegel*. 2 vols. Zurich: Europa, 1948. A major study of Hegel to the *Phenomenology* by a noted Marxist philosopher.

ROSENKRANZ, KARL. *G. W. F. Hegels Leben*. 1844. Reprint. Darmstadt: Wissenschaftliche Buchgesellschaft, 1972. A biography by one of Hegel's students, included in 1832 - 1845 edition of his works.

WIEDMANN, FRANZ. *Hegel*. Translated by Joachim Neugroschel. New York: Western Publishing, 1968. A brief illustrated biography.

3. Critical studies

AVINERI, SHLOMO. *Hegel's Theory of the Modern State*. London: Cambridge University Press, 1972. Highlights lesser known early political writings by Hegel.

BARTH, KARL. *Protestant Theology in the Nineteenth Century*. Valley Forge, Penn.: Judson Press, 1973. Contains a chapter on Hegel as well as several of his students and contemporaries.

BAUMANNS, PETER. *Fichtes ursprüngliches System: Sein Standort zwischen Kant und Hegel*. Stuttgart-Bad Canstatt: Frommann-Holzboog, 1972. Investigates how well Hegel understood the Fichte he criticized.

BEHLER, ERNST. *Friedrich Schlegel*. Hamburg: Rowohlt, 1966. Good study of the most representative romantic contemporary of Hegel.

BERNSTEIN, RICHARD. *Praxis and Action*. Philadelphia: University of Pennsylvania Press, 1971. Excellent on the Hegelian background of much post-Hegelian thought.

BETTI, EMILIO. *Die Hermeneutik als allgemeine Methodik der Geisteswissenschaften*. Tübingen: Mohr, 1962.

BLOCH, ERNST. *Naturrecht und menschliche Würde*. Frankfurt am Main: Suhrkamp, 1975. On the tradition of Roman law in the West.

————. *Subjekt-Objekt: Erläuterungen zu Hegel*. Frankfurt am Main: Suhrkamp, 1972. A major study by a noted contemporary German philosopher.

BRAZILL, W. J. *The Young Hegelians*. New Haven: Yale University Press, 1970. Good overview of the left-wing Hegelians in the decades after Hegel's death.

BRUFORD, W. H. *The German Tradition of Self-Cultivation*. London: Cambridge University Press, 1975. Traces the literary sources of German political irresponsibility, showing how historically Hegel lost in his struggle against Romanticism in Germany.

BUTLER, CLARK. "Hegel and Freud: A Comparison." *Philosophy and Phenomenological Research* 36 (1976), 505 - 22. Traces Hegelian themes in psychoanalysis.

————. "L'Hégélianisme interprété comme un matérialisme historique." *Hegel-Jahrbuch*, forthcoming.

————. "The Mind-Body Problem: A Non-Materilistic Identity Thesis." *Idealistic Studies* 2 (1972), 229 - 47. Defends panpsychism.

————. "On the Reducibility of Dialectical to Standard Logic." *The Personalist* 56 (1975), 414 - 31. Analyzes the concept of Hegelian dialectic presupposed in the text.

————. "Panpsychism: A Reconstruction of the Genetic Argument." *Idealistic Studies,* forthcoming.

————. "Technological Society and Its Counterculture: A Hegelian Analysis." *Inquiry* 18 (1975), 195 - 212. On recent American history.

CAIRD, EDWARD. *Hegel.* London: Blackwood, 1883. By a noted early British Hegelian.

CHOURAQUI, ANDRÉ. *La Pensée Juive.* Paris: Presses Universitaires de France, 1965.

CHRISTENSEN, DARREL, ed. *Hegel and the Philosophy of Religion.* The Wofford Symposium. The Hague: Nijhoff, 1970. Edited by founding president of Hegel Society of America.

COETZMANN, W. H., ed. *The American Hegelians: An Intellectual Episode in the History of Western America.* New York: Knopf, 1973. Selected writings by nineteenth-century, largely immigrant Hegelians.

COLLETTI, LUCIO. *Marxism and Hegel.* Atlantic Highlands, N.J.: Humanities Press, 1975. By a noted Italian Marxist philosopher.

DROZ, JACQUES. *Histoire des doctrines politiques en Allemagne.* Paris: Presses Universitaires de France, 1968. Sets Hegel in context of the history of German political thought.

EASTON, LOYD. *Hegel's First American Followers: The Ohio Hegelians.* Athens, Ohio: Ohio University Press, 1966.

ENGELS, FRIEDRICH. *The Origin of the Family, Private Property, and the State.* Translated by Eleanor Leacock. New York: International Publishers, 1971. One of my sources in reconstructing Hegelianism on a historical materialist basis.

FACKENHEIM, EMIL. *The Religious Dimension in Hegel's Thought.* Boston: Beacon Press, 1967. A sympathetic but critical study by a Jewish philosopher.

FINDLAY, J. N. *Hegel: A Re-examination.* New York: Humanities Press, 1958. Marks a return to Hegel by a mainstream English-speaking philosopher of note.

FLUSSER, DAVID. *Jesus.* Hamburg: Rowohlt, 1968. My major recent source on the life of Jesus.

FRANK, M., and KURTZ, G., ed. *Materialien zu Schellings philosophischen Anfängen.* Frankfurt am Main: Suhrkamp, 1975. Essays on the early Schelling.

FRANK, MANFRED. *Der unendliche Mangel an Sein.* Frankfurt am Main: Suhrkamp, 1975. Discussion of the late Schelling's influential criticism of Hegel.

FULDA, H. F., and HENRICH, D., ed. *Materialien zu Hegels*

Phänomenologie des Geistes. Frankfurt am Main: Suhrkamp, 1973. Essays on aspects of the *Phenomenology.*

GLASENAPP, HELMUTH VON. *Das Indienbild deutscher Denker.* Stuttgart: Koehler, 1960. Chapter on Hegel criticizes his appreciation of India.

GRAY, J. G. *Hegel and Greek Thought.* New York: Harper and Row, 1968. A short, well-balanced treatment.

GREENE, MURRAY. *Hegel on the Soul: A Speculative Anthropology.* The Hague: Nijhoff, 1972. Hegel on the prereflective, preconscious mind.

GRIMAL, PIERRE. *La Vie à Rome dans l'Antiquite.* Paris: Presses Universitaires de France, 1967.

HEIDEGGER, MARTIN. *Hegel's Concept of Experience.* New York: Harper and Row, 1970. A major twentieth-century German philosopher interprets the "Introduction" to Hegel's *Phenomenology.*

HEISS, ROBERT. *Hegel, Kierkegaard, Marx.* New York: Dell, 1975. Elementary; emphasizes differences in "dialectic" as viewed by the three thinkers.

HYPPOLITE, JEAN. *Genesis and Structure of Hegel's Phenomenology of Spirit.* Translated by S. Cherniak and J. Heckman. Evanston: Northwestern University Press, 1974. Most respected full-length commentary on *Phenomenology* by noted French Hegel scholar.

————. *Studies on Marx and Hegel.* Translated by J. O'Neill. New York: Basic Books, 1969.

IMBERT, JEAN. *Le Droit antique.* Paris: Presses Universitaires de France, 1966.

JANICAUD, DOMINIQUE. *Hegel et le destin de la Grèce.* Paris: Vrin, 1975. A massive study written from Heideggarian viewpoint.

JANSON, H. W. *The History of Art.* New York: Abrams, 1971.

KAINZ, HOWARD P. *Hegel's Phenomenology Part I: Analysis and Commentary.* University, Alabama: University of Alabama Press, 1976.

KAMINSKI, JACK. *Hegel on Art.* Albany: State University of New York Press, 1962. An elementary study of Hegel's aesthetics abstracted from its context in the entire Hegelian system.

KANTZENBACH, F. W. *Schleiermacher.* Hamburg: Rowohlt, 1975.

KAUFMANN, WALTER. *Hegel: A Reinterpretation.* New York: Doubleday, 1965. A breezy, topical, and very readable book on Hegel by an excellent Nietzsche scholar who discounts the dialectic and system.

KELLY, GEORGE A. *Idealism, Politics, and History: Sources of Hegelian Thought.* London: Cambridge University Press, 1969.

KOJÉVE, ALEXANDRE. *Introduction to the Reading of Hegel.* Translated by J. Nichols. New York: Basic Books, 1969. A passionate, sometimes compelling exposition of the *Phenomenology* stressing the master-slave dialectic; based on Paris lectures of the 1930s which exercised a decisive influence on French existentialism and neo-Marxism.

LAUER, QUENTIN. *A Reading of Hegel's Phenomenology of Spirit.* New York: Fordham University Press, 1976.

———. *Hegel's Idea of Philosophy*. New York: Fordham University Press, 1971.

LAUTH, REINHARD. *Die Entstehung von Schellings Identitätsphilosophie in der Auseinandersetzung mit Fichtes Wissenschaftslehre*. Munich: Alber, 1975. Excellent study of Schelling's (and indirectly Hegel's) philosophical beginnings in interaction with Fichte.

LEUZE, REINHARD. *Die ausserchristlichen Religionen bei Hegel*. Göttingen: Vanenhoeck and Ruprecht, 1975. Excellent study of Hegel's understanding of Oriental religions in relation both to his sources and contemporary knowledge I am indebted.

LOEWENBERG, JACOB. *Hegel's Phenomenology*. La Salle, Ill.: Open Court, 1965. A commentary in quaint dialogue form by a student of Josiah Royce.

LÖWITH, KARL. *From Hegel to Nietzsche*. New York: Doubleday, 1964. Critical history from neo-orthodox theological standpoint.

MacINTYRE, A., ed. *Hegel*. New York: Doubleday, 1972. Some good papers, but the anthology is too short to give representative samplings of Hegel scholarship as a whole.

MacKENZIE, MILLICENT. *Hegel's Educational Theory and Practice*. London: Sonnenschein, 1909.

McTAGGART, JOHN ELLIS. *Studies in Hegelian Cosmology*. London: Cambridge University Press, 1918. Unorthodox interpretation of Hegelianism as a pluralism by a noted British idealist.

MARCUSE, HERBERT. *Reason and Revolution*. Boston: Beacon Press, 1941. By the representative of the neo-Marxist "Frankfurt" school most widely read in the English-speaking world.

MARX, WERNER. *Hegel's Phenomenology of Spirit*. New York: Harper and Row, 1975.

MICHEL, ALAIN. *Histoire des doctrines politiques à Rome*. Paris: Presses Universitaires de France, 1971.

MURE, G. R. G. *An Introduction to Hegel*. London: Oxford University Press, 1970.

———. *The Philosophy of Hegel*. London: Oxford University Press, 1965.

———. *A Study of Hegel's Logic*. London: Oxford University Press, 1967. An excellent study by a long-standing British Hegel scholar.

NEGT, OSKAR, ed. *Aktualität und Folgen der Philosophie Hegels*. Frankfurt am Main: Suhrkamp, 1970. Contains several essays on Hegel in relation to trends in Marxist thought.

NOUGIER, LOUIS-RENE. *L'Economie prehistorique*. Paris: Presses Universitaires de France, 1970.

O'BRIEN, GEORGE D. *Hegel on Reason and History*. Chicago: University of Chicago Press, 1975.

O'MALLEY, J. J., ed. *Hegel and the History of Philosophy*. The Hague: Nijhoff, 1974. Drawn from 1972 Hegel Society of America conference.

———, et al., ed. *The Legacy of Hegel*. The Hague: Nijhoff, 1973.

OPPENHEIMER, FRANZ. *The State*. Translated by J. M. Gitterman. New York: Free Life, 1975. Important theory of origin of the state, using a master-slave dialectic reminiscent of Hegel.

OTTMANN, HORST HENNING. *Das Scheitern einer Einleitung in Hegels Philosophie: Eine Analyse der Phänomenologie des Geistes*. Munich: Pustet, 1973. Very clear study of the background of the *Phenomenology* in Hegel's Jena years.

NICOLIN, GÜNTHER, ed. *Hegel in Berichten seiner Zeitgenossen*. Hamburg: Meiner, 1970. Excerpts, largely from letters, on Hegel by those who knew him.

PALANQUE, JEAN-REMY. *Les Impérialisme antiques*. Paris: Presses Universitaires de France, 1967.

PAOLUCCI, ANNE. "Bradley and Hegel on Shakespeare." *Comparative Literature* 16 (1964), 211 - 25. Highly favorable evaluation of Hegel.

PELCZYNSKI, Z. A., ed. *Hegel's Political Philosophy*. London: Cambridge University Press, 1971.

PLANT, RAYMOND. *Hegel*. London: Allen and Unwin, 1973. First chapters on Hegel's development highly recommended. Hegel's early study of economic history is highlighted.

PÖGGELER, OTTO. "Philosophy in the Wake of Holderlin." *Man and World* 7 (1974), 158 - 76.

_____. *Hegels Idee einer Phänomenologie des Geistes*. Munich: Alber, 1973. Studies on composition and critical reception of *Phenomenology* by an outstanding scholar, who is also director of the Hegel-Archiv.

REIDEL, M., ed. *Materialien zu Hegels Rechtsphilosophie*. 2 vols. Frankfurt am Main: Suhrkamp, 1975. Volume 1 contains reviews on *Philosophy of Right* by Hegel's contemporaries.

REYBURN, HUGH A. *The Ethical Story of Hegel*. London: Oxford University Press, 1970.

RITTER, JOACHIM. *Hegel und die Französische Revolution*. Cologne: Westdeutscher Verlag, 1957. The most effective reply yet to Karl Popper's view of Hegel as an antiliberal reactionary.

ROSEN, STANLEY. *G. W. F. Hegel: An Introduction to the Science of Wisdom*. New Haven: Yale University Press, 1971. Difficult but rewarding study of Hegel in the history of philosophy.

ROTENSTREICH, NATHAN. *From Substance to Subject: Studies in Hegel*. The Hague: Nijhoff, 1974.

ROYCE, JOSIAH. *Lectures on Modern Idealism*. New Haven: Yale University Press, 1964. Elementary introduction to classical German philosophy; interesting comparison of the *Phenomenology* to a *Bildungsroman*.

SCHACHT, RICHARD. *Hegel and After: Studies in Continental Philosophy Between Kant and Sartre*. Pittsburgh: University of Pittsburgh Press, 1975.

SCHELLING, F. W. J. *Schriften von 1794 - 1798.* Darmstadt: Wissenschaftliche Buchgesellschaft, 1975. The early Schelling who most influenced Hegel.

SCHNABEL, FRANZ. *Deutsche Geschichte im neunzehnten Jahrhundert.* Freiburg: Herder, 1964 - . My own background reading on Hegel's context in nineteenth-century Germany.

SCHNADELBACH, HERBERT. *Geschichtsphilosophie nach Hegel: Die Probleme des Historismus.* Munich: Albert, 1974.

SHKLAR, JUDITH. *Freedom and Independence: A Study of the Political Ideas of Hegel's Phenomenology of Mind.* London: Cambridge University Press, 1976. Written by a political scientist for the uninitiated.

SIMON, MARCEL. *Les Premiers Chretiens.* Paris: Presses Universitaires de France, 1967.

SNOW, EDGAR. *Red Star Over China.* New York: Random House, 1968. On Mao Tse Tung.

SOBOUL, ALBERT. *Le Premier Empire.* Paris: Presses Universitaires de France, 1973.

———. *La Révolution Française.* Paris: Presses Universitaires de France, 1975

SOLL, IVAN. *An Introduction to Hegel's Metaphysics.* Chicago: University of Chicago Press, 1969.

STACE, W. T. *The Philosophy of Hegel.* New York: Dover, 1974. Follows the *Encyclopedia.* Clear, but perhaps overly schematic.

STEINKRAUS, WARREN E., ed. *New Studies in Hegel's Philosophy.* New York: Holt, Rinehart and Winston, 1974.

SZONDI, PETER. *Poetik und Geschichtsphilosophie.* Frankfurt am Main: Suhrkamp, 1974.

TAYLOR, CHARLES. *Hegel.* London: Cambridge University Press, 1975. A large-scale study by an established mainstream English-speaking philosopher.

VARENNE, JEAN. *Zarathustra et la tradition Mazdéene.* Paris: Seuil, 1966.

VIDALENC, JEAN. *La Restauration, 1814 - 1830.* Paris: Presses Universitaires de France, 1973.

VILLEY, MICHEL. *Le Droit Romain.* Paris: Presses Universitaires de France, 1964. Excellent on Roman law.

WALSH, W. H. *Hegelian Ethics.* New York: St. Martin's Press, 1969.

WEISS, F., ed. *Beyond Epistemology.* The Hague: Nijhoff, 1974. Essays by contemporary Anglo-American Hegel scholars.

WEISS, FREDERICK. *Hegel's Critiques of Aristotle's Philosophy of Mind.* The Hague: Nijhoff, 1969.

WILKINS, B. T. *Hegel's Philosophy of History.* Ithaca: Cornell University Press, 1974.

4. Periodicals

CLIO: An Interdisciplinary Journal of Literature, History and the

Philosophy of History. Beginning with volume 7 (Fall, 1977), published at Indiana University-Purdue University Fort Wayne Campus, under my coeditorship. Articles on Hegel in each issue.

Hegel Jahrbuch. (1961 -). Organ of the Internationale Hegel-Gesellschaft. Marxist orientation frequently represented.

Hegel-Studien. (1961 -). Affiliated with the Internationale Hegel-Vereinigung.

Idealistic Studies. (1971 -). Edited by Robert N. Beck at Clark University. Deals more broadly with the whole German Idealist tradition and its Anglo-American offshoots.

The Owl of Minerva. (1969 -). Newsletter edited by F. G. Weiss for the Hegel Society of America. Contains reviews and information on forthcoming books.

Recherches hégéliennes. (1970 -). Published by the *Centre de recherche et de documentation sur Hegel et Marx* at the University of Poitiers, France. Reports activities in Hegel research.

Index